Paul Thompson read History at Oxford and became a research fellow at Queen's College. In 1964 he joined the Department of Sociology in the new University of Essex where he is now Reader in Social History. His books include *Socialists, Liberals and Labour*, *The Work of William Morris* and *William Butterfield* and he edits *Oral History*. With Thea Vigne he has carried out the national interview study of family, work and community life before 1918 on which this book is based.

Paul Thompson

The Edwardians

Paladin

Granada Publishing Limited
Published in 1977 by Paladin
Frogmore, St Albans, Herts AL2 2NF

First published in Great Britain by
Weidenfeld and Nicolson Ltd 1975

Made and printed in Great Britain by
Richard Clay (The Chaucer Press) Ltd
Bungay, Suffolk
Set in Monotype Ehrhardt

In honour of the lives of those Edwardians who told their story to us, and to thank them all, this book is dedicated to

BOB JAGGARD
and
CLIFF HILLS

Contents

Acknowledgements

The author and publishers would like to thank the following for supplying photographs for use in this book:

The National Coal Board for plate 1; William Gordon Davis for plates 2, 7, 8, and 11; the Suffolk Photo Survey for plates 3 and 18; George Ewart Evans for plate 4; the Kodak Museum for plates 5a & b; the Radio Times Hulton Picture Library for plates 6, 9, 13, 14, 18, 19 and 21; the Gersheim Collection, Humanities Research Center, the University of Texas at Austin for plate 10; the Victoria and Albert Museum and John Freeman for plate 12; the Zetland County Library and Museum for plate 16; O. G. Jarman for plate 17; D. C. Harrod for plate 20; the London Transport Executive for plate 22; Hornsey Public Library for plate 23; Leeds City Libraries for plate 24; the Olney Collection for plate 25; the Greater London Council for plate 26; London Museum for plate 27; Edinburgh Library for plate 28; Mr Frank Benson, Mrs G. Whitelam, Mrs A. G. Hargrave, Mr P. Henry, Mrs Kent, Mr S. Ford for plates of Edwardians.

Preface

I have been helped by far more people than I can mention here: but above all by those Edwardians who agreed to be recorded for us; their interviewers; Thea Vigne as co-investigator and field-work supervisor; the special help of George Ewart Evans, Janet Parkin, Trevor Lummis, Ruth Hawthorn, Brenda Corti, Ann Burke, Thelma Crook, Reginald Collins, Michael Kidd, Carrol Hill, Marjorie English, Doris Redfern, Mary Prideaux, Jean Jacobs and Winifred Preece; and the financial support for the research project of the Social Science Research Council, the Nuffield Foundation, Nuffield College and the University of Essex.

The chapters on the family are to a considerable extent based on two articles by Thea Vigne, published in *New Society*, 5 October 1972, and the *Observer*, 24 June 1973.

I owe a great debt to discussion with many colleagues and friends, and above all those who were able to comment on the drafts for this text: Eric Hobsbawm, Thomas Pakenham, Anna Davin, Peter Townsend, Diana Barker, Raphael Samuel – and again, Thea Vigne, for this is a book founded on our joint work.

Introduction

I have three basic aims in this book. The first is quite simply to establish what I believe to be the most important dimensions of social change in the early twentieth century. This is more difficult than might be imagined. Of course there are countless aspects of change, which I shall scarcely mention, which are well enough documented – like dress fashions or types of motor car. But upon the issues which I have chosen, such as the distribution of wealth or the relationships between parents and children, the facts are much less clear, and where figures exist we shall often find them deceptive. I have also needed to concentrate upon a restricted range of issues. I have selected those which are fundamental to social structure – which determine the differing opportunities and rewards which people experience through their lives. These are, firstly, class structure, which is built up by and maintains the unequal distribution of money, food, shelter and other forms of sustenance; secondly, the physical social structure – the differences between regions, and between country, town and city; thirdly, distinctions between the sexes; and fourthly, distinctions between the various age groups.

Part One will set out the dimensions of inequality with these four fundamental measures in mind; and I shall sum up my conclusions on the facts of social change in the first three chapters of Part Four. I have not attempted to deal as thoroughly with any other issues, even though some were of central importance to many people's lives, but some attention is given, for example, to changes in work experience (in the chapters on 'The Economy', 'War' and 'Class'), leisure, religion, crime (all in the chapter on 'Escape') and education (in the chapter on

'Class'). Some of these – education for instance – would have been given more attention had I been writing about a period in which their development was more critical. The same may be said of the discussions of migration (in 'Country and Town') and of social mobility (in 'Escape'). I do not claim my fundamental dimensions of social structure to be in any sense exhaustive.

They are, however, deliberately related to my second aim. This is to suggest the main reasons for social change, and especially the extent to which conscious effort by Edwardians for social change was critical. This is the principal theme of Part Three, where I shall evaluate the chief instruments of change, conscious and unconscious: the economy; individual routes to escape or self-improvement; the collective pressures such as trade unionism, party politics and the feminist movement which culminated in the Edwardian crisis; and finally the drastic intervention of the First World War. Part Three is essentially an interpretation of the historical facts, but it will raise, if only implicitly, questions about the theory of social change. While it would require much more space to discuss this theory adequately, it would be wrong to leave it merely implicit. In the final chapter of Part Four I shall therefore sketch very briefly the theoretical position which underlies – and is supported by – the discussion in Part Three. Some readers may well wish to skip these pages, but I hope they may suggest to the sympathetic historian some further directions for exploration, and serve for the sociologist to identify my standpoint. I have conceived of this book as both sociology and history.

My last aim is to give a place, in this evaluation of general social change, to the contribution and experience of ordinary individuals. The discussion in Part Three will directly concern their contribution at many points, and the theoretical interpretation will again be brought together in the final chapter: also briefly, for the role of the individual in history is a matter of long debate hardly to be settled here. But I have tried at least to give a central place in the scheme to ordinary life experience. Several chapters, especially of Part One, rely heavily on direct quotation for evidence. And as an antidote to the simplifications with which I have had to outline the dimensions of social structure, Part One leads into a set of twelve accounts of childhood in real families – our 'Edwardians'. People will reappear at the end, with two more Edwardian families. They represent the untidy reality upon which, though too many scholastics would wish it forgotten, both theoretical sociology and historical myth rest. And I hope they will more than compensate for the relatively slight attention which I shall give to better-known public heroes.

I would justify in the same spirit the choice of social change as my general theme. The great political conflicts of these years were not manufactured, as we are sometimes led to believe, at Whitehall breakfast parties. They were manifestations of a deep self-questioning at all levels of society, which shadowed the confidence of Britain as still, seemingly, the world's most powerful nation. Innumerable unknown Edwardians gave their life's enthusiasm to the creation of a better society; a higher proportion, I suspect, than at any other time in Britain. Politics was for them a social faith. Men were 'confirmed in Liberal principles' or 'converted' to socialism. A young bricklayer's labourer's son in Oxford, for example, was one of thousands of recruits to the socialist movement at the turn of the century:

> 'And I'll tell you what made me turn a Socialist. Being a Freeman I should be a Conservative really, but I've seen boys when I went to school at St Thomas's, . . . I've seen one or two boys before they went into school at nine o'clock go round this back yard . . . and the people who lived in the back, if they had some stale bread, they'd chuck the stale bread in pieces to the birds out on to the grass, you see. Two of the boys used to come out early, pick up that bread and eat it, cause they'd got nothing to eat to go to school. And when I realized that, I thought to myself, well, England is supposed to be – it was – the most powerful and the richest country in the world, and yet – nothing could be done. Why not? And I tried to be a Socialist, and have been ever since.'[1]

Have there been rewards from such political faith?

Note on the Interview Method in Social History

The intrusion of machinery into the historian's craft, and the new title 'oral history', have perhaps made the use of tape-recorded interviews as evidence seem more novel than it is. Social investigators have long used interviews. There is an abundance of sociological discussion on the interview method, the sources of bias in it, and how these may be estimated and minimized; much more discussion, in fact, than of the bias similarly inherent in all written documentation. Historians have themselves also used interview material freely, not only in biography, but when printed in classic sources such as Henry Mayhew's *London Labour and the London Poor*, or the work of Booth and Rowntree. Interviews are also the basis of Royal Commissions, the census, registrations of birth, marriage and death and many other sources. Historians too easily believe, with Durkheim, in 'social facts as things'.[2] For example, we know for certain that early twentieth century marriage registers grossly under-represented the marriage rates of those youngest age groups who should have obtained parental consent. We know that food statistics, like those of the consumption of different kinds of fish, were distorted by the need to market new types of fish under old names. We know that the census definition of 'a room', used for measuring overcrowding, was a social one, which determined the exclusion of sculleries, and how thick a partition must be for one room to be counted as two. These social statistics thus do not represent absolute facts, any more than newspaper reports, private letters or published biographies. Like recorded interview material, they all represent, either from individual standpoints or aggregated, the *social perception* of facts; and all are in addition subject to social pressures from the context in which they are obtained. With these forms of evidence, what we receive is *social meaning*, and it is this which must be evaluated.

Retrospective evidence – whether from newspapers, court hearings, published biographies or recorded interviews – does not present any intrinsically different problems. The context of perception is separated from that of the presentation of the evidence, but the bias introduced by this later social context of presentation does not necessarily increase with time. Many social pressures against openness diminish in retrospect, and the last years of life for many people are a time of reflection and special candour. Nor is the problem of memory loss nearly as serious as is often believed. Memory loss is in fact concentrated during and immediately after the perception of an event. There are numerous old people who retain a remarkably full and accurate memory of their earlier years.

I have discussed these general issues elsewhere.[3] Here I simply want to add a comment on three frequent causes for suspicion of 'oral history'. Firstly, imprecise general questioning on the good – or bad – old days will encourage subjective impressions and retrospective bias; particular facts and detailed accounts of everyday events usually make much more useful evidence. Secondly, most people do not arrange their memories with dates as markers; calendar years do not matter to them as they do to historians. Thirdly, the more people are used to presenting a professional public image, the less likely their recollections are to be candid; politicians are therefore particularly difficult witnesses.

For our own research project we recorded some five hundred men and women, all born by 1906, and the earliest in 1872. We wanted to select a group representative as far as now possible of the Edwardian population as a whole, so that we devised a 'quota sample' – a list of categories of various proportions into which people had to fit in order to be counted. The sample was based on the 1911 census and it totalled 444 persons. The proportion of men and women was as in 1911; so were the proportions who had then been living in the countryside, the towns and the conurbations; and so too the balance between the main regions of England, Wales and Scotland. We tried to ensure a proper class distribution by dividing the sample into the six major occupational groups which are used elsewhere in this book. Those who were not working went in as dependents of the chief breadwinner in the household – normally the father or husband. We carried out more interviews than the total 444, partly because some turned out to belong to a different classification than expected, and partly because not all were sufficiently complete.

Although we wanted to encourage those whom we recorded to tell us their story, and tried to avoid imposing any rigid mould at the beginning of interviews, we did have a very long list of detailed points which we wanted to know about. These were essential for comparison, besides being intrinsically useful for securing a fuller story when a point had not been covered without a direct question being asked. Our interview schedule was some twenty pages long, and it normally required two or three recording sessions to complete each interview. We recorded a large number of the interviews ourselves, but the majority were carried out for us by interviewers specially selected for the project, and themselves coming from a variety of backgrounds. Together we found the Edwardians we recorded through many different means: personal contact, doctors' lists, welfare centres, visiting organizations, essay competitions, newspapers and even chance encounter. As far as possible we tried to counteract the social bias which the methods of contact could themselves introduce.

The plan turned out a more ambitious one than we imagined, so that at the time of writing some of the recordings had still to be transcribed. As a result, this book represents my first interpretation – and this is especially true of the rough estimates given, like those on page 85 – rather than a conclusion. Lastly, I should mention that quotations from interviews are not reworded, although some hesitations and repetitions are eliminated. Also, in order to protect evidence given us in confidence, in some cases I have changed the name of our Edwardians.

Part I
Dimensions of Inequality

1 Money

In the early twentieth century the open display of wealth was an essential element in the upper-class style of life. Wealth, birth and manners constituted the three prime qualifications for commanding obedience and respect from others. Although many of the rich already wintered abroad, most of their money was spent in Britain on highly visible comforts such as country houses, personal servants and lavish entertaining. And although death duties existed, they were not severe enough for tax evasion on a massive scale to have developed. Consequently we know more about the distribution of wealth in the Edwardian population than in contemporary Britain.

If we look at the raw statistics, the death duty figures for the 1900s, it appears that the richest 1 per cent of Edwardians dying owned over 40 per cent of the entire capital value left. But we can hardly rest satisfied with these figures. They underestimate the inequality for a number of reasons. To start with, they leave out nearly half of those who died, for only those who left sufficient property to make it worth while going through the process of swearing an affidavit were entered in the official returns. Chiozza Money, an Edwardian Liberal MP, made an allowance for this in his book *Riches and Poverty*, published in 1905, and drew his own estimate as the diagram[1] on page 22 shows.

But even this is an underestimate, for it fails to allow for the fact that most middle- and upper-class men did not reach their full wealth until their fifties, but younger men were less likely to die. Similarly women in general died later than men but were poorer.

A later calculation based on the whole population over the age of twenty-five concludes that the top 1 per cent of Edwardians in 1911–13 owned 69 per cent of the national capital.[2]

It may seem that we have made too heavy weather in reaching this calculation. A few of the difficulties in making an estimate

Table 1

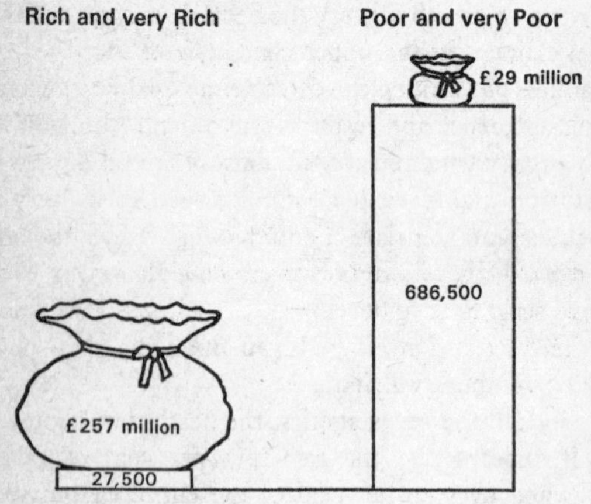

In an average year 27,500 persons die worth £257 million while 686,500 persons die worth only £29 million

of this kind have been mentioned, because although the basic facts are stark enough it is also important to see that any attempt to make comparisons with the distribution of wealth in other countries, or with Britain today, is a hazardous business. And even if we knew that the calculations had all been made on the same age groups with the same mortality allowances, we could never be sure how many estates have succeeded in evading the tax inspectors altogether. But we shall come back to this later.

In the Edwardian period this concentration of capital also represented a concentration of personal economic power. It was mostly held by male heads of families, and it consisted in the ownership of houses, land, railways, mines and businesses. Nine-tenths of the land was landlord-owned before 1914, rather than owner-occupied, and most of these landlords took a personal part in the administration of their property. Similarly the typical business organization was still the family firm. Employers and the self-employed made up one-eighth of the Edwardian work-force – twice as many as today. Capital wealth thus gave direct power to employ and to sack, to protect and to evict. If the Edwardians were disturbed by the growing power of anonymous state bureaucracy and the corporate capitalism of trusts and amalgamations, which they rightly saw as portents of the future, their own world remained dominated by the individual business-man or landlord. Indeed in the countryside, even within fifty miles of London, there were estate workers whose attitude to their employers was so personal as to be almost feudal in character:

> 'We used to live under people you know, those days . . . You were glad to go, to be under somebody, to feel you got somebody to cover you. You know, I couldn't tell you what . . . poverty there was, really there was a terrible lot of poverty in villages . . . They were glad enough to go to the soup kitchen and fetch soup. They used to give out soup three days a week to the poor . . . I wouldn't want to live the life over again, not those young days.'[3]

As with the distribution of wealth, so, if a little less drastically, with the distribution of earnings. In 1913–14 the average annual earnings of occupied men and women of all classes were £80. This average was the axis of a wide span. The salary of a High Court judge, for example, was £5,000; a charwoman's annual wage under £30. It is more illuminating, however, to divide the occupied population as a whole into groups, and compare the earnings of each group with the average, because we can then get a clear outline of the unequal distribution of earned income in terms of social class. As we shall want later on to see how much this has changed, we shall treat the overall average of £80 as 100, and express the average earnings of each group as percentages of this overall average. The result is the following table. For the present, we need only consider the first two columns:

Table 2. Occupational Class average earnings as *percentages* of the average for all occupational classes, men and women, 1913–14 and 1960[4]

	1913–14		*1960*	
	Men	*Women*	*Men*	*Women*
Higher professional	410	—	298	(209)
Lower professional	194	111	124	89
Managers	250	100	271	146
Foremen	141	71	149	88
Clerks	124	56	100	62
Skilled manual	124	55	117	58
Semi-skilled manual	86	62	85	50
Unskilled manual	79	35	79	41
Averages, all occupied men, all occupied women	115	63	118	64

Average entire workforce – all occupied men and women: 100.

There are two gaps in this table. Business employers are left out altogether because their earned incomes cannot be estimated. There is also no figure for higher professional women, because women were effectively barred from most work in this category. Nevertheless a clear pattern emerges. Higher professional men as a group have a striking advantage over all others. At the other extreme, women workers of all kinds are ill rewarded. The overall average wage of occupied women is well below that of an unskilled labouring man. One can see here the economic basis for the social confidence of the Edwardian upper middle classes, and for the general social dominance of men over women. Among manual workers, too, there is a distinct grading which gave force to the superiority claimed by the craftsman over the labourer. On the other hand, it can also be seen how the gap between their incomes could easily be closed by the presence of an additional earner, whether wife or son, in the family. Lastly, there is a significant overlap between manual and non-manual workers. The poor Edwardian clerk had a lower salary than the better paid skilled man.

To make full sense of this class inequality of income we need to attach some more precise names to these broad occupational groups. Who were they? And how numerous? The numbers can again be set out in a table.

Table 3. Occupational Status of the occupied population, England, Wales and Scotland 1911[5]

	Men	*Women*	*All*
Higher professional	1	0	1
Lower professional	2	6	3
Employers	8	4	7
Managers	4	2	3
Foremen	2	0	1
Clerks	5	3	5
Skilled manual	33	25	31
Semi-skilled manual	34	54	39
Unskilled manual	11	5	10
Total per cent	100	100	100
Number	12,900,000	5,400,000	18,300,000
Per cent all occupied	71	29	100

We can see that altogether nearly a third of the Edwardian workforce consisted of women, but the women tended to be clustered in the lower grades. Thus the top group of higher professionals, a mere one per cent of the entire workforce, was predictably almost entirely male: characteristically a clergyman, doctor or lawyer. The lower professional, typically a teacher, was by contrast more likely to be female. There was also a rising number of women clerks. Employers and managers were predominantly male: typically shopkeepers, followed by farmers, manufacturers and businessmen. Women in this group were mostly shop or boarding-house keepers. Employers and managers together made up half of the non-manual workforce. Foremen were a tiny group, almost as small as higher professionals and equally male. Of manual workers, the skilled occupations consisted above all of hewing coal, textile spinning and weaving, dressmaking, engineering, carpentry and painting. There was a large group of women workers here, but still more among the semi-skilled, who were typically domestic servants, agricultural labourers, horse drivers and shop assistants. Finally, the unskilled made up a smaller, largely male group of general labourers, builders' labourers, roadmen, scavengers, and railway labourers and porters. Because it cannot allow for inherited wealth, an occupational class structure is least meaningful with the uppermost and lowest groups. Very rich men, the top one per cent in terms of wealth, were formally unoccupied, 'gentlemen of independent means'. And at the other extreme very roughly two per cent of the population lived on the very barest resources, because the breadwinner of the family was too sick to work, or dead.

Here then are the bare economic foundations of inequality in early twentieth-century Britain. But how did such inequality affect men's lives?

2 Sustenance

The Edwardian well-to-do could literally look down on their social inferiors. They not only had the better of life, but they had more of it. They ate more, grew more and lived longer. Expectation of life in middle-class Hampstead was fifty years at birth, but in working-class Southwark only thirty-six years. In Edinburgh, Manchester and many other cities the general death rates for the most prosperous wards were half those of the poorest. You were four times more likely to develop tuberculosis in central Birmingham than in well-to-do suburban Edgbaston. The inequality, moreover, began at birth. In a healthy middle-class suburb, ninety-six of every hundred infants born would survive their first year of life. In a bad slum district, one in every three would be dead.

Some of the most striking facts emerged as a result of new assessments in these years. When conscription was introduced during the First World War, it was found that four out of five recruits had such bad teeth that they could not eat properly, and scarcely a third of all adult men could be classified as having a full normal standard of health and strength. The new school medical services similarly revealed that one in every six children was so undernourished, verminous or suffering from defective teeth or skin or eyes, as to be incapable of benefiting educationally from school attendance. And when they lined up the schoolchildren and measured them, it was found time and again that children from overcrowded homes were likely to be on average as much as ten pounds less in weight and five inches less in height than those from adequate dwellings, and middle-class children taller again.

In the poorest families the children usually went barefoot in summer and relied on police and other charities to find them boots to go to school. Their clothes were either hand-me-downs, or bought second-hand at rag markets and cheap sales. Their parents might have a best suit for weekends, but it was likely to be kept at the pawnbroker's during the week. The normal working-class family, at least in the towns, would be rather better provided than this. They would be able to buy new shoes and at least one complete set of new clothes each, even if week-day clothes would often be second-hand. The mass production of boot and clothing factories, selling their wares through multiple chain stores, had already found a growing working-class market. The well-paid craftsman, like the clerk, was likely to possess a good hat as well, and a fancy waistcoat on which to display his watch chain. But if this distanced him effectively from the ragged street urchin it was nothing to the equipment of the well-to-do.

It is hardly surprising that in an age which favoured conspicuous consumption by the rich, wealthy ladies were dressed with extraordinary expense, elaboration and variety. Their personal dressmakers and tailors supplied them with different clothes for morning, afternoon and evening; for teas, garden parties and balls; for being in the house, or going out shopping; for the sea, for motoring, for cycling or walking; for marriage and for mourning. With her abundant fur and lace trimmings and real or artificial flowers, and her giant hats, resting on hair constructions so ingeniously built up upon pads and wire frames that she was helpless without the personal assistance of a servant in dressing, the Edwardian lady was a triumph of artificiality and concealment. Conversely, rustling in her petticoats, tightly laced to throw out a grand, mature bosom, or, as fashion changed, helpless in a hobble skirt, she was clearly in a full sense an object of conspicuous consumption.

The Edwardian gentleman, too, needed a full wardrobe: a tweed suit for the country, frock coat for business, dinner jacket for the evening at home, tail coat for going out, and a series of boots, shirts, cuffs and waistcoats of different styles to match.

Gentlemen required special clothes for motoring, bicycling, yachting and other pastimes. They had to take notice of remarkably fine distinctions as to what dress was, or was not, appropriate for a particular moment. Brown boots, for example, could be worn at Ascot, but no nearer town. Like blue spotted ties, they were for country wear. In London itself one had to be careful in case one's dress was right for the place but wrong for the moment. 'In the park of a summer morning lounge suits and straw hats, Homburgs or bowlers, are very popular, and in summer quite as common as the regular silk hat and frock-coat,' advised the author of *Etiquette for Men*. 'But this is all changed with the luncheon hour. After that a frock, or morning coat, and silk hat should be worn, or the grey frock-coat suit.'[1] All this elaborate concern with clothing required not only spare time and cash on the part of the Edwardian lady and gentleman, but also sustained luxury trades, such as West End hatters and bespoke tailors, more in the style of personal service than manufacture.

As with clothing, so with food: the contrasts again run from luxurious personal service to less than the bare essentials. In his study of poverty in York, Seebohm Rowntree found 28 per cent of the city's population living below the nutritional standard which he calculated as necessary to maintain mere physical health. The proportion of school children in this situation was higher still, perhaps 40 per cent, because a single manual worker's wage was simply not sufficient to maintain a large family. Among the working classes a majority could in fact expect to experience poverty at three points in their lives. The first was in childhood, until they themselves or their brothers or sisters began to earn. A period of relative comfort would then follow, lasting into the first years of marriage. They would then sink back into poverty again as their family of young children grew. Once the children were old enough to work, the situation would again improve. Finally, as they grew old and sick in later years, poverty would strike again. Rowntree expressed these alternating periods of want and comparative plenty in a diagram:[2]

Table 4

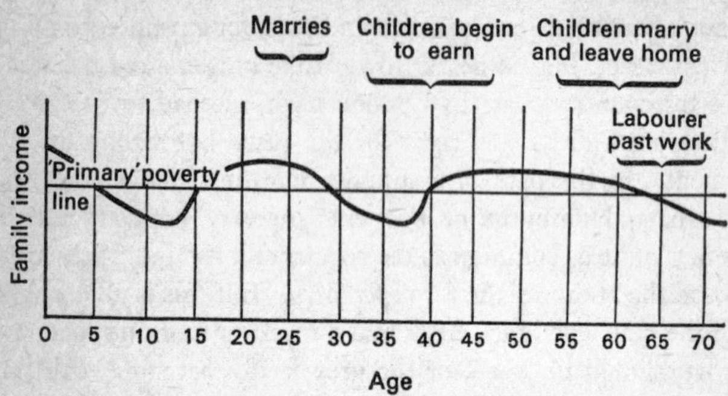

The worst effects of this cycle could in theory be escaped by the exercise of uncommon restraint. On a typical manual worker's wage, provided that the number of children did not rise above four (the national average for couples married in the 1890s) and that almost nothing was spent on drink or other pleasures, it was just possible to feed the whole family adequately. An abstemious craftsman would raise eight children in bare comfort; a regularly employed labourer, two. But no normal indulgences were permitted if these incomes were to be sufficient to provide the necessary food. As Rowntree himself warned:

> 'Let us clearly understand what "merely physical efficiency" means. A family living upon the scale allowed for in this estimate must never spend a penny on railway fare or omnibus. They must never go into the country unless they walk. They must never purchase a halfpenny newspaper or spend a penny to buy a ticket for a popular concert. They must write no letters to absent children, for they cannot afford to pay the postage. They must never contribute anything to their church or chapel, or give any help to a neighbour which costs them money. They cannot save, nor can they join sick club or Trade Union, because they cannot pay the necessary subscriptions. The children must have no pocket money for dolls, marbles, or sweets. The

father must smoke no tobacco, and must drink no beer. The mother must never buy any pretty clothes for herself or for her children, the character of the family wardrobe as for the family diet, being governed by the regulation, "Nothing must be bought but that which is absolutely necessary for the maintenance of physical health, and what is bought must be of the plainest and most economical description." Should a child fall ill, it must be attended by the parish doctor; should it die, it must be buried by the parish. Finally, the wage-earner must never be absent from his work for a single day.

'If any of these conditions are broken, the extra expenditure involved is met, *and can only be met*, by limiting the diet; or, in other words, by sacrificing physical efficiency.'[3]

Since the observance of these iron conditions implied abstention from most of the characteristic practices of Edwardian working-class life, it is hardly surprising that underfeeding was such a normal experience. There were innumerable Edwardian families in which only one good meal was eaten a day, and the source of supply was the regular sale of leftovers: broken eggs, stale bread, pieces of meat, bruised fruit, broken biscuits. In the poorest homes, if there were regular meals the children would stand at the table or sit on the floor because there were insufficient chairs, and they would eat with their hands or spoons because there were no knives or forks. The basis of their diet would be tea and bread with jam or dripping. If their father missed a few days' work, there would be no milk or sugar for the tea, and they might go to bed supperless and early, to keep warm. If the father was working, he probably set out himself in the early morning cold, and with an empty stomach.

'You didn't have much time to have anything first thing because you knew two hours afterwards you'd be home to breakfast. And it was very cold getting out, the mornings, yes. Of course us weren't dressed like the present-day ones you know, just scanty. Us could have done a bit more clothing and a bit more fire.'[4]

And there were many mothers who went short themselves in order to keep the rest of the family fed. An East London carter's daughter – Emmie Durham, one of our Edwardians – remembers how the irregularity of her father's work reduced them to killing the hens he kept, and even the pet rabbits:

> 'And the last one, it was a big white one, Billy we used to call it, beautiful thing. And my mother had no dinner one Sunday and he killed this rabbit. And my mother couldn't eat it. She said, "I'm not eating my Billy." And my dad was near to tears eating it . . . and gradually the fowls . . ., he killed them in the finish. Broke his heart but there. Money you see. We never starved . . . My mother went without herself for us, yes. I've known her to wipe the plate round with a drop of gravy, and tell my father she'd had her dinner, she'd never had any.'[5]

Nor, for a poor woman, was there much to look forward to in later years; perhaps a widow's dinner consisting just of two potatoes on the fire.

Rowntree recorded the weekly menus of some of the York families in poverty, as well as some in relative comfort, and a few from the professional and business middle class.[6] As a whole, judged by the subsistence standards of the world as a whole then or even today, they look ample enough. Indeed they should, for with the exception of the United States the working class of Britain was the best paid in the world. The amount of meat consumed is striking; and there is other evidence of the benefits of industrialization in the consumption of items such as bananas and tinned meats. Nevertheless, the differences between these menus are still more remarkable. The typical labourer's diet was in fact inferior to the week's menus at the local prison. Here is a day's meals of a casual labourer with three young children:

Breakfast Bread, butter, tea
Dinner Bacon, bread, butter, coffee
Tea Bread, butter, tea

Next, on the borderline between the working and middle class, the menu of a foreman with two children. The father 'occupies an allotment, and helps himself with vegetable growing':

Breakfast	Boiled bacon, bread, milk, tea
Dinner	Sheep's liver, potatoes, cauliflower, bread
Tea	Bread, butter, pastry, milk, tea
Supper	Gruel

Lastly, one of Rowntree's middle-class families, 'who are comfortably off (keeping from one to four servants) but who live simply'. This family with two children had abandoned high tea for dinner in southern English style. They may well have been waited on, dining fashionably, *à la Russe* – with each course served separately:

Breakfast	Fish, bread, toast, butter, marmalade, hot milk, cream, tea
Lunch	Soup, hot-pot, suet pudding, stewed prunes, cheese, bread, butter, biscuits, coffee, cream
Tea	Bread, butter, cakes, tea
Dinner	Out to dinner

Unlike most sociological investigators, Rowntree did not confine his attentions to the working class. Even so, his comparisons stopped well short of the rich. His families had weekly incomes ranging from eleven shillings (a widowed charwoman) to perhaps £10 at most. Arthur Ponsonby, a radical young aristocrat, was able to secure accounts from the households of some of his rich friends in the capital. He published the week's food budget for 'an "unemployed man", living in — Square, S.W., four in family and fourteen servants'. The tradesmen's food bills alone came to £60 12s 7d, and in addition, 'three hundred eggs were sent up from the country, as well as fruit, vegetables and a little poultry'. Much of this supply was pure waste; the family simply did not have the energy to eat it all. 'Quarts of cream are emptied down the sink, joints and birds only half eaten are thrown away, and the pig-tub receives a rich enough allowance of vegetables, fruit, and cakes to satisfy the appetite of a large family.' There were, indeed, single meals at which a rich household spent more money than the charwoman and her family had for the entire living expenses for two years. A dinner for twenty persons with the following menu cost £60:

Cantaloup Glacé
Tortue Claire
Bisque Nantua
Truites Saumonées Michigan
Mousse de Jambon à l'Escurial
Selle d'Agneau Montefiore
Poularde Strasbourgeoise
Salade Indienne
Cailles flanqués d'Ortolans
Asperges Verts. Sauce Mousseuse
Pêches Framboisines
Friandises
Fauchonettes Suisses
Hock, Claret, Port, Coffee, and Liqueurs[7]

Nor would this exhaust the household expenses for the evening. The servants would have eaten separately below stairs and the children in the nursery. There might even have been another separate group of upper servants eating in the housekeeper's room. And for the very rich, this household would itself be but one of several, occupied by the family in different phases of the season, each requiring a separate nucleus of servants. The town house was needed for the London season, from May until July. After an interval at a marine resort, perhaps yachting at Cowes, grouse shooting opened in August, and the rich moved northwards to the Scottish moors. They returned to the Midland and southern countryside in October for the hunting and county balls, which ran to February. After a brief Christmas in London, they then crossed to the continent for the remainder of the winter. Gambling at Monte Carlo was the most popular attraction, but King Edward VII himself favoured Biarritz. For an upper-class family the most convenient arrangement was to own houses in all these situations.

Some of these houses might be quite modest, such as the Mediterranean villa and the northern shooting box: perhaps no more than ten rooms. But the family's principal country house was more likely to possess over a hundred rooms, and if, as often, it had not been modernized and had no running water above the ground floor, it required more than fifty servants to run it comfortably. When we consider that less than one in ten Edwardian families had a single living-in servant, and that the average family cooked, ate and had their weekly wash in a tin bath all in the same living room, the social impact made by these great establishments is understandable. Indeed to some who participated in them, their masters took on a grace which was almost sacred: 'She'd been in service with titled people, and she thought it was very marvellous, if she met them out they'd shake hands with her.'[8]

By contrast with a wealthy family, the typical English working man's home in the early twentieth century was a brick or stone terrace house with a kitchen, a parlour at the front with perhaps a bay window, a lean-to scullery opening to a back yard or small garden, and three bedrooms above. The children slept two, three or more to a bed. If the house was a little smaller, a single bedroom divided by a curtain might have to suffice for separation of adolescent boys and girls. Downstairs, in the more prosperous homes, the kitchen was furnished with a linoleum floor, table and chairs, some prints and a wall dresser. There might be a gas stove in the scullery as well as an open fire and oven in the kitchen. In the parlour, generally reserved for use on Sundays or for visitors, would be a cushioned sofa, a piano, wall engravings, stuffed birds, a mantelpiece with china ornaments framing the clock, perhaps a small table with a cloth on which rested the family Bible, and lace curtains and a fern in the window.

Small enough by comparison with upper-class housing, it was nevertheless probably the highest national standard of housing in the world at the time. But once again, the variations in provision between the different social classes were as significant as the general standard. At one extreme, a peer's house might be several hundred yards from end to end. At the other, the poorest families lived in single rooms furnished with no more than orange boxes, and slept on the floor with old coats rather than bedclothes to cover them. Several thousands of Edwardians were actually homeless, sleeping in makeshift tents, caves in rubbish heaps from which they picked a living, barns and ricks in the country, doorways and arches in the cities. In London two thousand slept on the streets each night. Their presence shocked those who, like Lady Violet Brandon among our Edwardians, had come for the pleasures of the society season.

> 'Driving back in the early dawn from some wonderfully enjoyable dance and having terrible fun and suddenly seeing these terrible things you thought were just lumps of rags on the pavement or benches, and then seeing they were people ... "Keep on walking, darling, don't look round" – there was a tramp ... "Tramp" was a word that filled one with horror.'[9]

Apart from the extreme differences brought about by income, there was also a marked variety in the housing standards of different parts of the country. Much the best position was in the southern English towns, apart from London itself. Here the majority of houses had six or more rooms as well as a scullery, with running water and usually gas laid on, and increasingly often a bathroom as well. The old slum areas which existed were quite small. In northern industrial towns, on the other hand, the typical house was much smaller. In Lancashire it was a square house, with two or possibly three bedrooms above, and a front and back kitchen below. The front kitchen was the living room, with the range for cooking; the back kitchen was used as scullery, wash-house and larder. Instead of a back garden there was a yard, very often containing a smelly privy and refuse pit. In West Yorkshire there was not even a yard, for the normal house was a four- or five-room back-to-back terrace type, which was still being built in the 1900s. In almost all these northern towns more than a quarter of the houses had no drainage, so that excrement from the privies had to be shovelled out at intervals by sanitary gangs into barrows, and emptied from these into carts standing in the streets, a process creating overpowering stench. Although these undrained houses might otherwise be structurally sound, there would also normally be some older housing, perhaps a tenth of the town's total, built around narrow alleys and courts, with no damp courses, loose brick floors laid direct on the earth, roofs and gutters letting in the wet, ceilings bulging and wallpaper peeling off the damp walls, broken window panes stuffed with paper or rags. The only water supply might be a common tap in the yard, shared with other tenants. In Whitehaven the medical officer complained that the slum district had scarcely improved since the 1860s:

> 'Wherever one turns, whether out of the small or the large thoroughfares, one finds deplorable courts and alleys where the direct rays of the sun are but rarely seen, and where even its diffused light is often difficult of attainment. The alleys all too frequently consist of narrow channels often not more than three to three and a half feet across, on either side of which the houses face one another . . . The "over-looking" which is a consequence of this overcrowding of dwellings upon area necessitates the drawing down of blinds when anything approaching domestic privacy is desired.'[10]

The blinds drawn down for privacy were evidence that it was not only unrespectable families who found themselves living in slums. But it was an exhausting, exasperating battle trying to maintain a well-kept home in such a quarter. A Birmingham tenant complained:

> 'In the winter I fairly long for it to get dark, so I can light up. There's nothing to look at opposite but the windows, and I get that irritated, I want to pull their curtains down off them and wash them – not that it would do any good: you can't keep things clean here, they're no better next day.'

For the air was heavy with coal soot as well as reeking of refuse. The courts were noisy too:

> 'Every sound can be heard in the next house. We ourselves can hear those next door sweeten their tea – by that I mean we can hear them stirring it up. If the man comes home drunk at night, and uses filthy language, our children pick it all up.'[11]

Birmingham, with over 40,000 back-to-back houses, over 40,000 without any drainage or water tap, and nearly 60,000 without a separate sanitary facility, had the unhealthiest housing of any large English city in 1914. But for overcrowding London had a worse record: one-sixth of the city's entire population was living in housing with more than two people to each room. In spite of the very rapid development of northern and eastern working-class suburbs connected by cheap workman's trains and trams to the centre, and also the successive efforts to build model blocks of flats by philanthropic trusts and the London County Council, the amount of crowding, which had declined slightly in the late nineteenth century, was actually increasing in the 1900s. With the contrast between the prosperity of its new suburbs and the apparently insoluble decay of its inner slums, London in 1900 had already become one of the socially segregated conurbations which were to be characteristic of the mid twentieth-century world. The wealth of the West End and the City was ringed with a mixture of old courts and houses divided floor by floor, interspersed with well-intended but scarcely less daunting multi-storey blocks of model dwellings, designed like barracks, with common wash-houses in the yard, common staircases to balcony access, overflowing common dust-shoots, and batteries of common lavatories on the landings. Further out were square miles of ordinary working-class terrace housing: and then, where the hills began to lift the streets above the worst of the notorious winter yellow fog, pleasanter suburbs with gardens, where middle-class parents reared healthy children isolated from the problems of the majority. Yet, at least for the commuting fathers, this very isolation bred social guilt and fear:

> 'Every day, swung high upon embankments or buried deep in tubes underground, he hurries through the region where the creature lives. He gazes darkly from his pleasant hill villa upon the huge and smoky area of tumbled tenements which stretches at his feet. He is dimly distrustful of the forces fermenting in this uncouth laboratory.'[12]

Well might he fear. But bad as it was, London was not the most overcrowded city in Britain. On Tyneside, and throughout Scotland, housing expectations were altogether lower than in southern England. Indeed almost half of the entire Scottish population lived overcrowded. Half the Scottish housing stock consisted of one- or two-room houses. In towns of all sizes blocks of flats were common, so that young children had either to stay indoors all day or play unsupervised in the yards or the dark access passages. With the tenement itself containing no more than two fair-sized rooms with bed recesses opening off them, cooking, eating, washing, the drying of clothes and sleeping had to take place in the same rooms. For copulation, for childbirth or for death, little privacy was possible. Respectability for most Scottish families was only won through the exercise of severe self-discipline. The housing situation was worst in Glasgow, where three-quarters of the city's population lived in a central area of seven and a half square miles, in which the average density was 117 persons per acre. In the most overcrowded districts houses were 'ticketed' by the council in an attempt to control numbers, and families subjected to regular night raids by inspectors with lanterns and notebooks. But rehousing had scarcely begun.

If the housing was worse in Scottish than English cities, so was it in the Scottish countryside. Certainly there was a great deal of unsatisfactory rural housing in England. Few cottages had more than two bedrooms, leaking roofs and damp brick or earth floors were common, and even in model villages there was no drainage, no refuse collection and no running water. A candle or oil lamp was the only light. Water came from unreliable wells, or streams contaminated by sewage. The lack of facilities made the typical colliery village especially unpleasant, with its terraced housing looking across unmade mud streets to batteries of stinking ashpits and open privy-middens, overflowing at intervals when the contractors failed to empty them. But the Scottish miner, while provided with no better sanitation, could expect merely two rooms in his cottage. So could the farm labourer's family. Unmarried Scottish farm labourers were still worse off, for they slept communally in outbuildings. Yet at least they could expect to be dry. On the subsistence farms of the Outer Hebrides, the 'black house', once typical of the whole Highland region, remained normal.

Black houses were built by the crofters themselves of stones gathered from the moors, the walls several feet thick and filled with peat, the roof rafters of driftwood, the thatch of barley straw tied down with heather. The crofters had no mortar, and because driftwood was scarce they rested the roof on the inner instead of the outside edge of the wall. The rain came in by the exposed top of the wall, so that even if the thatch was sound the walls were dripping. The family kept dry at night by sleeping in roofed box beds in the end room of the house. In the middle room, set in a ring of stones in the centre of the floor, was a peat fire, whose smoke drifted up into the thatch. Here families and neighbours sat through the long winter evenings sewing, mending nets, telling stories, debating and singing. In the third room, beyond a partition which did not usually meet the roof, the cattle were kept for the winter. They helped to keep the house warm as well as providing valued manure for the croft in spring. In the spring too the smoke-impregnated thatch would be taken off for use as manure. Some black houses were 'improved', with boarded walls and a chimney in the middle room, but the older were without doubt the most elementary houses in Britain:

'Often they have no chimney, and sometimes no window; the floor is a bog, and a few boxes, with a plank supported

> by stones for a seat, is all the furniture except the unwholesome shut-in beds. Cleanliness is impossible, with a soot covering the roof overhead, wet mud for floor, and, except in the very rare fine days, chickens, and perhaps a sick sheep or even a cow or horse, for fellow-occupants.'

Confronted by the windswept, treeless landscape in which these houses stood, 'a wilderness of rock and standing water' not even divided into fields, the crofters' grain and potatoes rotting in the wet ground, one can understand the Edwardian traveller concluding: 'Nowhere in our proud Empire is there a spot more desolate, grim, hopelessly poverty-stricken.'[13]

Certainly there was in early twentieth-century Britain, as today, a gradient of poverty which ran from the south to the far north, a geographical distribution of inequality underlying and partly independent of inequality by social class. Nevertheless, one suspects that this imperial traveller had spent less time investigating the inner slums than the outer islands. One measure of what modest benefits had yet reached the British people from more than a century of industrialization and urbanization, and a measure also of the inequalities of British society, is the fact that the average working-class family in 1900 was still poorer in certain essentials than the subsistence farmers of the crofting counties. To argue this one does not need to cite the consolations of an ancient community culture, to juxtapose, from our 'Edwardians', the lives of Peter Henry and Will Thorn, or to contrast the defects of the black house, which at least stood free to the wind and the sky, with the gruesome suffocation of an environment like 'Coffin Close' in the Anderston district of Glasgow, its sunk flats approached by 'passages pitch dark on the brightest day, so that only by feeling along the walls can one discover the doors . . . In all these closes the stairs are filthy and evil-smelling, water-closets constantly choked, and foul water running down the stairs, sickly cats everywhere spreading disease . . .'[14]

However unpleasant, fortunately 'Coffin Close' was an extreme example of urban conditions in Edwardian Britain. What is more significant is that the *average* family was still less healthy and less well fed than those of the crofting counties. And in three of those counties, Argyll, Orkney and Shetland, where black houses had largely given way to two-room cottages, the chances of an infant surviving its first year were twice as good as the entire English average; three times as good as in such cradles of wealth as the cotton towns of Preston and Burnley, the potteries, many Durham mining towns; five times as good as for a child born in a London workhouse.

3 Country and Town

Britain in the 1900s was the most urbanized country in the world. Under a quarter of its people lived in rural districts and a mere seven per cent of its workforce was engaged in agriculture. The great wave of rural immigration into the towns was near its end. Already the populations of Germany and the United States, now challenging British industrial supremacy, had well surpassed Britain's forty-four millions, but a third of their workers still remained on the land. Ruthless urbanization had been one of the foundations of Britain's greater wealth.

Left to the mercies of the market, unprotected by state subsidies, the Edwardian countryside was economically and socially moribund. The country houses it is true kept their old splendour, assisted by infusions of industrial money. Great landed families such as the Churchills, Cecils and Greys continued to supply some of the nation's political leaders. They could still employ gardeners to pick up leaves from their mile-long avenues and village girls to staff their mansions. As Lady Bountifuls, distributors of winter blankets, coal and soup, landowners' wives claimed a natural right to interfere with the lives of village families, and took any challenge to that right as ungrateful insolence:

> 'My wife's father lived up in Over Grafton and most of the houses belonged to the Hawkins people, it was an estate you see. But my wife's father didn't work for Hawkins. He worked down at the mill, doing the dye work, and he rented a house up there. Well now, the old Lady Hawkins, she used to go round and give advice here and there to the people who worked for them, and she'd go round and pull the pot

lids off to see what they was cooking, and all things like that. And if they were having a meal at the dinner time and she went into any of the houses, she expected them to sit upright like the soldier does when the officer goes round at mealtime. She expected them to do that. And she went into my father-in-law's place one time and they were having a dinner. She expected them to do the same. Of course they were nothing to do with her actually, and the eldest brother went on with his dinner, and the others, they sort of half sat up and half went on. "Well," she said, "you rude boy" ... and she took his plate off him ... Oh, that was a terrible thing, see.'[1]

But if the social supremacy of the country houses was being maintained, it was equally significant that the great epoch of country-house building had ended with the collapse of agricultural prices in the 1870s. The rare new houses built for Edwardian landowners no longer boasted their novelty as had those of their mid-Victorian predecessors. They were discreet, irregular, looking as old as a new house could. Since land was no longer much of a source of wealth, the country house was valued more as a symbol of ancestry than of economic power. Old walls were thus more fashionable than new. With this change the landed aristocracy abandoned their leadership of English taste.

As they ceased building new houses for themselves, so they put less of their money into new model cottages and model farmsteads. Some had to cut their rents in order to get tenants to take their farms. With less money coming in, they merely kept the existing barns and houses in bare repair. Their farmers were a demoralized class. It was now cheaper to ship grain produced by homesteaders on the American prairie than to grow it in East Anglia. Four-fifths of Britain's wheat was imported. The countryside was dominated by grassland, for cattle and sheep were now the best-paying farm products. The north and west were thus less affected by the depression than the south and east, which had grown rich on corn-growing – one reason for the contrasting stories, among our Edwardians, of Peter Henry and

Fred Mills. But with refrigeration, even two-fifths of the meat eaten was brought in from abroad. There had been some development of milk farming linked to railway delivery, but very little of production for the potential city market in butter, eggs, bacon and poultry. The typical farmer preferred to concentrate on those traditional cash products which still paid, and to make ends meet by spending as little money as he could. He took on less labour. The unemployed could take the railway to the town. The wages of the farm labourers who remained were the lowest of any large occupational group. Except in the family farm regions of the north and west, where single farmhands still lived in, the average labourer's income was less than enough to maintain his family and himself in mere physical efficiency. In sickness or old age he could only choose between dependence upon an arrogant patronage or a humiliating Poor Law relief. Most labourers swallowed their pride and hid their smouldering anger in a servile but stubborn taciturnity. They worked in an English countryside which was never more beautiful or quiet, the great uncut hedges, abundant with flowers and small animals, arching over the empty lanes: the beauty of decay.

Although the life had drained out of southern English villages before 1914, they were still isolated enough for much of the old rural culture to survive: crafts, home-made wines, foods and medicines, superstitions, dialects, a canny observation of nature, poaching. A farmer could have a horse and cart and his children bicycles, but the labourer's family were still confined to walking distance. Unless they took a Sunday newspaper, their only taste of mass entertainment would be the annual travelling fair. The rare political speaker on tour would present the only public alternative to the views offered from the pulpit. Even a visit to the neighbouring market town could be something of a momentous event.

In isolated regions traditional cultures had survived more fully still. Language was one indication of this. English had to be taught as a second language to Shetland children, in most of Wales and in the Gaelic-speaking Hebrides. Many aspects of the economy and culture of such regions remained astonishingly archaic: open fields with family strips rotated by lot, the renting of land in return for labour services, the grinding of corn by stone hand querns, the barter of handwoven cloth, the use of eggs instead of coin as currency. There was a time span in the culture of Edwardian Britain itself comparable to that between the contemporary western city and a village of the under-developed world. At Cambridge Rutherford had already begun his work on the atom. At the same time families still survived on St Kilda, paying the rent for their inaccessible Atlantic out-crop by the barter of the cloth their women wove from the island sheep's wool. They lived off the flesh and eggs of seabirds captured from the cliffs, brushed their floors with seabirds' wings and burned seabird oil in their lamps. Like early Christians, they divided their harvest according to need, and spent long hours with their missionary, chanting the strange medieval dirge of the Gaelic psalms. Their only regular contact with the outside world was when steamers brought tourists to gape at them.

The ordinary contrast between town and country was much less sharp than this; but it is hardly surprising that a steady stream of country children made for the towns as soon as they left school. Young women could find work as servants in middle-class homes. Young men could follow when they had picked up one of the building trades, or learnt to handle a horse. Alternatively they could take up an occupation for which the knack of deference was a qualification, as in the army, the police or the railway service. The current of migration affected all classes: among our 'Edwardians', Peter Henry, Will Askham, even Lady Violet Brandon, as well as Fred Mills. What differences would they find in life in the towns?

To move from a southern country village into London was certainly to see a startling transformation. London with its seven million people was the largest city in the world, cosmopolitan as an international capital and seaport. Birmingham, Glasgow, Liverpool and Manchester, with nearly a million each, were also great cities by the standards of the 1900s. They followed London in its pattern of suburban spread, travel to work by train and tram and residential separation of classes. The cutting of direct personal contact between the classes was already, as we have seen, fostering fears of class hostility. And there were visible enough grounds for hostility in the astonishing contrasts between the poverty of London's slums and the affluent parades and service trades of its West End. Indeed this range of city social worlds – from Brandons and Fulfords down to Thorns – will be one of the themes of our 'Edwardians'. But an equally important aspect of the cities was their fluidity. Migration continued within them, as well as into them. Settled working-class neighbourhoods and middle-class suburbs were certainly developing, but there was still frequent movement in search of work and housing. This hindered the development of class community feeling, and thus probably class consciousness, in the cities: as, among our 'Edwardians', with a working-class family like the Durhams.

The cities also provided, through a different kind of movement, an important anticipation of the late twentieth century. Britain in the 1900s was by modern standards an ethnically homogeneous society. Even immigration from Ireland had dwindled to the point at which the Irish-born numbered only one per cent of the entire population. Alien immigrants did not quite reach this figure. The largest group among them was Jewish, driven by persecution from Eastern Europe. They had, however, settled in the cities, concentrated in small inner districts, in a pattern which foreshadowed later waves of immigration, not only through overcrowded housing and competition with older residents for already poorly paid work, but also in their uneven path towards social integration, marked by considerable social prejudice and political protest. Still smaller numerically, there were also already, in a few of the early twentieth-century ports, black communities; and partly because of their significance for the present, one of our 'Edwardians' will be Harriet Vincent.

Another, who also looks to the future, is Sidney Ford. The emergence of clerical workers as a distinctive social group is very much a phenomenon of the years around 1900, especially in London, where they were more numerous than in the industrial north, and where residential social segregation helped particular suburbs like Lewisham to develop the reputation of being strongholds of the lower middle and upper working class. 'To the superior mind,' wrote T. W. H. Crosland, author of *The Suburbans*, in 1905, 'in fact, "suburban" is a sort of label which may be properly applied to pretty well everything on the earth that is ill-conditioned, undesirable and unholy': tasteless people, oyster bars, small shops, free libraries, Methodist chapels and so on. He could perhaps have added recitals, debating societies, drama and sports clubs, for there is certainly evidence that very varied voluntary activities flourished in the suburbs. Much of this was similar to the culture of the prosperous working class in industrial towns. But Crosland feared that the commuting of so many workers out of the suburb, leaving a weekday population chiefly of women and children, must sap the nascent local community. He also portrayed, in a nice imaginative passage, the effect of such ecological arrangements on family relationships:

> 'When the gentleman of the house arrives he is usually grumpy. That upstart Jones has been browbeating him at the office. "Nostrils" has gone down at Kempton Park, and the gentleman's week's lunch-money has gone with it. Or the train has been fogged up for a whole twenty minutes . . . He sinks into his well-cracked, saddle-bag, gent's arm-chair as one who has the cares of all the world upon him. He inquires why it is that "the damned dinner" is never ready, despite the fact that there are three women in the house . . . He pronounces the soup to be filth . . . The *Daily Telegraph* may well say that marriage is a failure . . .'[2]

The cities, then, looked to the future. But the suburbs constituted but one section of them, and the cities as a whole still provided for a minority. The typical Edwardian lived in the smaller industrial or country towns, which altogether accounted for half of the national population. These towns also varied a great deal in social character. Market towns shared much of the spirit of the countryside upon which they depended. Seaside towns, as well as Oxford and Cambridge and the remaining inland spas, were dominated by their numerous middle-class residents. With the need for middle-class patronage, both working men and shopkeepers learned to be obsequious. Industrial towns tended to be less hierarchical in atmosphere, but here again there were marked differences between towns. Edwardian towns normally concentrated upon a single type of industry. In some, both men and women could earn well, as in the textile towns of the north and the boot, hat and hosiery towns of the Midlands. In the iron and steel and coal towns, on the other hand, the rough, highly paid work was almost entirely carried out by men. Ports were again distinctive, offering plentiful low-paid factory work for women, the wives and daughters of impoverished dockers. These differing economic opportunities affected the type of community and family life which developed.

There was also the effect of time. In older towns established networks had developed, both of patronage and of neighbouring. This was less so in the new boom districts, such as those parts of South Wales and South Yorkshire where mining was rapidly expanding. Here there would be large numbers of young men lodging with families, outnumbering the local young women, and liable to seek consolation in drink, religion or politics.

Lastly, there was the effect of size. Edwardian towns as a whole were far smaller and denser than today. Even from central London the countryside was only two hours away on foot, half an hour on a bicycle. And while the modern city imposes its pattern of housing and cars imperviously across the countryside, the early twentieth-century town was much more obviously dependent upon the land from which it grew. While the principal form of transport remained the horse, constant supplies of hay had to be brought in, and large numbers of horses stabled within the town. There were a quarter of a million horses in London alone, dragging rattling carts and carriages across the stone sets, their droppings swept aside by crossing sweepers and picked up for sale by ingenious poor boys. There were also considerable numbers of cattle kept by dairymen. Many families too, often drawn recently into the town but retaining country tastes in food, kept hens, rabbits, pigeons and even pigs in their back yards. But all this was more possible in the smaller towns, where there was more likely to be the space for animals, and it was easier to pick up food for them. In a really dense city district, migrants from the country would only keep in touch with their backgrounds by spending holidays with relatives who had remained in the village. The smallest industrial towns, by contrast, not merely allowed them to continue many rural habits, but often even provided a social structure of the village type in which the landed squire was replaced by the mill-owner. The old rural underworld could also continue. A pottery town like Hanley was congested enough within its bounds:

> 'The houses of the town are small, and are closely packed along the narrow streets. Here and there, at irregular intervals, rise the upper parts of the pottery ovens, which constitute the characteristic feature of the town, and above these rise great chimney shafts. At places on the north-west outskirts are tall colliery headings, the rusty roofs of iron foundry sheds, and, still further away, the wide grounds of a brick works, with deeply dug clay pits. The smoke and steam, which are the accompaniment of the local industry, have given to many parts of the town an atmosphere of grime and neglect.'[3]

Nevertheless, it was only a few minutes from the dense terraces to the open fields. A miner with too many children to feed easily could always find help from that quarter:

> 'My father's had many a rabbit from pub off poachers. Oh aye. Perhaps a price of a pint of beer he's bought a rabbit off somebody who's a bit stuck. Oh they used to take 'em in pubs you know, rabbits to sell, have a pint or a couple of pints for one. Oh yes, there's a fair lot of poachers about here, we had. They used to come round selling them Sunday mornings. Aye, got 'em slung over the shoulder. He'd go out all Saturday night, perhaps all Friday night, and he's come round. Oh aye, did that regular.'[4]

For all that, the towns were a different world. There were the facilities like running water, gas and more recently electricity; public baths and public libraries. The streets were noisy with horse traffic, trams and the new motor buses, and in the north the clatter of workpeople's clogs. There were bakeries, cookshops and restaurants, street markets, Co-operative stores and the branches of cheap chain stores. Salesmen toured the sidestreets offering cockles, kippers, muffins and coal. During the day crowds of children played street football, pitch and toss, or with marbles, hoops and skipping ropes, fleeing at the sight of the policeman on his regular beat. At night the men could be seen 'congregating at the street corners, rattling about anything. There wasna much drinking done in the week. But at weekends there was plenty.'[5] On Saturday nights the town streets would be packed with men emptying from the pubs, women finishing their pay-night shopping, and adolescent boys and girls strolling to and fro in the 'monkey parade', eyeing each other hopefully. There was plenty of indoor entertainment for them too: music halls, an increasing number of cinemas and also church and chapel activities such as concerts, debates and lantern shows.

Then, as today, there were great inequalities in the public facilities provided in towns, so that for example, while well-to-do Edinburgh had an acre of public open space for every 130 of its people, in the working-class steel town of Middlesbrough there was only an acre for every 1,040 inhabitants. But a working-class town in the era before radio and television was less at a disadvantage in entertainment than today. There would be visits from famous touring theatre and opera companies as well as music hall performers. There was also a flourishing local musical life, with choirs and brass bands competing at regional festivals. A Darlington furnaceman's daughter recalls with regret the days of chapel concerts, Co-operative lectures on Shakespeare and the classics, local choirs and bands:

'I could name nearly half a dozen choirs. Male voice choirs and mixed choirs. And orchestras. There was a chamber orchestra, a Darlington orchestra. There was a Miss Kate Jackson that used to take pupils for violin, she used to have an orchestra. And they were all very thriving. The Co-operative movement in those days was not just a shopping movement, it was also an educational movement ...

Looking back, there was far more culture, what I would call cultural activities in Darlington than there are now. It's very starved of cultural activities now.'[6]

It was indeed perhaps – for this is an impression, and not an analysis from our survey evidence – such relatively small industrial towns, rather than the big cities, which manifested the most fully developed working-class urban culture in the early twentieth century. Certainly in mining and steel districts, and where there was manufacturing such as textiles, engineering or shipbuilding requiring a substantial skilled workforce, there were relatively good regular earnings to be had. There was thus an economic basis upon which an organized culture of church, chapel, friendly society and trade union could be built. Families could afford to buy a piano and new Sunday suits; men to drink with their workmates, or put an offering in the chapel collecting dish, or both. Some of these more prosperous working-class families were too anxious for privacy and respectability to encourage frequent calling and company. But those who wanted to welcome friends had the spare chairs and food needed for entertaining. Neighbours would drop in for tea, or for cards and singsongs at the piano in the evenings. Children would be running in and out without ceremony. A Keighley child's neighbour 'had a harmonium in their house and if they wanted me to go in they used to knock you see, knock at the wall . . . Oh, I weren't two minutes before I was in there.'[7] One of our 'Edwardians', Gwen Davies, a Welsh tin rollerman's daughter, remembers her mother's motto: 'To be rich in friends was to be rich indeed.'[8]

Generous neighbouring, besides bringing intrinsic pleasures, brought a security which these relatively well-paid families needed. It provided another kind of insurance against the possibility of unemployment which haunted even a regular worker such as a railwayman:

'I remember in those days [my father] was slightly going grey, he went grey very quickly. And he used to try and

> change his hair, dyes wasn't out in those days, and the soot from the chimney he used to get that, mix it with butter and put it on, and of a weekend his hair was snow white because he'd washed it. He did that to appear younger because if you looked older your job was finished. It seemed you were getting old you couldn't get on. He was always afraid it would put him out.'[9]

Workmates who collected money for an injured friend, or passed the hat round in the pub to pay the fine of a convicted drunk, knew that they might find themselves in the same difficulty. There was a similar understanding which made even an aloof artisan's wife believe in helping a neighbour in trouble:

> 'My mother never did a lot of gossiping. She never went in a lot of people's houses, never . . . [But] see anybody what were ill. Now they wouldn't have to ask me mother. "Oh Mrs So-an-So's ill." No sooner me mother knew, she'd go in and she'd knock at door, "Can I do anything for you? Can I mop your flags? Can I do a bit of baking for you? Do a bit of cleaning?" '[10]

Some households exchanged help on a regular basis. But it would be a mistake to overemphasize the element of neat calculation in neighbouring relationships. There were many cases in which help went far beyond any return which could be anticipated. Small families, for example, would lend a bedroom for children from large ones rent-free. A mother with several daughters would send one regularly, and again free, to clean for an old couple. Conversely, in many cases help was not in fact given free. It was quite common to pay even a relative for assistance. And there were also many families who found in a moment of need, such as a confinement, that neither neighbours nor relatives were prepared to give any significant help. 'They all had their own families to look after.'[11] Even a crisis as great as the death of a parent might bring no response. A Staffordshire brickmaker's son remembered the abrupt change when his father died. The family had kept the front room for

> 'when relatives called or someone like that, you see, and when my father died of course the relatives didn't seem to cling to you as well, it was a case of what we used to term soldier on and do the best you can . . . *When your father died, had you any help at all from friends or relatives or were you more or less left?* Oh no, left, left. My mother, she had a little bit of club money, of course . . .'[12]

She was only able to support the family by working as a washer-woman, and with help from the Board of Guardians.

No firm lines can be drawn to separate the different styles of life within the urban working classes, for each merged into the next. Even the generally recognized distinction between the rough and respectable was a flexible one, raised or lowered according to the standpoint of the observer. Nevertheless there was a wide gap between these industrial neighbourhoods and the ubiquitous poverty of the inner city slum. Working-class families here – Will Thorn is an example from our 'Edwardians' – had the bare resources to live from day to day. They could not afford to subscribe to trade unions or friendly societies. They were not interested in church attendance unless it brought them gifts such as free boots, soup and coal. Friends could not be invited in, because there was nothing to give them. The men, characteristically labouring at the docks, transport or building, were chronically under-employed. Because they went to work unfed and were often not strong enough to finish a full day, they were taken on and paid by the hour only. They spent hours waiting at places of call in the hope of a chance of earning. Foremen would pick from the crowd before them with the disdain of cattle dealers, or throw the work tokens among the men so that they could fight for them, or set up a degrading competition such as a race to seize three shovels set up against a wall. In times of depression, and in the winter season, there was still less work, even for the labourers' women who were employed in sweated hand trades such as boxmaking, sack-making and slopwork (cheap garment-making). During the 1900s, when the government first set up local distress committees, the applicants for relief in many inner city working-class districts represented more than a third of all families.

Mass poverty supported a peculiarly systematic economy. Very little that could be re-used was wasted. Children picked from street gutters, rubbish heaps and river banks. They crawled under market stalls to look for fallen food, and queued at public houses and restaurants for the day's leftovers. When a London horse died, its body was meticulously divided. Its skin was taken for leather, its bones boiled for oil and then ground for manure, its flesh cooked for cats' meat. Even its feet were taken apart, the skin and hoof for the glue factory, the bone for the buttonmaker and the old shoes for the farrier. Women, as patient, cheap workers, were especially used for refuse work. At contractors' and local authority refuse dumps they stood in lines, each with a sieve and several baskets.

> 'As the carts bringing the refuse enter the yard they are emptied in front of each woman in turn, and a man is employed to spade the refuse into the sieves. After sifting out all the dust the women then sort the remainder into different baskets, separating carefully the ashes, china, paper, tins, glass bottles, corks and "soft core".'[13]

Each was disposed of differently. The dust was sent by barge to brickfields for mixing into brick clay; china and hard core were used for roads; paper and soft core for manure; tins for ship ballast; glass for emery paper, and so on. In a society in which labour was so cheap, there was no doubt that it paid to recycle waste.

There was another face to the culture of poverty, to which contemporary observers gave rather more attention. The poorer working class may have been less often brought together through the exchange of services in their neighbours' houses, but they certainly formed an active social community on the streets. Like many of the very similar features of black ghetto poverty in American cities today, this was seen as evidence of hereditary degeneration and incapacity. The critics forgot that even the poor need fun and hope to make life bearable, and that their overcrowded rooms forced them to act out their social lives on the streets. Children would break into dancing in the street and families sit out on their doorsteps chatting. Men who could not get work were seen as loafers if they stood at the street corners, dissolute if they entered the pubs. Still worse were the mothers who drank or fought in public in their nightdresses, shrieking as they pulled each other's hair. The brave outdoor preachers who struggled for their souls were obviously fighting a losing battle:

> 'Walk down Union Street on any Saturday night. The bright electric globes, the warm glow of the gas lamps, where, to the braying of the Salvation Army bands, a motley crowd surges to and fro. There is the blue of the sailors, the red of the soldiers, and the gauds and fripperies of innumerable women. Through the windows of many chapels pious anthems go upwards, through the swing-doors of the countless public-houses noisy ribaldries abound. King Beer and Queen Gin hold high revelries within a stone's throw of where pale women count the coppers that are to feed their children for a whole week to come.'[14]

Should not such fecklessness alone justify the strictest meanness when such families approached the Relieving Officer?

4 Childhood

It was a man's world, despite poverty; at least so long as a man's strength lasted. Adult men had the lion's share of the national income. They alone had the vote. As fathers they were heads of household in law. And there were many families in the early twentieth century which seemed to observe among themselves the same hierarchy of privilege and command which characterized society as a whole: 'I've seen people walking out together with the husband walking two paces in front of the wife ... The children tailing behind them too.'[1] Was this typical of the Edwardian family? Was the father so much king, the children and mother so separate and subordinate, as this public procession suggests?

Certainly the ordinary Edwardian parent was not much troubled by notions of family democracy or equal rights for children. The common assumption was a relationship of mutual obligation between parents and children which distinctly resembled that between master and servant. Parents provided food, clothing and shelter as best they could: in return, children owed respect and obedience until they set up homes of their own. Parents of all social classes demanded respect. A London packing-case maker recalled that he wanted his children to behave 'in a deferential sort of way, you know. We've got to be respected.'[2] On the other side, a Nottingham child's view of his parents was characteristic: 'They was your father and mother – you respected them as mother and father, aye.'[3]

It is also true, although less universally so, that in many families this respect focused upon the father, especially when he was the only breadwinner. In a small working-class house there was not much room for a man to relax after a hard day's work if children were about, so that many mothers, like a London sheet metal worker's wife,

> 'tried to get them to bed before my husband came home – of course, he would be half past six to seven – if I could get them to bed beforehand. Or perhaps Alec might be up – but the two younger ones I'd always get to bed. 'Cause a man don't want yarney children when they come home to a meal.'[4]

There were other households in which the children ate their evening meal with their parents, but under conditions which reduced to a minimum any possible friction with their father's needs. In a skilled engineer's home in Lancashire, for example,

> 'at night, when they'd all come in, me father'd come home from work and he'd pick *Bolton Evening News* up while tea was being set on the table ... He sat in rocking chair and when he said go you started ... Then we'd all sit down, have our tea and then there was no talking. And then he'd come away from table and we came away then. Now anybody wanted pick up that paper they could while he had a smoke; then when he finished that pipe of bacca that paper must be on the table ready to him starting reading. He had a matter of half an hour to glance through paper at night time and then when he'd finished with it, when he was getting washed like for night you could all have a look at it. If you were in – cos you used like get out as quick as you could after you'd had your tea, because if you stayed in and you started making any noise you were upstairs.'[5]

The father here was an under-foreman and the mother well enough off to employ a weekly washerwoman. The children had to call her Auntie Meg to avoid any suggestion that in terms of social class they were not 'all on one footing'. Nevertheless, in some senses the atmosphere here was more like a lower-middle-class than an ordinary working-class household. With some paid help, it was more understandable that the men should sit back when they came home. Even the boys were being prepared for such a future, for while the girls cleaned their own bedroom, the mother looked after the boys' room. The boys thus had more freedom from an early age. But this at once opened them to a world of influences very distant from those of the middle class, for, like the overwhelming majority of working-class children, they played outside 'with a gang of lads round t'houses, round corner . . . Play in't street. In't back street, in't front street or at bottom there was spare ground down there.'[6]

In a typical working-class family, children did not come out into the street just to play. As they grew older they would be expected, not only to play a part in the household tasks of cleaning, washing and preparing fuel, but also to earn money from other houses.

> 'These high class people, cleaning the silvers in their homes, after school. Go home and get a cup of tea and come down, tap on the door, "Can I come in madam?" Soon as they recognise you, "Oh come on boy, here's the silver, in the front room ready for you on the table." ' They learned to harden themselves to rebuffs as they went looking for odd jobs: 'Get away, boy, that's our gate, get away' – or even, 'Get off footpath, let me come by you.'[7]

There were coppers to be earned in many ways: running errands, washing steps and windowsills, minding babies, catching vermin, delivering milk or meat, selling papers or matches in the street, cab ducking or carrying bags for strangers. Most parents regarded such children's earnings as a valuable supplement to the family income, and expected most of it to be handed over. It was the same with a child's first full-time earnings after leaving school: a wage of perhaps five shillings would be presented to the parents, and simply a few pennies returned as pocket money.

If parents made use of their children to subsidize the family income, in doing so they helped to free their children of their own influence. On the streets, as in the school playgrounds, a remarkably independent children's culture flourished, with its own secret pacts and passwords, ancient rhymes and adaptations from Edwardian music halls, old seasons and new fashions. This children's culture was in its own way as savage, competitive and hierarchical as that of adults. Boys generally had to learn to fight their way to respect, and there were some places in which male pride was so emphasized that a boy could only play with his own sister in the privacy of the home. 'I never used to play with the sister outside, if I did that I should be called a "cissie" in them days, aye.'[8] But this culture did give children some small means of retaliation against adults. All over Britain the common street games included such tricks as running down a street knocking doors (knock down ginger), tapping on a window with a needle tied to a piece of cotton, and pushing cabbage smokebombs into letterboxes. Avaricious pedestrians would be led on by parcels left on the pavement on the end of a cotton, which would be jerked as they reached to pick up the find. Irritable neighbours would be provoked to quarrel by so tying their doors together that opening one banged the knocker of the other. Even the noisome street privy had its assets for children, who would surprise a sitting enemy by stealthily opening a back flap and thrusting a burning candle under his naked backside, to the victim's angry cry: 'Nobody's goin' to set my arse afire. I'll get the police.'[9]

The borderline between rough and respectable behaviour was much less clear in the children's street culture than in the adult world. Few children, for example, would have been ashamed of being caught stealing apples. If they found themselves among a group who 'brought ourselves up' because their parents were too preoccupied or drunken to take close care of them, their activities might move towards delinquency: window breaking, jumping at girls, or stealing from their own parents:

> 'Me friends, the whole gang of us, the one that used to stand near the shop door – his mother and father . . . used to come home on a Friday night drunk and what this young fellow used to do, rifle their pockets. Take so much out and on Saturday afternoon he'd come and we'd all go for a walk

then, along the river bank, that was Irwell river . . . and he'd buy a load of these cigarettes, Turkish, Russian, and buy a load of toffee, cakes. And then we'd go along like lords along the river puffing away these fancy Russian cigarettes, red tipped ones, golden tipped – and have a good feed. It was all stolen money. They'd never miss it.'[10]

In spite of these dangers, only a minority of working-class parents attempted to restrict their children's choice of playmates. Girls were more often restricted than boys, but even with the daughters of skilled men restriction was less common than free choice. Working-class parents in general did not have an elaborate view of their responsibilities for the moral education of their children. Most of them tried to inculcate the virtues of truthfulness, cleanliness and respectability in conduct and manners. Only a small minority were prepared to tolerate swearing. Most refused to allow children to hear any discussion of sex, and for this reason would not explain the facts of life to them, or in some cases even permit them to read newspapers. But few of them had the time and energy, even given the inclination, to enter into moral refinements or provide spiritual frills. These were largely left to the Sunday school teachers and, to a lesser extent, the elementary school. This was distinctly different from typical middle-class parents, who were less likely to support Sunday schools, preferring to give their children religious instruction themselves. Their larger houses and the help of servants gave them more daily respite from their children's company, and Sundays were taken as an opportunity for expressing parental concern. With the more harassed working-class couple, by contrast, even in the cities where church-going was a minority habit among adults, Sunday school attendance was almost universally insisted upon if only because it could provide them with their only certain hour of privacy in the whole week.

How far did most Edwardians regard the giving of affection as a parental duty? It has been suggested by the sociologists John and Elizabeth Newson that 'a relationship of real friendship' between parents and children is a new possibility resulting from the more flexible attitudes of contemporary parents to discipline.[11] In fact there can be little doubt that the most distant parents were to be found among the well-to-do, even though these parents were much more likely to use reasoning rather than physical punishment to enforce their authority. A child in such households would often be handed over from infancy to the care of a nurse, and would sleep, wash, eat and play for most of the day in its own nursery quarters, leading an entirely separate life from its parents. Only at the end of each day after nursery tea would it be brought down to the drawing room, scrubbed and in clean clothes, to spend half an hour with its mother. Boys, and increasingly girls, would later on be still further distanced by being sent to a boarding school, from which the only legitimate contact with parents would be a weekly letter and a visit once in three months. Well-to-do children were financially absolutely dependent upon their parents, who expected to support them through education, help them find a career and very often set them up in business as well as endow them in other ways. But emotionally these children were as likely to find support and friendship in a servant as a parent. A Lancashire doctor's daughter felt so distant from her father that: 'once I remember I was very worried about my mother because she wasn't well; and rather than talk to him, I wrote him a letter and left it for him in the surgery. I was still at home; but I wrote this letter, rather than talk to him.'[12]

There were some middle-class mothers, perhaps an increasing number, who spent much more time in the nursery, or encouraged their children to play throughout the house; and among the less well-off the daughters were more likely to be brought closer to their mother through working together in the house. But in working-class families, by contrast, it was normal for children to share in the work of the house, and for a mother to give her own care and attention, especially to a sick child or an infant. At a time when many more children's illnesses resulted in death, sickness usually brought out all the tenderness and patient nursing that parents could give. Babies, too, were generally given ready affection. They were not normally disciplined before they could toddle, and, except in certain districts such as cotton towns where married women commonly worked in factories, a majority of mothers still breast-fed their infants. Many mothers did not wean suckling babies for a year or even two years, and recall the pleasure of nursing:

> 'When they were born I used to cuddle them up – 'cause you can love them then, can't you? When they got bigger, well ... And when they got married – well they don't belong to you.'[13]

Nor was it so uncommon for working-class parents, despite their long hours of work in the home and outside, to find time to be close to their children when they were no longer babies. We could cite Gwen Davies from our 'Edwardians'. A Wiltshire cowman's son provides another instance of real friendship between himself and his father, a widower:

> 'We was one: him and me was one. I'd always go to him with any troubles, and he used to listen and if he could help me he did and when we sit on the couch like we did (we had a big old-fashioned sofa) he used to put his arm all round my shoulders. We used to sit there sometimes of an evening, cuddled up to him.'[14]

There was, however, undoubtedly another attitude to the display of affection which was also widespread among working-class families. Self-control here was as much valued as among middle-class public schoolboys: 'None of us wears his heart on our sleeves. We was brought up to keep us moans and us groans to ourselves.'[15] It seems that families which deliberately sought to inhibit the expression of feeling in this way were commoner in the north. Frank Benson's will be an example. The impact of evangelical puritanism on the industrial working classes may provide part of the explanation, but equally the hardships of industrial work itself may have left a deep scar on life within the family. It is certainly clear that some of the most distant parents were those who resented being trapped in a bitter struggle for a decent living.

Some were the mothers of large families who had to work full-time as well for ten hours in a mill, or take in sweated factory outwork, to make ends meet. They would find it difficult to show affection for children whose existence itself was partly responsible for their situation. 'My mother nursed a bit of bitterness because she had a big family and would have liked to have done different . . . Me mother used to be upset when she used to see her sister with only two and we'd the houseful.' Her resentment was likely to be all the more – as we shall find with the Durhams and the Toweys – if her difficulties were partly due to a husband who not merely earned little, but spent much of what little he earned on drink:

> 'Very bitter my mother. Because she used to say to him, that he could do better and what he spent on beer he could have provided her with a dashed good meal . . . Oh he was full of the joys of spring, were me father. Used to come home and play the piano and sing like a lark. And me mother used to just play the devil with him.'[16]

A woman had little choice but to put up with such a man, for if she found herself entirely without his earnings, either through permanent injury, or through death or desertion, her situation was in many ways still worse. Probably the children fared best when they were taken over by grandparents. If they were sent to an aunt, they were much less likely to be welcomed; while if their mother married again, they often found themselves openly disliked by a harsh stepfather, especially if the mother chose a second man with the same failings as the first: 'He was a piece of a rotter. He used to drink and come home and knock me mother about. And if we used to stick up for her he used to say, "Well you'll have to clear out". He just wanted his own four.'[17] The experiences of some Edwardian children at the hands of step-parents, and even of their grandparents, is sufficient to cure any nostalgia for an earlier age in which more children – principally because a parent died – were partly brought up by relatives and others outside their parents' household. Conversely, the fate of some of those whose parents struggled on could be equally bitter. One Liverpool woman had married a Scots seaman, later a docker, who disappeared for long periods drinking his small earnings. They 'had kids like rabbits', altogether nineteen, of whom only seven lived to adulthood. The father deserted, but she tracked him down to London. She earned money taking in washing, especially from ships. Eventually he stopped working altogether after an accident, and she had to face the further humiliations of dealing with the Relieving Officer:

> 'This chap come down and she took the clothes off us and washed them and put them on the line see, to air. Cos we did have something she put on us anyway. And this fellow come down, he'd a stick and he said, "Oh", he said, "you're not destitute," he said, "you've got clothes on the line," he said, "and you've got a plate of fish and meat," he said. So she said, "Yes," she said, "you know how much that cost," she said, "that cost me fourpence." . . . "Oh," he said, "you're not destitute, you'd better come up to the committee." Oh they were beasts them days, absolute beasts they were . . . really cruel to people. You daren't have a mat on the floor. Cos we only had orange boxes for tables and chairs you see, with covers on them.'

No wonder that this mother, fighting against such odds to bring up her surviving children decently, was a stern figure at the family table:

> 'She was very strict . . . She'd have a little stick, a little thing what they called a cat o' nine tails on the table and if we was all sitting down to our meals then we mustn't speak, you had to get on with your meals, and no putting off your plate on the other one's plate what you didn't like – not to put it on that plate, you'd got to eat it. You had to eat it.'[18]

The strictness of Edwardian parents did not, however, necessarily imply abundant physical punishment, as is often believed.

It is not true that families in which children were given a 'good hiding for the least thing' were common.[19] The truth is that they did not need to, because their authority was rarely openly challenged. The experience of a shop manager was typical:

> 'I only ever hit my youngest lad once. They never had a real thrashing, and the only time it was, he brushed some bread on the floor, and I said, "Pick it up." And he wouldn't. And I made him pick it up because I knew that I had to be master. But they never got a thrashing otherwise.'[20]

There were also many artisan households, no less strict, in which the father commanded undisputed obedience: 'He never hit us. Well, he'd no need to hit us with the telling off he give us . . . He didn't tell us twice.'[21]

There was also a significant number of labouring families, especially in the countryside, rather less severe, in which the children were never physically punished. 'We knew when Dad spoke that was it. They never laid a hand on us.'[22] M. E. Loane, a nurse who worked extensively in the southern countryside and towns, wrote how the extent of harshness in working-class homes was greatly exaggerated: 'In all my experience I doubt if I have come across as many as twelve cruelly used children; not one of those was persistently ill-treated.'[23]

Charles Booth observed similarly from his experience of London that working-class children were 'more likely to suffer from spoiling than from harshness'.[24] In the industrial north and Midlands, on the other hand, there was almost certainly a more frequent use of slapping and also of severer forms of chastisement. One of the immeasurable costs of the industrial revolution, indeed, may in this way have been wrought indiscriminately on the bodies of children.

Probably the freest, if not always the least punished Edwardian children, were those from the very poorest, 'roughest' city families. They brought themselves up on the street, because there was too little room at home for themselves and their parents, when they were not out working or drinking. These children relied for clothing less on their parents than on charity and the police. For food they depended on free mission suppers, soup kitchens, school meals, restaurant leavings, begging and stealing. And long before they left school, they could earn enough to free them of financial dependence on their parents. A South London boy, son of a coal heaver, who 'fetched ourself up' in this way, described his parents as 'two of the biggest drunkards in Waterloo and Blackfriars'. He was the youngest of a family of thirteen children dispersed among various relatives and truant schools. While his parents moved between pub, workhouse and prison, he was out selling papers and pushing a barrow vending hearthstone and vinegar. He developed a method of simulating ringworm on his skin which successfully deceived the school authorities:

> 'I was away from school three or four months at a time. Yes. Over Covent Garden with a sack, a sackful of broken-up wood, you know, flower boxes, back over Waterloo Bridge, down Tenison Street, where Waterloo station is now, knock at door, "Firewood, ma'am?" "How much?" "Twopence the bagful." "No, give you a penny or three halfpence." "No." "All right." Shoot it down the area and back over the Garden four or five times and earn about eightpence, or something like. Used to go over Bert's, Farringdon Street, next to Earl's Corner, a packet of envelopes and paper in a pub – 'cause you was allowed in – we used to play on the sawdust in pubs then – envelopes and paper penny a packet. I'd sell a packet – I'd earned fourpence out of that. Back again for another – that's how we used to get hold of money. No, we never used to get anything out of our parents – nor pocket money anyway. They never had enough for their beer.'[25]

Here we have a type of independence essentially resulting from the powerlessness of parents who had themselves abandoned or failed in the fight to keep a home together in an unequal society. But at the other end of the social scale there was another significant minority of children whose upbringing also seemed less restrictive than was normal, at least at first impression. They came from upper- and middle-class families whose abundance of resources made it as easy to smother a child with the apparent kindness of professional diagnoses as to drill it in the traditional manner. Here was the vanguard of future fashion:

> 'Punishment is taboo. Long moral lectures, full of well-balanced argument, interspersed with an occasional intimation that the lecturer has been deeply grieved and hurt, are, if I understand the advice tendered to the managers of modern nurseries, to take the place of old-fashioned punishments. Before even these mild correctives are administered, a doctor must be called in to see if the fault is due to some defect of health; and, generally speaking, the business of correcting thumb-sucking, nail-biting, small tempers, or the vagaries of some seven-year-old lady . . . will occupy the entire time and attention of one medical specialist, one ethical lecturer, two parents, and a nurse . . .[26]

It is however an interesting and possibly highly significant paradox that the most generally 'progressive' parents in Edwardian Britain were to be found in a particularly 'primitive' region. Among the families of the Shetland crofters children were treated less unequally than anywhere else in Britain. Here too the authority of parents was accepted, but it was imposed with reasoning rather than punishment. It was the only part of the country in which physical punishment was not socially approved. On the crofts, on which parents often lived with grandparents, children shared in the work from an early age. At the common table, like adults, they were not forced to eat food they did not want, their conversation was welcomed, and when they had finished they could leave without asking. They also shared in the common social life of the community, including even dances. There were very few public houses, but instead men and women called frequently on each other, customarily walking into the house without a knock on the door. When there was company, Shetland children stayed up late, like Peter Henry, with their parents round the fire, perhaps making kishies (baskets) as they talked together.

It is not easy to explain customs so much more gentle, generous, indeed, civilized towards children than those of the ordinary British family of all classes. One can only observe that the Shetlanders had been unaffected by industrialization and urbanization, and less than most of the north by religious puritanism; that there was less class stratification within their communities; and that just as the dimensions of inequality between adults and children were reduced, so the position of women in their families was also in some respects unusually favourable. We may have here the survival of old rural traditions, which had also lingered to a lesser extent in southern England. Alternatively, the peculiar economy of the crofter-fishermen, combined with the shift to smaller families, may have generated patterns special to the last hundred years. For the moment we know too little of the history of childhood to do more than speculate.

5 Youth

Tension between young and middle-aged adults is no new development of the late twentieth century. It was well set in by the Edwardian era, and indeed long before it. By their mid teens young adults were able to earn and were sexually mature, but they had not yet taken on the burden of maintaining a household of their own. Physically and economically they were ready for independence. Their moral education was formally complete, for few continued to attend Sunday School once they started work: 'I wouldn't lower me dignity. I was finished with that.'[1] Yet it was in the interests of their parents, who had so far supported them, now to share something of their growing capacity to earn, and so to retain control of them within the family. They wanted also to ensure that when their children married they could take pride, and sometimes assurance for their own comfort in old age, in the spouse chosen. For both reasons, they did not want their children to rush into sexual experience and hasty marriage. There was thus an immediate possibility of conflict between parents and their own teenage children. There was also a wider tension between the generations. The middle-aged were jealous of young adults for their freedom, and for their opportunities for success at work and in sexual love.

They were also frightened by the independent youth culture which they saw on the street – the corner groups, and the notorious if less common city gangs of 'scuttlers', 'ikeys', 'hooligans' and 'peaky blinders', who fought over girls with belts and bottles, and assaulted vulnerable pedestrians in the dark. These gangs would attack a drunkard and 'probably leave him insensible in the gutter. If they cannot trip a man or knock him down, they kick or use the buckles of belts . . . They will use knife, poker, fork or anything.'[2] And as today, there was a distinctive dress style which made the youth culture more readily identified and criticized. At the street corner, or the 'monkey parade', the weekend mating promenade which parodied the social display of the Sunday church parade of respectable adults, youth displayed the symbolic provocation of brass buckled belts, 'the peaked cap, hair curled well over the forehead, white neck-scarf, bell-bottomed trousers and sharp-pointed clogs with heavy brass nails, which formed the uniform of their class'.[3] Nor were boys the only offenders: 'What would our grandmothers have thought of girls, sixteen or eighteen, parading the fair alone, dressed in jockey-caps . . . imitation open jackets and waistcoats, and smoking cigars or cigarettes?'[4]

Faced by this threat, the older generation sought to impose its authority with some vigour. The street culture was attacked directly by the police, and indirectly by removing children to schools, and keeping them there longer and longer. Until 1890 a child could not be forced to stay in school beyond the age of ten, but by 1900 the official leaving age was fourteen. When they were allowed to go to full-time work, teenagers were confined to the worst paid and most menial roles. And so successful was the pressure of various techniques for delaying their sexual fulfilment that the mean age of marriage, at any rate, in the early twentieth century was higher than at any other time in British history: twenty-seven for men and twenty-five for women, in contrast to twenty-four and twenty-two today. For the typical Edwardian the gap between leaving school and the full independence of marriage was twice as long as it is today.

To a considerable extent adults were able to succeed in this counter-attack against the freedom of youth without resorting to the use of violence. Among the well-to-do, few boys protested at their incarceration in monastic schools, followed by segregated university colleges, until they were in their twenties; while girls at best covertly evaded the constant chaperonage which was designed to prevent them from ever walking alone, or being in privacy with a young man, before they were securely contracted to marriage. Similarly, the adult sons of clerks and artisans accepted that they should be in by specified hours. At twenty-one they might be given the privilege of a housekey with the severe warning: 'Remember this is your home and don't abuse it.'[5] Girls, even in their twenties, were less likely to be given this kind of freedom, and when they were courting it was their father who decreed when the evening's pleasure should end:

> 'Me father told me husband – well, he were my young man at that time – "Our bedtime's ten o'clock" – and it was sort of like it or lump it. He said to me, "I can take the hint." '[6]

Most young adults preferred not to risk the punishment that parents still believed themselves right to inflict. One girl of seventeen who came in half an hour late from the cinema remembers the reaction of her usually mild father:

> ' "I'll give you ten o'clock at night! Get up those stairs – you go out no more this week." And I was so surprised when he hit me with his slipper, I turned round and got another one.'[7]

Nevertheless there were many teenagers who frequently had to accept being disciplined by informal violence from adults: from the police, from employers, from schoolteachers, from parents, sometimes in bewildering succession. One Essex youth worked before starting school as the kitchen boy at a farm, cleaning boots among his tasks. The farmer's son would give him a cigarette if he told him when the farmer had his best boots cleaned, for 'he knew he'd gone to London, you see, on business, which enabled him to have the day off going on the spree'. The unfortunate kitchen boy one morning

> 'was smoking in the woodshed, chopping sticks, when the farmer caught me and picked up a twig end and give me – not a thrashing because I just bolted, but he caught me three times ... [I came home, crying, to father, who said] "What did he hit you for?" I said, "Because I was smoking" ... so he give me a clip with his hand ... a back-

hander right across me cheek. And off I went to school crying. By that time, you see, it had gone ten . . . and that's where the headmaster was strict . . . so we got one on each hand, then, the cane on each hand.'[8]

Farmers were perhaps the employers most likely to strike a boy whom they employed; in the less hierarchical community of the towns, parents might protest. Nevertheless, here too a boy was firmly put in his place at work. At first he was allowed to do little more than odd jobs, cleaning, running errands and fetching food and drink like a servant. He could not start either labouring work or training for a skilled craft before he was sixteen. If he did become an apprentice (by the 1900s a practice confined to few trades), he was liable to ritual humiliations: being sent on false errands, forced to carry out useless tasks, subjected to tricks and often to a form of sexual violation such as having his balls blacked. He was expected to know his place, not to offer his opinion to men who had served their time. And if he dared to cheek a foreman, he was certainly likely to get a backhander.

There is no doubt, however, that the most persistently violent Edwardian adults in their treatment of teenagers were school-teachers. Caning in school was ubiquitous. Innumerable children who had been firmly but gently brought up at home experienced corporal punishment for the first time at school. Children were liable to be caned, not merely for talking in class, or for being late for school, or more serious offences, but for not getting their answers right, for speaking Welsh or a dialect in the playground, even for coughing. Teachers would not only use the cane, and in Scotland the tawse, but would slap, pull hair, throw books and slates, tie children to radiators, or make them stand for hours holding their petticoats above their heads. Most of these teachers were simply acting within the educational conventions of the day, but the number who showed signs of definite im-balance was considerable. There was the headmaster who was prepared to beat an entire school of three hundred when he could not find out who had broken a window; another, who endearingly referred to the cane hung from the end of his mantelshelf as 'Miss Sweetlips'. At a rough guess, a good quarter of Edwardian children left school to harbour resentments against their teachers for the rest of their lives:

> 'I didn't like the schoolmaster. He was a sadist. He enjoyed beating . . . One boy, he was the most poor, miserable boy and he had the most dreadful chilblains, all cracks on his hands and they were all purple and bleeding and he had to go up to have slashes across his hands. The schoolmaster would beat him. All sadistic you know. I'm sick with it, I get almost into a state of frenzy with passion when I think back on what one had to tolerate and one wouldn't run from it, we might as well have been in a concentration camp.'[9]

Not all teenagers took this kind of treatment without resistance. They tried to protect themselves by padding their trousers, or rubbing lotions on their hands, and they counter-attacked by calling teachers names, making faces, flicking darts, throwing inkwells and sometimes fighting back in teams. Some persuaded parents to allow them to change school. Others simply played truant.

On the streets teenagers were less easy to catch, and their characteristic relationship with the police was one of tip and run. In general, rather than prosecute for loitering, obstruction and gambling, the police preferred to punish with a flick of their gloves or cape. On the other side younger children were organized to provide an early warning system, while the older boys played football, or pitch and toss for pennies. Sometimes these gambling groups were quite elaborately set up. Sheffield newspaper boys, a parliamentary committee was told, were

> 'living a life of lawlessness – in fact a state of juvenile brigandage. They are highly organized in their own way. There is a private gambling club run by street traders behind a certain ice-cream shop where through a regular system of insurance, fines for gambling, theft, etc., are met out of the common fund.'[10]

Another situation in which ingenious youthful combination was quite common was the cinema. Teenagers had numerous devices for slipping in free (as also to the music hall), and in quite a few cinemas they used the cover of darkness to create general uproar. It was partly the gloom, as well as its comparative novelty, which made the cinema in the 1900s a focus for adult anxiety about the sexual morality of youth. There were reports published by bodies such as the National Council of Public Morals deploring what these unsupervised groups of young people might be led to think of in such conditions. Such busybody speculations were one aspect of what was often the final tussle between parents and youth: choice of sexual partner.

Working-class parents, unless so insensitive in wielding their authority that a child decided to flee to independent lodgings (a relatively rare occurrence), could control a teenager's choice of friends and behaviour with them at home, and could restrict their hours out; but they could not have much direct influence on whom they met. Well-to-do parents would invite carefully selected young guests to parties and dances. Working parents at best could encourage their children to continue with the social life of church and chapel, or join a respectable youth club. Some also welcomed friends home. Girls, if only because they could earn less and might be expected to help more at home, were perhaps less independent of parental control. But the contrast should not be exaggerated: indeed we shall see from our 'Edwardians' that Gwen Davies's parents, who hoped her to marry a minister, were no better able to influence her choice than Frank Benson's; while Emmie Durham certainly married no better for being kept two years at home. For both girls and boys the commonest way of making contact with the opposite sex was by chance, in the street, the park, or on parade:

> 'After tea, the bright boys wash, clean their boots, and change into their "second-best" attire, and stroll forth, either to a picture palace or to the second house of the Balham Hippodrome; perchance, if the gods be favourable, to an assignation on South Side Clapham Common; sometimes to saunter, in company with others, up and down that

parade until they "click" with one of the "birds". The girls are out on much the same programme. They, too, promenade until they "click" with someone, and are escorted to a picture palace or hall or chocolate shop. Usually it is a picture palace, for, in Acacia Grove, mothers are very strict as to the hours at which their young daughters shall be in. Half-past ten is the general rule...

'As the boys pass the likely girls they glance, and, if not rebuffed, offer wide smiles. But they do not stop. At the second meeting, however, they smile again and touch hands in passing, or cry over the shoulder some current witticism, as "'Snice night, Ethel!" or "I should shay sho!"

'And Ethel and Lucy will swing round, challengingly, with scraping feet, and cry, "Oooh!" The boys linger at the corner, looking back, and the girls, too, look back. Ethel asks Lucy, "Shall we?" and Lucy says, "Ooh – I d'no'," and by that time the boys have drawn level with them... "Well – shall we stroll 'cross the Common?" "I don't mind." Then boys and girls move forward together... They have "got off".'[11]

What followed is, inevitably, more a matter for speculation. It does seem that the typical town boy normally took to serious courting before his late teens, although of course there were many who began later, or earlier still; the girl was likely to be a little younger; and courting itself quite often sprang from an earlier acquaintance, sometimes from childhood. For most the parade simply led at first to chatting, nudging and walking arm in arm. Later on, a steadily courting couple would be allowed to sit in privacy in the front room. They might sometimes be engaged for several years. But among the poorer working classes, marriage in the early twenties was common, and it was probably often hurried by premarital conception. Charles Booth believed that in London:

'With the lowest classes premarital relations are very common, perhaps even usual. Amongst the girls themselves nothing is thought of it if no consequences result; and very

> little if they do, should marriage follow, and more pity than reprobation if it does not. As a rule the young people, after a few experiments, pair off and then are faithful, and usually end by marrying . . . I do not know exactly how far upwards in the social scale this view of sexual morality extends, but I believe it to constitute one of the clearest lines of demarcation between upper and lower in the working class. I do not suppose that young men of the better working class are any more virtuous . . . [but] the girls, though not ignorant of evil, are full of pride, and a fall from the paths of virtue is a very serious matter for their families and themselves; serious enough to bring very great pressure on the man concerned, who is most likely to be well known. In such cases, however, a prompt marriage may probably hide all.'[12]

In view of the late age of marriage and not infrequently long engagements of the Edwardian years, there cannot be any doubt that as a whole this was a time of striking sexual self-restraint among young adults. Contrary to what was often asserted, migration to the towns probably resulted in stricter sexual morality, partly because those who chose to move often had aspirations to a higher standard of living and respectability, but also because there was much less privacy, less secret open space in the towns, so that the social pressures against extramarital sexual relationships were more effective. These pressures were particularly strong in the early twentieth century, for they carried the cumulative weight of three generations of Victorian puritanism, affecting the working classes both directly through church and chapel teaching and indirectly through middle-class influence. Thus the general illegitimacy ratio, as a percentage of all live births, had fallen from 6 per cent in the mid nineteenth century to 4 per cent in the 1900s, despite later marriage. More recently it has risen again, and now stands at 8 per cent. Figures for the proportion of first pregnancies conceived before marriage, although less reliable, follow the same trend, falling from around 40 per cent in the early nineteenth century to under 20 per cent in the early twentieth century.

It is true that these figures do not allow for the spread of contraception, especially in the towns. But the fact is that for most Edwardians the only acceptable contraceptive techniques were either withdrawal during intercourse or complete abstention. Mechanical techniques were known, both through covert advertising and through talk at work, but they suffered from their association with prostitutes. Information was passed between women in the shops too, punctuating comments on excessively large families: 'She's the eldest of six, isn't it awful.'[13] Nevertheless, under 10 per cent of working-class couples married before 1918 ever used mechanical contraceptives.[14] They were more likely to have resorted to abortifacients such as lead-plaster. But there can be no doubt that both the fall in illegitimacy and the fall in the number of children born within marriage from the mid nineteenth century was achieved by restraint. Edwardian adults, whether married or not, were having less sexual intercourse.

In one respect this fact itself constitutes the most remarkable triumph of adult authority over youth. But in truth adults were as much victims of the denial of sexual expressiveness as youth. A surprising number of women, working-class as well as middle-class, entered marriage in complete ignorance of its physical aspects, and even up to the hour of their first childbirth so misunderstood the facts of life that they expected the baby to be born through their navel. Women were neither exposed to expectations of physical pleasure from sex as today, nor offered advice as to how it might be achieved. Many were understandably scared of conceiving more children. The factory talk of unresponsive wives remembered by Robert Roberts may well have represented common experience. A young brassmoulder grumbles that in the

> 'very lists of love . . . "She goes an' asks me not to forget to leave twopence for the gas." A second man's wife will not stop chewing an apple during sex, while a third insists on full clothing – "It's about as exciting . . . as posting a letter" . . . Another, a sad little man, complained that not only did his wife take no interest in the proceedings, but

she also insisted on a regular emolument of sixpence per session.'[15]

Certainly there must have been many more contented couples than these in every social group. But it is interesting that a more open sexual spontaneity was to be found especially at the extreme ends of the Edwardian social scale. Among the rich, although their own unmarried women were closely protected, a young man's sowing of wild oats in other fields was winked at. For married aristocratic women too in certain circles, including the court of Edward VII, discreet adultery was acceptable, and indeed the hostesses of Vita Sackville-West's *The Edwardians* actually planned for it in their allocation of bedrooms. At the other extreme, we have already seen Charles Booth's view of the poorest London working-class youth. In the countryside the working classes as a whole had been rather less affected by Victorian notions of sexual respectability. Illegitimacy rates were markedly higher than in the towns. In rural Wales and Highland Scotland the practice of bundling, or courting in bed, continued, with the connivance of girls' parents. Bundling was customarily limited to cuddling, but even this was shocking by middle-class English standards. In the English countryside the practice was only a memory, perhaps because youth could no longer be trusted. Certainly Spike Mays's portrait of Essex youth is not one of sexual innocence. Children learnt the facts of life early, partly by watching animals:

> 'Human refinements were gleaned – mostly on Sunday afternoons – through the absorbing pastime of playing gooseberry on courting couples. There being little incentive or scope for the more usual pastime of train spotting – there were but four trains per weekday upon the single-line track – careful records were mentally made of the sexual prowess of the "engaged", the "steadies" and the "casuals".
>
> 'Many local girls had practical experience before puberty . . . sometimes with schoolboys, but more often with uncles and cousins. Nor were they in the least ashamed. Some even bragged about their personal experiences.'

His own first opportunity came in 1918 at the age of eleven, lying in a wood with a fellow schoolgirl who chided him: 'What are you a-lookin' like that for, then? Are ye frit? Doant you worry, bor. I dunnit afore!'[16] That time, he did not take his chance. Nor did most Edwardian youth. They had their sphere of freedom, certainly; but it was a world in which adult authority generally prevailed.

6 Men and Women: Adulthood and Old Age

The dimensions of inequality among adults were defined by sex and age as well as social class. A working man enjoyed his most prosperous years in his twenties. Both skilled men who had completed their training and labourers in full strength were at the height of their earning powers, and if they had married their families were still small enough not to drag them back into poverty. A prospect of a higher income in later years was only open for the few who crossed into the middle classes, either through setting up on their own or by becoming foremen.

For many working-class women too these were the best years. At the age of twenty two-thirds of women were at work. Although they were paid far less than men, their wages gave them a brief feeling of independence. The daughter of a drunken Lancashire building craftsman, for example, a harsh man who beat his wife as well as his children, could dream of a fresh start:

> 'When I was fetching a bit of money in, especially when I started for sixteen, I started being a bit cheeky you know then, saying . . . well I'm going to leave home and take me money with me and all this . . . and he used to give me a bat if he could . . . I used to think, ooh I'd love to get me mam on her own and we'd get a room, you know, away from it all.'[1]

Even during these working years, however, few women could aspire to any equality with the position of men. They were systematically excluded from all the best-paid occupations. The higher professionals, lawyers, doctors and clergy, were almost entirely male; among manual workers, boilermakers, engine drivers, cotton spinners and coalminers were equally exclusive. The grounds for this exclusion were purely social. Women had already shown that they could train for the professions, and the range of manual work in which they were employed did in practice include both skilled crafts and heavy labouring. When their abilities were needed, during the First World War, they proved fully capable of all kinds of work. But normally, even in the working classes, women were expected to display some of the physical and mental weakness of the ideal 'lady'. They were encouraged to choose work because it was clean and the company was respectable rather than because the earnings were good, so that the daughters of artisans became court dress-makers or shop assistants rather than factory girls. Where both men and women were employed in workshops, official factory inspectors attempted to segregate the sexes. Indeed a steel-worker, who thought his mates 'rough, crude and tough', was surprised to find when women were taken on in the war, 'that type of women was nearly as bad as the men'.[2]

For the daughters of the well-to-do, no paid work was thought suitable. Lady Violet Bonham-Carter recalled

> 'as a child, asking my governess how I was going to spend my life . . . Her answer came without a moment's hesitation. "Until you are eighteen you will do lessons." "And afterwards?" "And afterwards you will do *nothing*" . . . The deep river, the Rubicon which flowed between, was called "Coming Out" . . . One day one had a pigtail down one's back – short skirts which barely cleared the knees. The next day, hair piled high on top of one's head . . . It used to be a sin to be vain – but now it became a sin to be plain . . . "Lessons" were of course thrown to the winds . . . In fact I remember being warned by a well-wisher to *conceal* any knowledge I *had* managed to acquire . . . "Men are afraid of clever girls".'[3]

The chief business of the upper-class girl was to dance and dine until she married. Afterwards, she might become a hostess herself, or, if she preferred, a recluse. It was a life of leisure rather than of freedom. The protections which social convention imposed on a lady ruled out many forms of sport as well as work, and in many ways prevented her from exploring the world independently. The two Brangwyn sisters of *Women in Love*, Midland teachers, stand by the lake of Crich the coal-owner, in which Gerald Crich, the heir, bathes, naked:

> 'God, what it is to be a man!' she cried.
> 'What?' exclaimed Ursula in surprise.
> 'The freedom, the liberty, the mobility!' cried Gudrun, strangely flushed and brilliant. 'You're a man, you want to do a thing, you do it. You haven't the *thousand* obstacles a women has in front of her . . .
> 'Supposing I want to swim up that water. It is impossible, it is one of the impossibilities of life, for me to take my clothes off now and jump in. But isn't it *ridiculous*, doesn't it simply prevent our living!'[4]

Not many women had sufficient leisure to become concerned at such restrictions. Marriage, if less luxurious than for the upper-class lady, was to be the principal career of most working- and middle-class women. Many of them, moreover, did not enjoy a very different experience in the relatively free years before marriage. In some families one daughter had to become the housekeeper, either because the mother worked or because she was ill or dead. For example a Staffordshire pottery thrower's daughter had lost her mother when she was two. Her father managed for some years with the help of his sister-in-law, but she was a severe woman and the two were never close; when they went out, as for a walk, they always went separately. At sixteen the daughter took over as her father's housekeeper:

> 'I would have liked to have gone to work. Because I was alone a lot and I would have liked to have gone out because I think that there was more enjoyment out of going out to work . . . I used to envy girls that went out to work. You hadn't got the company.'[5]

A woman in this situation was working as an unpaid servant. And it is also significant that of those women who were employed in paid work, a full third were domestic servants, cleaning, cooking, carrying coal and water up and slops down stairs, serving food and opening doors for the middle and upper classes. In the single-servant household, which was the commonest situation in the early twentieth century, it was a lonely, demanding, never-ending occupation: 'Oh all the hours God Almighty sent, if they wanted you up in the middle of the night they did. Nobody had set hours in service.'[6] Domestic service was widely regarded as the occupation which provided the best training for marriage: a start to a life's career confined to housework.

Only one in ten Edwardian married women were in paid occupations, as against a third today. The principal reason for the difference is demographic. Edwardian women married later, had more children and died earlier. They married in their mid rather than their early twenties and had three or four children. Larger families were still very common. A working-class mother was not usually free of her children before she was fifty-five, by which time she had a dozen years to live. Today with a typical family of two children, independent when she is little above forty, a wife now has more than thirty independent years ahead. If Edwardian husbands did not like their wives to go out to work when they could afford not to, it was partly because they had a full job at home.

It must not be assumed from this that Edwardian men and women were peculiarly rigid in their separation of roles. It is widely believed that Edwardian husbands, unlike their successors, were never expected to help their wives with housework. Sociologists have written that

> 'Marriage today is ideally envisaged as a partnership . . . To most younger husbands, washing up is no longer a sign of henpeckery . . . and in the home, many of the traditional distinctions between what used to be considered women's work and men's work are wearing rather thin.'[7]

Well-to-do Edwardian husbands certainly did not help in the house, because their wives could afford servants, and the disappearance of servants may well have forced a dramatic realignment of roles in many middle-class families. It is also true that a very large number, perhaps two-thirds, of working-class husbands, gave scarcely any more assistance. In some cases this was reasonable, because they were out at work for twelve or more hours a day, or worked shifts. In other families the mother had more aid than she needed from her daughters. Other fathers simply felt that as chief breadwinner they deserved to be waited on; and for those who took this attitude, there were social conventions which supported them:

> 'It was illegal for a man to ever use needle and cotton in those days ... A boy wasn't supposed to bake, he wasn't supposed to wash up, he wasn't supposed to make beds.'[8]

But the truth is that in the privacy of their homes many working-class husbands ignored the conventional prohibitions imposed by a male-dominated society. For probably a quarter, marriage could be described as partnership.

It seems likely that the most rigid segregation of roles in the house took place in regions dominated by heavy industry, such as mining, where men's work was entirely segregated and physically exhausting. Very often there was little paid work available in these districts for women, who consequently came to be expected to devote themselves to the servicing of the male earners. Indeed their tasks became so taken for granted that they were almost depersonalized. A South Welsh woman thought of her five brothers as 'the colliers':

> 'I used to get up at half past five in the morning and put four colliers out ... We had to clean even the colliers' shoes, on a Saturday afternoon, and oil them ready for Monday ... They were working then on a Saturday and they'd come home to bath. Well you'd have to clean up after that ... I remember one day. My mother had gone on holiday I

think. And my brother Tom, he was bathing, and I wanted to go somewhere, and he tipped the tub with the water so I had to clean all that up.'

Besides expecting women to clean up after them, the miners wanted their backs washed for them. Nor was this service confined to women of the family:

'There was a family next door but one to us, and if their mother or the daughter wasn't there, they'd shout to me, "Olive! Come and wash my back!" And I'd go in and wash their backs. Yes, men.'[9]

This ritual could provide one of the few points of interest in a wearing day. The worst situation of all was where the pits worked night shifts, as in County Durham, and the men might be setting off to work at different hours. A miner's wife here could find herself working twenty hours in twenty-four:

'The day began at 3 a.m. when the eldest son, a hewer, made his breakfast, took his "bait" put up the night before and went on shift at 4. Mother, if awake, would try and snatch an hour's sleep before preparing a younger son, a datal worker, whose shift started at 6 a.m. He would no sooner be off than Father would be coming in for breakfast and "bath", his shift ending at 6 a.m. He had started his shift at 10 p.m. the previous night . . .

Next the three children had to be got up and prepared for school; dinner prepared for the eldest son returning after 11 and then the children back for their mid-day meal; three more sons prepared to go on shift at 2 p.m. Soon after that the son who went on shift at 6 a.m. would be back needing a meal and bath; and then the children home from school.

'On top of this continual round all the washing "laundry" was done at home as well as baking. There was no bought bread in northern mining villages in those days. The bread was all baked at home. This took sacks and sacks of flour.

> 'Then she had to prepare for Father going on shift at 10 p.m.
>
> 'The next preparation was the biggest of the day. After 10 p.m. the three sons who had gone on shift at 2 p.m. would be home. Not only had Mother to prepare their meals on the kitchen fire, but she also had to boil the water for their bath in pan and kettle. Altogether it would take anything up to two hours before they were all bathed, which they took successively in a tin on the hearth in front of the fire. It was always after midnight before they were all off to bed. This was the end of a normal day and the alarm clock would ring again at 3 a.m. for another day.'[10]

Fortunately the continuing tradition for members of the same family to join the same work team, which was observed both in the mines and the mills, made such an extreme burden the exception rather than the rule.

The heavy industrial areas present one extreme. The reverse pattern, of men and women quite commonly sharing in household work, was most likely to be found where an unusually high proportion of women worked, as in the textile districts. According to a Factory Inspector, in the Potteries

> 'a woman is looked upon as lazy unless she takes her share in contributing to the family income. In Staffordshire the men and boys appear to willingly do their part in the domestic work of the house, and it is no uncommon sight to see a man cleaning and sweeping, caring for the children or even putting them to bed, on the evenings when the women were engaged with the family washing.'[11]

One Longton wife who had been a cup sponger was married to a miner, but he would help with both house and children:

> 'I've seen him bath 'em. Seen him bath 'em, oh aye, when they were new . . . He'd do the cooking perhaps – well he'd help with the cooking any road. Aye, and then he always used to make the beds . . . Aye, make the fires. Oh he wasn't a bad old stick.'[12]

In the countryside, where it had been normal for women as well as men to work as agricultural labourers until the late nineteenth century, there were also many adaptable husbands. A Wiltshire baker's assistant, for example, would 'do the dusting, polishing floors, do all that, do all the garden', although his wife did not work and had no children.[13] Another instance, from our Edwardians, is Fred Mills's father. And in the Shetland islands roles were especially flexible. Almost a third of the crofts were tenanted by women, a far higher proportion than among farmers elsewhere. There was none of the segregated world of male clubs and pubs normal even in the countryside. The crofting–fishing economy took the men away for frequent periods on the boats, leaving the women in charge of the crofts; while at sea, the men learnt to cook and clean for themselves. It may be that the withdrawal of men from housework, like the exclusion of women from many spheres of paid work, was a relatively recent tradition of the industrializing nineteenth century.

Certainly this must be true of the segregation of the social lives of married men and women, for this depended upon the existence of a world of separate facilities into which the man could withdraw: clubs, friendly societies, trade unions and public houses. Beer houses had sprung up in the countryside from the 1830s, but the full range was confined to the towns. Conversely, it was also principally in the towns that a good organized basis for a mutual social life was offered by chapels and churches. But generally, active neighbouring or frequent contact with relatives could provide a social network either for the wife, or, if the husband preferred to spend his free time at home, for both. In some families, couples would call on couples; in others, the man would have his friends at work, the wife among women relatives and neighbours. In the early twentieth century these two different tendencies were probably almost equally common. The patterns are, of course, less neat in real life than in theory. Our Edwardians include several mixed patterns, as well as contrasts like the Davieses and the Thorns. But the home-centred working-class husband is certainly not a new phenomenon of the more affluent late twentieth century.

Understandably such quiet husbands received much less public attention at the time than the small but justly notorious minority of Edwardian husbands who exercised what they believed to be their right to beat and kick their wives. Here was a situation in which the inequality of the sexes was manifest. Women had had no effective remedy against such treatment until separation orders from magistrates became possible in the 1890s, and many wives preferred to suffer rather than to go to law against their husbands. A solicitor, unsuccessfully defending a husband against an application for separation, could argue that 'in Blackburn and Wigan it is the usual thing for the husband, when he comes home at night, to give his wife a kicking and beating'.[14] And although separation orders were now available to any seriously maltreated wife, and women no longer forfeited their property to their husbands on marriage, the inequality of husband and wife before the law was still striking. Divorce was available to a husband on the simple adultery of his wife, but his wife could only divorce a husband whose adultery was aggravated by cruelty or desertion. Divorce was in any case so expensive that only the well-to-do could afford it. Working-class spouses who wished to remarry could only resort to pretence, although this would be condoned by the neighbourhood if their grounds were sufficiently reasonable. Occasional wife-sales also took place, giving a traditional sanction to the exchange, as well as compensation for the former husband. In the law courts husbands also had the right to damages for abduction. Wives, however, did not have this right, nor were there traditional husband-sales. A married woman was still in important respects the property of her husband, as well as being subject to his orders. The children were also legally his rather than hers, and if the couple separated the man had the first claim to them.

Petitions for divorce were a rarity in the 1900s. Separations, however, were ten times as common. As a separation is now more often followed by a divorce – how often is unknown – the combined separation and divorce rates in 1970 suggest that legally recognized breakdowns are now six to ten times more common than in the 1900s. No doubt many more separations then remained informal. In the peerage a full third of the marriages of the 1900s were to end in divorce. But in every other social class most Edwardian couples, for better or for worse, were to stay together.

Whether companionable or bitter, every marriage followed a cycle. At first the birth of each new child brought more strain. Then as the children began to earn an easier phase followed. Finally, as their children left home and they grew older themselves, parents normally entered a phase of gradual economic and social contraction. Working-class couples lost both the earnings and the company of their children. Middle-class parents were less likely to lose income, but they commonly had to spend money in setting up their children in house and business perhaps in another district. Once grandchildren had been born, grandparents could also provide practical help in child care, especially if they lived near by. A close bond might continue between grandmother and daughter. But before long, especially in the years before the introduction of old age pensions, the need for help would be reversed, as the grandfather ceased to be strong enough for regular work. At this point the ageing couple would slip helplessly towards extreme poverty. They had reached a stage at which once again, as in childhood, the inequalities of age overshadowed those of sex.

Because of the higher death rates of the early twentieth century, it was in fact only a minority of Edwardians who lived long enough to meet this crisis of old age. Men especially were more likely to die before their mid sixties. Altogether a mere 5 per cent of the national population was aged over sixty-five, in contrast to 13 per cent today. Of those who lived, half were widowed; and if Rowntree's information for York is typical, nearly half shared a household with their children or grandchildren, generally unmarried. A quarter took in paid lodgers – a practice which, in contrast to sharing with relatives, is today very rare. Nearly one in ten was reduced to living in the workhouse. It is true that old people in the workhouses were generally either ill, or had lost contact with their relatives. Nevertheless, by the age of seventy, one Edwardian in five was a pauper; and of those who lived to seventy-five, almost one in three. An old person's chance of actually dying in the workhouse in the years before a national health service was still higher.

The rough diet of the workhouse, a rhythm of broth, boiled bacon and dumplings, was good enough by the meagre standards of the Edwardian poor. But the old, since they were not given false teeth, could hardly eat it; and the price of the diet was the degrading regimentation shown in George Sims's picture of a workhouse dinner from *Living London*. Even as a visitor, the East London socialist George Lansbury was so shocked by his first encounter with the workhouse that he gave a large part of his political life to improving its conditions:

> 'My first visit to the workhouse was a memorable one. Going down the narrow lane, ringing the bell, waiting while an official with a not too pleasant face looked through a grating to see who was there, and hearing his unpleasant voice – of course, he did not know me – made it easy for me to understand why the poor dreaded and hated these places, and made me in a flash realize how all these prison or bastille sort of surroundings were organized for the purpose of making self-respecting, decent people endure any suffering rather than enter.
>
> 'It was not necessary to write up the words "Abandon hope all ye who enter here". Officials, receiving ward, hard forms, whitewashed walls, keys dangling at the waist of those who spoke to you, huge books for name, history, etc., searching, and then being stripped and bathed in a communal tub, and the final crowning indignity of being dressed in clothes which had been worn by lots of other people, hideous to look at, ill-fitting and coarse – everything possible was done to inflict mental and moral degradation.
>
> 'The place was clean: brass knobs and floors were polished, but of goodwill, kindliness, there was none.'[15]

It was in such a setting that an ordinary Edwardian who had lived his full lifespan might end his days. It was perhaps best for men that they died first.

Part II
Edwardians

We have so far seen the dimensions of Edwardian social structure as generalities. Let us now look at them through the voices of twelve individual Edwardians. In 1900 the oldest was ten, and one, the youngest, not yet born.[1] It would have been possible to have also included older Edwardians, but we have chosen from this single age group partly because recollections of childhood and youth are generally the clearest, but also because it will allow straightforward comparisons between their stories. The relationships within each family, its members' experience and perceptions of the outside social world, will reveal some of the uniqueness inherent in every life story. But at the same time the differences which we shall find between them will be partly due to the fact that they came from a range of social classes, of regions, and from country, town and city. We shall begin at the top of the social scale and move gradually downwards. At the same time we shall move backwards and forwards between country, city and industrial town, and from London to the north. Our Edwardians do not constitute any kind of sample. But their voices will represent the contrasts in social experience, the dimensions of inequality, which underlay the moves for social change in Edwardian Britain. They will also show the web of connections between social classes, age groups, the two sexes, which held the social fabric together, and contributed to the shaping and limitation of that change.

7 Upper and Middle Class

Lady Violet Brandon

We begin with a childhood from the upper classes. Unlike any of those which follow, it is essentially detached from any local setting. The family belongs to an upper-class society which is national rather than local, and follows its seasonal migrations. The parents represent two contrasting strands in the Edwardian aristocracy, each quite typical of the period: the father rather more conventionally old-fashioned, and the mother tending to withdraw from the performance of public social duties which had become less of an upper-class obligation. And the scale on which their family life was conducted was not abnormal for the time.

Lady Violet Brandon was the daughter of a Marquis. Her father's ancestral home, which was in Norfolk, was too large for her to be able to count the number of rooms it contained. There were two grand halls, a large and a small dining room, a library, a muniment room, parlours, innumerable bedrooms including a 'bachelor's row' for guests, nursery, schoolroom, servants' hall, steward's room, lamp room, china room, laundry and so on. So vast indeed were the distances inside the house that at mealtimes the lamp man 'dragged an enormous sort of truck with the food, because it was a long way from the dining room to the kitchen'. It was also difficult to keep track of the numerous grades of servants and estate staff. They were headed by the agent, a hunting gentleman in his own right, and the housekeeper, a 'terrifying lady in purple satin'. There were also the butler, footmen, valets, governess, nurse, cook and numerous grades of maids from the ladies' maids to the still room and kitchen maids. Nor was this the only Brandon family home. They had taken another country house on an Irish estate. They had a house in London. And for many years, they also had a Mediterranean villa. They normally spent, in fact, only the autumn in Norfolk, after the London season and before going to winter abroad. It was not surprising that Lady Violet was little aware of the social world outside the estate gates and knew nothing of the poverty of other country children. Her mother took little part in country life, and did not involve herself in the charitable works which many ladies of her social standing still felt their duty. 'She did so hate Norfolk and really English climate and English life.' As a result, Lady Violet 'only knew the retainers, gamekeepers and this and that, people around, gardeners and so on, who were employed and well off'; the people at the lodge gate and the groom who 'touched his hat as you got into the carriage and out of the carriage and that sort of thing'.

The Marquis's five children lived a life which was both luxurious and also restricted. In this they were quite typical of their social class. The four girls received their whole education at home from governesses and companions; an education including foreign languages, art and literature. A private music teacher taught them the piano and violin. There was also a private tutor for their brother, until he was sent away to Eton. At mealtimes as young children they normally ate separately from both parents and servants too, either in the schoolroom, or earlier in the nursery. They were unusually well fed by Edwardian standards: on beef steak, mutton chops, milk, cake, biscuits, and so on, and sometimes even red wine. They ate with the nurse or governess, waited on by the most junior under-footman.

They rarely saw their mother except when 'we went down scrubbed up after tea', or occasionally in the garden, or sometimes in London when she was in her finery with 'some famous beauties who came round all dressed up for a Court ball'. She was a distant if admired figure. 'We were frightened of her, quite frightened of her I think. But we did adore her.' Of their father the Marquis they saw even less, for he would be frequently away, speaking in elections, shooting or coursing at other country houses, or yachting at Cowes.

The children's nurse was thus a crucial figure. In one case, at least, a seriously mistaken choice was made, at a time when the girls were left for some time in Ireland. As parents the Marchioness and Marquis used no corporal punishment, but this nurse, until she was eventually found out by the estate factor, would frequently get drunk and beat the children. After she had been sacked 'my mother said that we must have a course of spoiling' and an older nanny came, who stayed with them five years. They came to love her very much, as a second mother. 'We were all in tears for several weeks after she left. Because we were so attached to her.'

The servants thus provided to a certain extent substitute parents and playmates. This was quite common in households of this kind. There were occasions, such as birthdays, when the children were able to enjoy the company of others of their own age and social class. Their parties were elaborate occasions, complete with conjurors and old-fashioned dances.

> 'Quite often the parties took the form of "cotillions" where you got presents ... You might be given gold cigarette cases, gold lighters and things at a cotillion. Somebody went round with the tray of what they called "favours", these presents, and then the young men if they asked somebody to dance, to cotillion with them, they gave them this favour, gave them this present. And the same thing happened to the girls.'

But mostly the children made their own fun in the great house. 'Being four sisters like that we were very self-sufficient. Didn't have a tremendous lot of outside friends.' They formed their own secret society, the Bolingbroke Republic, with officers, meetings, elaborate rules of conduct and fines. Or they would

> 'gallop madly through the passages being "pursued" by people ... saving somebody or – it was always connected with some story ... But I was alone a good deal and had a lot of imaginary games which I played on my own. And my father [and mother] were frightfully amused

if they came unobserved on me fighting a duel with a tree or something like that. I can remember being deeply humiliated because I discovered they'd been watching my game, when I was fencing madly with an imaginary opponent. And one rather minded finding out that they'd been watching, and probably laughing.'

As they grew older, however, they could more easily share pleasures with their parents. Their mother read aloud to them from Thackeray, Dickens and Shakespeare; they began to ride with their father; they would all play tennis, or whist, papers games, charades, or billiards, or just sit talking. Sometimes the Marquis would lead a family sing-song. 'He loved singing, he liked to have singing bouts, but it was singing Tor-roo-li-oo-le-i-day, and naval songs, and Gilbert and Sullivan. Oh yes, yes, we used to do a lot of yelling together.'

Outside the family, contacts remained restricted. The Marchioness, for example, was not interested in church activities – an attitude which was growing more common among the Edwardian wealthy. Indeed Lady Violet was astonished by her first experience of family prayers – now a declining convention – at a great aunt's house: 'thrilled by the sight of all the behinds, the butler and everybody, while they bent over their chairs'. The girls were not taken to London during the social season until they began to be presented at court, and especially when abroad led a very quiet life, 'like living in a nunnery'. Some young men would come down to house shooting parties in Norfolk, but they were very much of the same social type. The family had some social contact with professional people, but none with industrialists, and little even with the world of finance. 'I think by then it was quite alright to be in the City . . . I suppose banks were always respectable were they?'

All this was to change, Lady Violet hoped, when she was launched on the London social scene. 'It was something I looked forward to tremendously . . . There was a great sort of excitement spread about coming out, and you thought you were going to be free. We knew very few young men in our ordinary life till we came out.' And in some ways coming out did mark a drastic change: the introduction to a round of dinner parties, dances, calling with cards, and country house visits; to the world of political controversy; even to an awareness, amidst all this social splendour, of the poverty to be seen in London. But even so, restrictions continued. At dinners, seating was by order of precedent, and as the daughter of a Marquis this too often resulted in her being placed next to an elderly host. At dances her mother insisted, through close questioning, that she observe the convention of continually changing partners. And although she sometimes secured a rather gay cousin as her chaperon, she was never allowed to go out alone, even for a walk in the London parks. A chaperon, a sister, or a maid had always to be with her. For Lady Violet, as for many women of her class, the real end to restriction came from an unexpected quarter: war. In August 1914, for the first time in her life, she found herself at work, as a hospital nurse; with less leisure, but with the full freedom of an adult. 'Within two months of the war, I was fighting my way home through Vauxhall Bridge Road, alone, at night.'

Grace Fulford

Because the same landowners led Edwardian society in the capital and the country, Lady Violet Brandon's childhood has already taken us to the city. The middle classes were much more localized. The place in which they lived could influence their social lives as much as their occupation. Our first middle-class childhood is from a well-to-do professional family from London, and it is here that the biggest single concentration of professionals was to be found. But there were also many others scattered through the countryside and provincial towns, frequently leading an isolated existence. We need to remember that the daughter of such a doctor or clergyman could have presented a very different picture from this family from London.

The Fulfords belonged to that upper section of the middle classes who kept living-in servants, and followed the rituals of upper-class 'society' as far as their means allowed. The family, for example, participated in the weekly display of local elegance in the suburban park close to their house:

> 'And of course every Sunday it was church parade. The whole of that drive round the park was filled with victorias and traps and carriages and the ladies would get out all beautifully dressed after coming from church and parade round that lake.'

Mrs Fulford held a monthly At Home and exchanged calls with cards. Her daughter Grace had her own printed cards at the age of fifteen. 'Copperplate card. We used to distribute them to all the boys.'

Grace Fulford, whose education began at a private school 'for the daughters of professional gentlemen only', where she was instructed in vowel sounds and deportment, and taught to curtsey and walk with books on her head, grew up with a clear perception of the social hierarchy and her own place in it:

> 'There was a class distinction. Definitely. There was the working class and middle class and the aristocrats. But you were beginning to lose it . . . You got a lot of people who were beginning to make a lot of money; we used to call them the "parvenus". They'd no breeding, but plenty of money.'

By origin the Fulfords 'were a county family. None of them worked until my great-grandfather died . . . except in politics and that sort of thing. They were the backbone, they were the real aristocracy.' Her own generation, however, were

> 'middle-class . . . [along with] mostly successful business-men and professional gentlemen. Bankers, insurance; especially inside insurance – not so much the agents, they came a rather lower grade . . . Master builders, I suppose would have been considered more in the middle class, but the actual workmen themselves – railwaymen – and their

families, extremely respectable, nice class of people, but still they were considered the working class.'

Grace Fulford was taught to treat such lower social grades with courtesy and respect, but also with distance:

> 'My father had one trite saying, and that was, "Courtesy costs nothing, but it opens the door to many opportunities." And he was right. If we were heard talking to the servants as if they were dirt like sometimes you do if you're a bit young, we were very quickly reprimanded. Treat them with proper respect.
>
> 'Children were taught to be selective. They usually chose their own kind – people who were one sort from a speaking point of view. We were taught to judge by that. Because some of these poor people, you know, they were quite capable of washing . . . but when they opened their mouths you could tell that they weren't so educated . . .'

The Fulfords themselves were a household of ten: four girls, one boy, parents, a nurse, a parlourmaid and a cook-general. Their house, recently built on a smallish plot like the others in the same street, rose three floors, with a nursery at the top, three other bedrooms, a bathroom, and kitchen, scullery, drawing room, dining room and study. Their standard of living is well suggested by their meals. Except on Sundays, when parents and children ate together, the parents would eat in the dining room, children in the nursery with the nurse and the other two servants in the kitchen. The children's mid-day meal would include such dishes as 'a boar's head boiled with caper sauce'. In the afternoon there would be a tea of 'little tiny slivers of bread that you could blow away like that – fancy cakes and very often home-made cake'. Finally there would be a dinner, such as steak, chips, sweet, cheese and biscuits. Sometimes, as the children grew older, there was wine; and there was always plentiful fresh fruit: pears, apples and grapes.

Like many middle-class families, the Fulfords were considerably assisted in reaching this degree of comfort by the support of their grandparents. Mr Fulford worked all his life as an actuary, for the same insurance house in which both his own father and grandfather had been prominent. When he married as 'a young man on a small salary' his parents-in-law bought a first house for his wife. 'That was in her name. The second house was dad's. And they provided her with a couple of maids and all coal and light bills were paid by them, for the first ten years. Gave them a good start.' More remarkably, when Grace's elder brother proved delicate, they removed him and brought him up themselves. And they continued to send up weekly food baskets and even once provided a complete new set of china and curtains while they were away on a holiday.

With such plentiful help, and a weekly washerwoman and a gardener as well as the living-in servants, neither the children nor their mother had many household tasks. The girls were taught to sew and knit at school, which became useful later in life 'as the servant shortage became a menace'. They occasionally helped about the house. The boys 'didn't have any tasks to do, not even clean their own boots'. And the nurse relieved their mother of much of the work of looking after them as young children. Mrs Fulford would see the baby at bathing time in the morning, and perhaps for an hour or two in the late afternoon. The consequent lack of sufficient occupation told on Mrs Fulford, like many other middle-class women. 'I think she had too much time on her hands, you see; intelligent woman, and her life of ease was bad for her.' Eventually she became depressed and withdrawn, and her life more and more separated from that of her husband. Earlier on their social life focused on the family weekend: 'visitors and relations had a way of popping in on Sunday.' As time went on Mrs Fulford saw her local friends on weekday afternoons, and Mr Fulford saw his business friends at work or at bowls, or at the Conservative Club. He liked to invite friends home for chess or cards, 'but she couldn't bear it . . . I don't think either of them liked each other's friends very much.' Their interests also diverged in other ways. Bottled up in the office all day, Mr Fulford enjoyed outdoor recreation. On hot summer nights he would sleep in a tent in the garden. And sometimes at the end of a day's work 'dad would come in and he'd say . . . "What about putting on your hat and coming for a walk round the houses – a bit of a promonation?" She'd say, "What on earth do I want to walk round the houses for? I see enough of them all day. No, I'm going off to the theatre." '

Understandably, Mr Fulford sometimes looked over his shoulder to keep his morale up. Once on a steamer outing he allowed Grace to fall off a chair and bang her mouth while he was engaged in winking and lifting his hat in another direction. 'Oh, he didn't pass a pretty girl easily.'

The separations in the Fulford household, between servants and family, parents and children, husband and wife, were all commonly found in many well-to-do Edwardian households. But there is another side to their family life, an element of closeness and gaiety, which is more typical of middle-class and relatively prosperous working-class families than of those at either end of the social scale. As a mother, Mrs Fulford was

'easy to talk to . . . She could be angry but she could always show a lot of affection . . . I'd go and talk to her about the different boys I knew and that sort of thing . . . [We] never went to bed without mother came and kissed us goodnight. And dad usually did too . . . I can remember dad tickling me, yes, oh yes. And I can remember the youngsters, younger than I, they used to clamber on his knee.'

As they grew older he would take them out cycling, or to the zoo. At home he would play rounders or cards, or join in singing while Mrs Fulford played the piano. With their mother they went to the theatre, concerts and cinema. And they would all go, taking maid and nurse with them, on summer holidays in the country or at the seaside. The children also had the servants as playmates; and many local friends, whom they would see at children's parties, on Saturday walks or on Sunday. The children enjoyed church. 'It became a habit and then it became a pleasure because you met the people you knew.' These same friends later provided plentiful sweethearts. 'There was no shortage of boys believe me.' And the active school life of a girls' High School included lectures, lantern shows and debates. For the young Grace Fulford, there was 'never a dull moment'.

Her parents also took a personal responsibility for her training and education which may well have been peculiar to middle-class families at this time. A series of carefully selected schools led to a private college, where Grace learnt general subjects, including typewriting 'for a hobby ... He wanted us to make good marriages, he never thought of us going into business.' Home discipline, normally verbal but occasionally with a cane, was reserved to the parents; the servants were not permitted to chastise the children. Censorship of the information which the children received was also attempted. 'We rather resented it, always being sent out when grown up people were talking.' Mr Fulford kept his bookcase locked and the children were not supposed to read the newspapers. 'I used to get them on the quiet sometimes. Say there was a spicy murder ... But we weren't allowed to.' The relationship intended was clearly indicated when they ate together, the children sitting up straight, eating everything on their plates, 'seen and not heard'.

But the careful intentions of Grace Fulford's parents were partly undermined by the servants, who, for example, would deliberately throw away fat which the children would not eat, so that it could not be given to them again to eat at the next meal. Mr Fulford's attempts to ensure that his teenage daughters were in bed were similarly foiled by collusion. The various maids

> 'used to shield us right and left ... when I was courting ... Dad'd go out ... and he'd say, "Is Miss Grace in?" "Yes, sir, I think I heard her go up to her bedroom a short time ago." I'd come in a quarter of an hour later, she'd be round the side entrance: "Your father's been inquiring for you. I told him you were in bed – be quick and get upstairs and get your hat off." Oh yes, we were ever so friendly with all the maids.'

The maids were sympathetic partly because they too were in moral subordination to the mistress of the house. They also were supposed not to listen to the conversations of Mr and Mrs Fulford and their friends, and on their nights out might be told that their dress was 'most unsuitable' or not to go near the barracks. They always had to be in again by ten o'clock. And in the house, their recreations had to be appropriate to their station. Mrs Fulford once had to dismiss two newly-engaged maids who had started to practise music in their room, so that

> 'the strains of a violin came downstairs. She said, "Where on earth is that coming from?" – waiting for afternoon tea you see. Goes upstairs, there's one of them – it's an easel up in the bedroom with music on it and there she was playing away and the other one sitting back in her chair with her feet on an ottoman cushion. Oh, they went faster than they came in.'

After a fourteen-hour day of cleaning floors and grates and boots, serving meals, making beds, answering the door, continually answering bells rung by the family for more water in their bedrooms, more coal and so on, such restrictions could rankle.

As it happened, however, the critical courtship in Grace Fulford's life did not develop through the assistance of the maids. A young man appeared who sensed how to play Mr Fulford's game. He had been introduced to Grace on a previous occasion, but first got talking to her one evening when she was sitting by herself in the park near her home.

> '[He] ended by asking me if I'd go out with him to a musical on the Saturday. Well at that time I was not allowed out after half past eight. So I said to him . . . "Good gracious no. My father'd have a fit if I asked." Do you know what he did? He wrote to my father. I thought I was in for a good wigging. Dad came down to breakfast one morning and he said, "Grace, I want to speak to you in the study." I wondered what on earth I'd done. In his study I went. He said, "I've had a letter from a young gentleman called Hargrave." So I thought I was in for a "what cheek – what is he writing to you about?" He said, "Now don't talk

> like that. When a gentleman approaches me in a gentlemanly manner I treat him as a gentleman." And apparently he'd written to him to ask if he could take me out to the music hall on the house in the evening. And I said, "Can I go?" So surprised. So he said, "Yes," he said, "I've told your mother to answer it and say that providing he fetches you and brings you home . . ."'

It was young Hargrave whom Grace Fulford was to marry. At eighteen – unusually young for a girl of her class – she started a new home of her own. And her father bought them their furniture, just as he, on marriage, had been helped to set up house by his own parents-in-law.

Sidney Ford

There were other families, lower down in the middle class, who looked up to a social existence like that of the Fulfords as an ideal. Their own experience was barer and frequently lonelier. The father was often a clerk, or a 'high-class' shopkeeper or branch manager, drawn to the standards of respectability of clients, customers or an employer whom he assisted, yet without the income and security to maintain them. Such a family could rarely afford even a single living-in servant, and they often led a very private and restricted, if intimate, family life. They formed an intermediary class between manual workers and professionals which was of growing importance, especially in the middle-class towns, and in the city suburbs. It is indeed in London again that we find our third family.

For much of Sidney Ford's childhood, his parents had to struggle to provide for him. The couple had only one other child who survived, a younger brother. But they had married young, without resources. 'It was a runaway marriage . . . They were very much in love and they set up home together on just what very little they could scrape together.' Then, after Sidney had been born, Mr Ford lost his job as a junior clerk. They were forced to move from a flat into rooms and 'things got so bad that there was a time when I really was crying because I was hungry'.

It was over a year, 'through the good offices of a friend of the church, that my father really got put on his feet again and introduced to an employer, Tempest and Company, the confectioners, where he obtained another situation'. He stayed with this company as a clerk-typist until joining the army during the First World War. The war, with a soldier's allowance instead of his clerical income, brought another straitened, if less drastic time, and there was to be a third period after the war when, like many ex-soldiers, Mr Ford suffered a temporary nervous collapse which left him unable to work.

Mr Ford's own family could have helped to alleviate some of these crises. Very likely they did meet some of the inevitable debts, and certainly later on helped pay for Sidney's education. But they could only provide modest assistance. Mr Ford's father came from a West Country glove manufacturing family, had joined the Merchant Navy, and eventually retired to north London, where 'they weren't wealthy, they weren't poor. They were very, very thrifty, and there was nothing elaborate in their home at all.' There was, in addition, a rift between Mr Ford's parents and his wife. Perhaps she felt that they looked down on her for her humbler social origins. Certainly she disapproved of their manners, of the old couple's quarrelsome domestic life – so that at one stage they lived on separate floors not speaking to each other – and also of her father-in-law's attachment to rum. 'He carried out his old sailor's habit, last thing at night he always had his tot of rum and it used to smell the room out. I can smell that rum now . . . My mother didn't get on with either of them very well.'

Mrs Ford came originally from the north, and she had been a domestic servant. It is ironic that the conflict came from her commitment to just those middle-class values which she had espoused. In bringing up her own children

> 'there was a certain enforcement of discipline and general manners which was something perhaps my mother had never been taught, herself. She'd picked it up from being in service and what was done in nice households and she tried to introduce it into her own.'

There were also advantages, in view of the family's financial difficulties, in a humbler social origin. Mrs Ford had not been educated to be a middle-class lady who regarded paid work as degrading. During their first difficulties she worked as a cook; in the war as a grocer's shop assistant. Later she tried dress-making, and then succeeded in running a boarding establishment. Sidney helped increasingly with the housework. 'I had to do the chores. I had to go and queue up for the bread and the meat.' Fortunately Mrs Ford's own parents were now living near by, and they would look after the younger boy.

In spite of Mrs Ford's earnings and some help from each side of the family, there was little money to spare at the best of times. There was a period of four years in which they were able to live very pleasantly in an ample six-roomed house on the fringe of north-east London, letting off one room to a lodger. They had a bathroom, and a garden in which to grow vegetables. But their good fortune was ended by the war, and they returned to the housing conditions which were typical of Sidney's childhood: a divided house in a part of Hackney, once fashionable, and still respectable, although in gradual decline. Here they rented a top floor, with a large living-room, a kitchen and a bedroom. Later on another room on the floor below was also included, but they had to share the landlady's scullery for washing and bathing. This close contact might have caused considerable antagonism, for the landlady and her husband spent most of their weekends in the public houses, 'and two of their daughters used to work as barmaids . . . [But] we got on quite well with her. Although it's rather surprising.'

By middle-class standards the Fords' diet also was restricted. They began the day with a breakfast of porridge, tea and toast or bread. 'You could have either bread and butter or bread and jam, you didn't have both. [And] one talks of butter, but invariably it was margarine . . . from the Home and Colonial.' The children had a midday dinner, which would be reheated for Mr Ford in the evening. 'But the meals were rather sparse, two penn'orth of bones stewed down into broth with peas and lentils . . . Boiled mutton and pearl barley as a soup . . . Even weekends it was often a steak pie, we didn't seem to run to joints.' The end of the week was especially thin. 'Probably Friday there would be cheese. Saturday dinner was always a makeshift dinner.' There was little for the children later; tea, with occasionally on Sundays a kipper, and then 'my last little supper drink with my father as he had his meal'.

It was an economic diet, supplemented chiefly by extras which could be obtained free, such as home-made blackberry jam, and once even home-made wine, which the Fords did not seem to have realized was alcoholic. The food was, moreover, distributed equally. This was not a household in which the principal earner was given special favours. 'My mother and father shared equally. My father was a very obstinate man and if he thought that my mother hadn't got her share he would make sure that they got more or less equal.'

This is an attitude which, probably like many men of his class, he maintained in other aspects of domestic life. His wife could afford no paid help in the house. He was prepared when necessary to cook, and he would help regularly with washing up and with child care, reading and telling the children stories, playing parlour games, flying kites. They would all go out for Saturday picnics. Later he would play the violin with Sidney. And even when his boys were infants, he was one of those clerks who can be found portrayed in contemporary literature pushing prams. 'It was unusual, perhaps, in those days. Men didn't do it so much.' The average family, of course, was less likely to possess a pram at that time. Indeed the pram – like the children's clothes, some made at home but some bought, and Sidney's bicycle, and the birthday parties to which he could invite guests – shows that the Fords, if in reduced circumstances by their own standards, were far from absolute poverty. Later they were even able to provide Sidney, as a teenager, with a week's holiday by the sea or in the country.

Although both parents took a close interest in the children, it was Mrs Ford who was 'the dominating personality . . . Father wasn't quite so forceful.' She was very demonstratively affectionate, but also quick to give corporal or other punishments.

Sidney was 'constantly checked'. She emphasized manners, was horrified by swearwords and kept him from playing in the streets. But her main intention was much more positive.

> 'All the time she was looking for me to improve my mind. She did her best as far as education was concerned . . . It was a Christian home and basically there was a very strong moral atmosphere and it was these Christian virtues that were always put in front of you . . . They expected obedience . . . and they expected me to respond to their plans for me and also to return any affection that was shown.'

His parents took a close interest in his progress at the local council school, and 'they were very concerned if you brought home a bad report'. They encouraged him to read, and helped to guide his choice. There were books in the house, as well as a daily paper and magazines such as *Home Notes* and missionary journals. A Sunday school lending library was used, rather than the public library. 'The books in the house were very much edited by my mother. I was only allowed to read good books and I was only allowed to read religious books on Sundays.'

The heart of this education, and indeed of the family's whole cultural and social life, was the Methodist chapel. The Fords were probably quite representative of the more active Edwardian Nonconformists. They were convinced teetotallers, but they were prepared to play cards provided no money was at stake, and they were keen theatre-goers. Their other main recreations were church receptions and concerts. At home they said grace at meals and daily family prayers. On weekdays the children attended scripture classes, the Band of Hope and a church boys' club with sports facilities. On Sundays the family went three times to church. Sunday afternoon was used to visit relatives or friends, but 'they were usually people who frequented church on an evening and so we all went together in the evening'.

Social relationships were therefore on the basis of common interest, rather than with those who chanced to be neighbours. They had scarcely any social contact with adherents of other religious denominations. 'Chapel was chapel and the church was church . . . The word "Catholic" was almost anathema.' This did not mean, however, as it might easily have done, that the Fords only mixed in a narrow social circle. Like many Nonconformists at this time, they were enthusiastic Liberals with a strong social conscience. As their own children grew older, they took up mission work in a near-by slum district, and in particular the visiting and assistance of crippled children. 'This seemed to be their main hobby – their main activity.' It took them out frequently at night. They also brought many of the children to their own home, especially girls in need of help.

Through these slum girls, and also through his visits to the mission, Sidney was brought into sharp contact with another social class. 'It was like walking from the West End into the East End, almost – a different world.' The children there were, 'ragged – no shoes, no socks; very largely unwanted and neglected.' His parents showed him one of the causes:

> 'At the end of this narrow street, there was a public house named the Black Bull and it seemed to me as a youngster that practically every man that lived down that particular area was usually drunk, and I think it gave me a horror of the effects of alcohol. And that is something that has remained with me all my life.'

Here were others who were really destitute, whom the Fords could help. 'They were very very genial, I think, to these other people . . . Mother wasn't afraid of the poorer people.' But this did not change her general attitude to social class. Mr Ford, with his middle-class background, met his social superiors with some confidence. 'He would be more prepared to – with due deference – meet them on their own level. He would try to be man-to-man with them, but very polite with it.' But Mrs Ford continued to feel her own social inferiority.

> 'She would say that "I'm not as good as they are" . . . She could take a roomful of East End women and she could preside over their meeting and she could keep them in order and talk to them and hold her own, but the moment she was

confronted, shall we say, by somebody with a little bit of a title or even not as high as that, she just went to bits . . . I put it down to her parlourmaid days, where she was "Yes, ma'am; no, ma'am." Curtsey when you go in the room and when you come out of the room.'

Sidney Ford was also brought up to an essentially similar view of society: to admire people 'of very high breeding, and people who were well off and . . . people who spoke very nicely and used correct English, and one tried to copy them, sometimes with very poor results, really'. In holding such a view the Fords were not uncommon among the clerical lower middle class. Their active mission work marks them out from the ordinary Nonconformist family, so that they broke out from a social experience which would have otherwise been more home-centred. But their concern for social improvement, and its association with personal social mobility, may well be typical. It could bring success, even without the resources for completing secondary education. Sidney Ford followed his father into office work, but he was to rise well beyond the level of an Edwardian clerk; a career which may have been less colourful than he could at times have wished, but achieved the security which had been his parents' ambition for him.

'I've been very grateful for it . . . I'm now reaping the fruits of – shall we say the years of monotony, by the things that a secure job has . . .'

8 The Borderline

Peter Henry

With the Fords we are already close to the borderline between the middle and working class. There were some chapel-going upper-working-class families whose lives were in most respects very similar. There also were many Edwardians who were in middle-class occupations, managing commercial enterprises and holding property, yet who were drawn more directly, through work and residence, towards a working-class way of life. Market shopkeepers, publicans, small manufacturers and dealers, and small farmers are all examples. Two of our Edwardians come from families of this kind. The first, however, represents a rural way of life which was receding; while the second is more relevant to the urban life of the future. We move, first, to the region which was the most remote in Edwardian Britain from the industrial and commercial influences of the city: the Scottish north.

Early twentieth-century British agriculture could be divided into two broad regions. In southern and eastern England, and in parts of eastern Scotland, arable farming predominated, and depended for labour upon a landless rural working class. The farm labourers and farmers of this region together accounted for some two-thirds of the entire agricultural workforce. The remaining third occupied the second, geographically much larger, northern and western region, which was characterized by pasture. Here the families of farmers themselves provided most of the necessary labour.

It was at the northernmost fringe of this immense and relatively unpopulated family farming region that Peter Henry was born, at Greentown, Walls, in Shetland. His family were crofters, typical in combining farming with other occupations, and in farming partly for subsistence and partly for the market. The extended family in which he was brought up was also relatively common in the crofting region of north-west Scotland. It was headed by Peter Henry's grandfather, who combined crofting with fishing, and was also a boatbuilder and housebuilder. He had built the house in which the family lived. The main room was a long kitchen, with an open peat fire, where the family cooked and ate, but there was also a second room decorated as a sitting room for 'very special strangers', and a garret up in the rafters. Peter Henry was the only child, but the household also included, besides his grandparents, three single aunts and an uncle. He never knew his own father, but his mother lived in the house for his first years, until she moved away on marrying into another crofting family. A second uncle also came at intervals between working away as a ploughman and at sea. They slept as best they could: there were two enclosed box beds in the kitchen and an ordinary bed, another bed in the sitting room and another in the garret. Two of the aunts shared a bed.

Crofts were too small for the sheep and cattle raised on them to bring much of a cash income, but their produce underpinned the family's standard of living. Some of their clothes and shoes were bought new – 'they wouldn't humble themselves to buy second-hand clothes'. Others were home-made: slippers of cowhide, called 'rivalins', and a range of garments knitted from their own sheep's wool. 'Right from the sheep's back the knitted garment was all processed through at home; carded and spun and all that at home.' Similarly with food. Breakfast would be of home-baked bread, and bacon, butter and eggs from the croft. The main midday meal would consist of mutton from the croft and fish caught from their own boat, fresh at some seasons of the year, dried or salted at others. It might be boiled or stewed, and served with potatoes, cabbages and turnips. Salads, fresh fruit or cheese were never seen. For the tea there would be eggs, bread, oatcakes and home-made rhubarb jam. Tea for drinking had to be bought, but a child could drink milk from the croft.

It was a monotonous, but by Edwardian standards a nutritious and plentiful diet.

The meal was served, in the typical local manner, in a big central dish set in the middle of the family table, with the child allowed to talk and little fuss made about table manners. He could leave the table when he wished, without asking. 'No, they're not fussy at all . . . I couldn't say that ours was a very strict home.' Peter Henry's upbringing was, indeed, a mild one in several ways by the standards of any other part of Britain. He was disciplined by reasoning rather than by corporal punishment. Even for such a serious misdeed as window-breaking on a Sunday he was not beaten. 'I many a time got a severe telling off but never to use the hand.' Nor was he subjected to many rules. At bedtime, for example,

> 'there were none of this – go to bed at eight o'clock or something like that. No, no, no, there was nothing that you could – if there was something going on in this house, a lot of people in and the like, that was nothing unusual you might have been up to midnight.'

He was allowed to join in the conversation of visitors too. 'Occasionally they would have said, "Oh, wait till so-and-so's spoken," but generally speaking we weren't kept down in that.' And although the child's part in adult social life was linked to his share in the family's work, he was not given a set of strict tasks. He helped chiefly with the animals, feeding the hens, ducks, pig and geese, keeping a grazing cow from 'going in among the corn and the turnips or the potatoes . . . I would sit with that cow for maybe hours.' In winter there were lambs inside the house:

> 'You had lots of days with snow and suchlike and you just kept them in and fed them, hand-fed them. And with these lambs around the croft I was always interested.'

The work roles of the two sexes were also flexible. This was again characteristic of the locality. Two of the women normally worked outside on the croft, while the men would help inside with washing, making fires, decorating, mending shoes and looking after the boy, reading and telling him stories. His uncle, who had a wooden leg, worked in a carpentry shop on the croft. The boy would 'spend a tremendous amount of time in his workshop, joiner shop . . . In my very early days I got as much book training from my uncle as ever I got from the teacher.' His uncle taught him to read, and gave him much more encouragement than the southern teachers at the school, where he felt 'too much tied down'.

Leisure was informal too. Children played freely on the crofts, but unlike town children they played no team games such as football. The family attended Church of Scotland services, and there was sometimes a church concert, and an annual Sunday School outing, but little else. There was no active local political life, and no clubs. There was one bar in the district, but few of the crofters went to it, and only the ploughman uncle from the Henry family. Afterwards, 'if they wanted him to come in and be nice and quiet, I was sent out to meet him. And he would pick me up and come in as quiet as a lamb.'

Perhaps two or three times a year families would gather for a funeral or a wedding, the latter very festive occasions with dancing continuing for several days. But the most important regular community occasions were connected with work: the fishermen's annual regatta, and the quarterly cattle sales.

> 'You see, our folks came from the island of Papa Stour really . . . Now when the cattle sales was on, which by the way was a very special day, they had to swim these cattle out from Papa Stour. And they would stay then one night in Sandness . . . [You might] see anything from a dozen to twenty cattle tethered in our croft for the night and an equal number of people attending them. Some were getting down in the house, some were lying on the couches, or maybe even stretched out on the floor . . .
>
> 'And they went away very early in the morning. There was no auction sales then, it was just a case of the buyers came along and they looked at the animals and they bought them,

by independent bargain between the two . . . And by about midday then the selling part of it was all passed and then . . . right until teatime it was just a crowd of young folk walking around for maybe a mile or so on each side and meeting each other and having a joke with each other and such like. Or maybe couples pairing off and were walking away. Then very very often you called at some house before you went home and a few more gradually gathered in some house which was in your route and you ended up maybe with somebody having a fiddle and you had a dance. So that was really a big day, the cattle sale day was.'

The young gathered in some of these houses quite frequently for an evening. 'There was one or two houses which was very very much sought after, houses where they could play a fiddle.' Parents do not appear to have imposed any regular hours. Very occasionally, too, the boys might go on to join a group of girls who had been carding wool in a croft barn, straw pellets or 'flatchies' would be brought out, and a night of romping ensue, the boys rolling and jumping over the girls. This was known as a 'flatchie carding'. Alternatively, there might again be dancing.

This linking of work and leisure was typical of all generations. In the scattered crofting community, especially on the long, isolated winter evenings,

> 'there was very little social life around unless a few gathered together – well, grandfather was probably repairing herring nets . . . The womenfolks gathered in and took their knitting and suchlike. Then of course all these ghost stories of things of that kind went very high then.'

Visiting was openly welcomed, an attitude symbolized by the local convention of entering a neighbour's house without knocking. Neighbours also constantly exchanged help, such as in harvesting: 'Say they were behind with their croft work or something like that, the rest of the crowd around would gather and help them – and they would have been insulted if you had said pay. Oh no, no, no, no.'

Although by comparison with an urban community the crofters were close to the same standard of life, some needed more help than others. Those with large families of young children were worse off, and so were the old, who were given much of their food by neighbours. There were a few landless families, cottars, 'in pretty dire straits'. The Henry family were among the more prosperous, and their relatively new house with its wood and felt roof instead of the old-fashioned thatch signified their standing. Other families were their superiors:

> 'There was a lot of class distinctions, oh definitely . . . Oh the shopkeeper, the minister, the schoolteacher, the likes of these people were definitely in the better class . . . You would never have dreamed of taking them as equals. No, they was a step above you.'

On the other hand, they did not observe the deference to social superiors normal elsewhere in rural Britain. Crofters were not brought up to touch the cap or call those a step above them 'sir'. Recognition was rather through avoidance. Professionals did not visit the crofters' homes in the evening. If their paths crossed on the road, 'you felt more like just trying to pass them by, you know, you're a different class, you don't want to bother me and I don't want to bother with you so to speak'. The local landowner was the most aloof of all, an occasional visitor from England whose house could only be reached by a launch. 'I don't think he would have mixed much with any of them . . . A lot of his life I think it was spent in Bradford. He had a lot to do with wool mills in Bradford, yes.'

The crofting community stood, in fact, in a curious halfway position. It was integrated with the British social and economic system, but not fully digested. The cash crops of the islands, sheep, cattle, fish and clothing, had been drawn into the national market. The local superior class represented national interests: the industrialist turned landowner, the minister, the teacher, the shipping agent who was the local wholesaler. The crofters, moreover, suspected that there was some intrinsic merit in the economic ways which such people represented. Peter

Henry was taken on by the shipping agent as a clerk and goods checker:

> 'Jobs under an employer were just a thing almost unheard of . . . They were just engaged round their own croft and suchlike, but get work outside of the home and under an employer and just at a specified job – you thought yourself somebody then.'

Nevertheless, among themselves the crofters maintained an essentially egalitarian society, with no marked work specialization and a strong convention of unpaid mutual help. The local economic system was still elementary enough for eggs to be used as a form of currency in the shops. For essentials the crofts were still largely self-sufficient, and few depended on an employer for work or wages. And since the 1880s, with their tenancies legally protected at low rents, the crofters had been freed of their former dependence upon the landowners. The community could be egalitarian not only because the crofters themselves were unusually homogeneous, but also because they depended so little on their class superiors.

Harriet Vincent

Still on the borderline between the middle and working classes, we now return to the towns, to a family whose business brought them into inescapable contact with the poorest section of the working class. They kept a boarding house and store in a port district. Here the class line is at its most distant from the standards of well-to-do society.

They also introduce among our Edwardians one dimension of social inequality which we have otherwise mentioned only briefly, because its effect was more generally felt in the Empire than in Britain itself. Immigrants were a very small proportion of the Edwardian population. The majority, while certainly liable to suffer ethnic prejudice, were not, being Irish, Jewish, or perhaps Italian or French, vulnerable to colour discrimination. In the ports, however, small black communities could be found.

The social history of each of these various immigrant groups has a significance far greater today than would have seemed probable then. It would be little more than a guess to suggest how the story which follows is typical, and how it is exceptional, of racial as distinct from class relationships. It is more simply a claim for a social history which very much needs to be written.

It was in Bute Town, close to the docks in Cardiff, that Harriet Vincent was born in a boarding house for seamen. Bute Town was a port district with a typical mixture of nationalities and colour; and also a typical reputation for being rough. The seamen staying in the Vincent house were generally West Indian; for although Mrs Vincent was Welsh, born locally, daughter of a skilled sea pilot, her husband was black, and his family originated from the West Indies, although he himself had been born in Nova Scotia. Mr Vincent had started his working life as a seaman.

> 'He was going to sea when he came to Cardiff, came here first. And then he was going to sea as cook and steward. And he gave it up, he was a confectioner and baker for a long time. He used to go around with a cart selling his bread. Then he gave that up when he opened the boarding house, and we kept a boarding house for years after . . . I was born in a boarding house.'

It was at first a small establishment, but this was not the only function of the corner house, which also operated as a cook shop, selling teas and hot pea soup. 'The children when they came home from school came in for jugs of pea soup.' As a small girl Harriet helped serve in the shop; and like the boarding house, it proved a successful enterprise.

It was impossible for a family to escape all the consequences of living in a poor quarter. Mrs Vincent gave birth to fourteen children. Only six lived, and of these only two boys and two girls survived their childhoods. But the family itself had a distinctly middle-class standard of life. They employed two servants. They were well dressed. 'I had all my clothes made in the dressmaker's . . . Bought everything that we wanted – boots or anything like that we wanted. Nothing secondhand.' Mr Vincent would take them to buy footwear, Mrs Vincent clothing – 'at town, in town'. Mr Vincent had his suits made by a Scots tailor, with whom he would converse in Gaelic – a language he had perhaps picked up during an earlier stay ashore in Glasgow. The family similarly ate extremely well: a cooked breakfast, such as saltfish and potatoes, bacon, or tripe and onions; mid-day dinner, meat, vegetables and sweet; for tea, cakes, bread and cheese; and finally a supper of biscuits and hot milk. They bought fresh fruit and vegetables, and had eggs from their own hens in the yard. 'We always had plenty to eat.' These meals, moreover, were eaten with formality: grace said, the children sitting up, holding their knives and forks correctly, not talking, eating what they were given, and staying until the meal was finished. As was quite common in lower middle-class households, the servants ate with the family. There was also a definite attempt to insulate the children from some of the social dangers of their surroundings.

The Vincent boarding house had started in one six-room corner house. 'We had only a few men then.' Later, however, it became quite a large establishment, moving further down the street.

> 'My father had two houses, and he had them knocked into one. And the bedrooms was upstairs, and through the yard wall that we could get around . . . Six [bedrooms upstairs and six rooms downstairs] . . . Only the front bedrooms in the one house were let to the boarders, the others we used downstairs for ourselves. It was like a big room, we could put five single beds in it. Well then there was the other room that we could put five in and that was ten beds. And we had two in another bedroom, and one in a smaller bed-room. See, single beds for the men, . . . all seamen, seamen boarders . . . We dare not go in there. In fact he wouldn't let us in there. We weren't allowed in that part where the men were . . .
>
> 'My sister and I slept in the small bedroom and the boys slept in the middle bedroom.

'[In the other house, father and mother were downstairs, and the other two rooms] – oh well we used them, my grandmother – well after my grandfather died, my mother took her on, she had the middle room downstairs.'

Although the two sisters normally slept together, there was a stage when Harriet shared her bed with a servant girl whose home was in Newport. 'We had a double bed ... She was alright. She'd taken me out sometimes – the Empire.'

Normally the servants lived locally, and as was usual in lower-middle-class homes, the whole family helped with the work. There was a washerwoman who came twice a week, and two daily girls for ordinary housework.

'My father used to do the cooking for the men. And mind he wouldn't let my mother get up in the morning. He used to let her stay in bed till he gave all the men their breakfast. Then she got up, then we'd all have breakfast together as a family ...

'My mother used to help a lot. I used to do the washing when I got bigger. We had [the girls] mostly for scrubbing because my mother couldn't kneel very much, she used to have rheumatic fever ... It was my job to clean all the shoes, every Saturday. When I came home from school in the evening I had to help with the back kitchen and clean the knives and forks. We all had something to do ... [My youngest sister] I nearly brought her up because my mother was in bed, she used to have gout. I had to look after her then when my mother was bad. Wash her and dress her, and wash all her clothes. ... [My younger brother] used to go to the pub where they used to have horses. He was always on a horse. The stable up there, like top of the street, Gladstone Street. He'd go around with my father's waistcoats on.'

The dominating spirit in the busy household, however, was Mr Vincent.

'If my father would go to the docks with men sometimes taking their clothes to the ships, my mother would do the cooking, in the afternoons. But always my father done the most – made pastry and everything.

'And he had only one hand. His right hand was off, from his wrist, from an accident in a saw mill in Canada. Before he ever came to England. Do everything with it, make bread, anything. He cut the boys' hair – my mother used to tie a comb round his wrist there, and he'd comb them and cut. He had the power in his other hand. Only a stump. We used to call it "Joey" when we was kids. He used to laugh a lot with us. But if he hit you with it you'd know it. Oh my God. Hard.'

Mr Vincent was the stronger disciplinarian of the two parents. He alone would cane them, although this was 'very rare, very rare'. Their mother 'never raised her hand to none of us ... She was very affectionate ... a wonderful mother'. While Mrs Vincent was a non-practising Anglican, Mr Vincent was a keen Nonconformist. He hated swearing, and was a teetotaller. On Fridays he insisted that the family should eat only fish, a practice which he had continued after working for a short time for a monastery in Canada. On Sundays no games or scrubbing were permitted, and in the evening he would conduct his own service with the children. 'He'd have a big book on the table specially and we had to be stuck there. Oh – three times church Sunday. And then sit down Sunday night and sing hymns with him.' Even on weekday evenings he would sometimes read the Bible aloud to them. Books in the house were chiefly religious, and 'we wasn't allowed to read much newspapers ... You couldn't say yes or no to my father, or mother. Dare not answer them. Couldn't stop in the room if he was speaking to the women. You go in the room but he only look at you and you get out quick.'

There was a certain conflict between such standards of strictness and the role the Vincents played as figures in the local community. They partly solved this by the home-centred privacy of their own leisure. They scarcely ever went out. Mr Vincent spent his evenings 'just sitting, that's all. Sometimes he'd play patience. He never drank in his life, never drank anything. He didn't sport about – he didn't like – he was more religious than ever. I never known my father to drink. Nor curse.' Mrs Vincent 'never was outside the home'. She had two sisters who 'only lived across the road. One kept the shop on the corner.' These called often, and before they married – also to West Indians – they would stay the night. Her parents were close by too. 'I used to go down to see them, and they used to come up to us . . . My father made a lot of cake and that and I used to take them down.' One neighbour would call for tea, but there were few other visitors. In the evening Harriet 'used to crochet a lot. My mother taught me how to crochet and we used to make anti-macassars for the chairs.' They would also have family parties at birthdays and Christmas. One sister played the piano. 'We had an old battered gramophone, till we had a music box. We were all allowed to sing and that, we had a good day. Plenty to eat.'

But however private they might wish to keep themselves, there were two strong reasons preventing the Vincents from cutting themselves off from the neighbourhood. They were among its natural leaders, important customers of the shops and small employers themselves. And, the Vincents, as a respectable mixed marriage in a racially mixed community, were among those who especially helped to hold it together. Conversely, outbreaks of racial tension were peculiarly threatening to them. Tension affected Bute Town in two ways. Socially, the normal local situation was one of tolerance. In the bars, the street outing, the shops, the churches, there was no customary segregation. 'They went all mixed, oh all mixed. There was nothing like that.' Children of different nationalities played together: 'the white girls was my mates.' Nevertheless when work was short there was undoubtedly discrimination: 'very dark ones couldn't get a job.' As in most ports, there was a great deal of drunkenness and frequent fighting, often between households of different nationality. In bad times these fights would bring economic conflict into the open.

'It would be the drink. They were quite different sober . . . [Neighbours] were the protagonists – against each other.

And one'd be cursing the other. Of course there was plenty of fights between them. I've seen plenty of them.'

It was these fights which gave Bute Town its reputation for roughness, and its derogatory nickname, 'Tiger Bay'. And this reputation, in turn, created a tension between the Bute Town community as a whole, and the surrounding South Welsh population. It would flare up particularly when a big crowd had been drawn to the near-by football ground.

'The Welshmen used to come down here often used to fight ... They attack – now – now and again you get it ... It was just that they didn't like the coloureds ... It was very nasty, used to have big fights sometimes. Every time there'd be a football match or anything – when they'd come down on a holiday there's sure to be a row before they go back.'

To the Bute Towners, this external hostility was much more dangerous. Indeed, it helped to make them into a single community. Harriet Vincent knew about class differences: for example, that the ships' captains in Loudon Square 'thought they were better than the others'. But she was much more aware of colour distinction. And the emphasis in her upbringing was upon the essential equality of all.

'I used to say, "Well I can't call one black nor I can't call one white. My father was black, my mother was white, and I had to respect both." That's what I always said ... So I can't make no difference.'

Mr Vincent's attitude was similar. 'You had to respect everybody. My father tell you, "If you give respect you can command it."' In this spirit he would organize help for less fortunate neighbours.

'If anybody was in trouble we all helped one another. Many times I've gone round collecting for people that had –

somebody died you know and perhaps they was short, I've gone out collecting for the funeral many times like that.'

And he received respect himself. 'Plenty of that. They respected my father a lot.' He was the Grand Master of a friendly society lodge. Both black and white families wanted his presence at a funeral. 'He used to go to all the funerals and head all the funerals. When anyone died they'd come for him to head the funeral . . . Used to wear his top hat and his coat, used to look well.'

Social leadership brought no conflict with his own standards of conduct. But it made it hard for him to prevent the assimilation of the children with their poorer neighbours. 'They didn't mind who you played with, not as long as you looked after yourself.' The Vincents could scarcely afford to practise discrimination. As she grew older, Harriet would explore the city with her local friends, on foot and bicycle, visiting museums and cinemas. When the children had a party, too, local guests, and even the seamen boarders, might be included. 'Some of the men sometimes used to play the guitar and if they had a party amongst themselves they'd play for us.'

Thus Harriet, despite her parents' middle-class economic situation and family life, was growing up as a member of a working-class community. This contradiction was acutely revealed when, as a teenager of fifteen, she was taken by her father to the local Oddfellows Lodge dance.

'So he took me with him. And when they come along with the drinks he said, "None for her mind, give her a lemonade." Well – I started getting – if I wanted to dance with anybody I'd have to get out of his way. No, not with anybody. Oh he was very strict, my father was. No, not with anybody. There were his friends out of the lodge, well that I could dance with them. No, no outsiders.'

On other occasions, when she did not go to a dance as her father's guest, he would nevertheless wait for her outside in the street, to take her safely home afterwards. But in fact it was not one of the men from the Oddfellows Lodge whom she chose. She married a friend of one of her father's boarders, a black West Indian from Barbados, at the age of eighteen. This was her first marriage. They went to live up in the Rhondda, in lodgings. Work in the coalfield was plentiful and another West Indian friend found him a job in a pit, pushing drams. They stayed there four years. 'He didn't like it though, he didn't stick it long. And we came back, he went to sea again, he died at sea. We were only married about five years. Not quite five.' Harriet was a widow three years before her second marriage, once again to a seaman from Barbados, who had been a boarder of the Vincents. 'I knew him before I knew my first husband.' It was a big wedding, with a 'pair of greys and three pairs of chestnuts, at St Mary's . . . My mother stripped the big room upstairs and we had all the people up there dancing. And he was a good husband.'

Judged by occupations, Harriet Vincent passed on marriage from middle class to working class; but she might not have noticed herself. Our remaining childhoods are all working-class; less prosperous than the Vincents, but with much else in common.

9 Working Class: the Skilled

Frank Benson

Nearly a third of all occupied Edwardians were skilled workers. Such a large group concealed many variations. At the top were those small groups of skilled men who earned more than the average clerk, and had kept control of entry into their trade through apprenticeship. Some were in old crafts, like glass-making, or the most modern section of an old craft, like news-paper compositing; others were in sections within modern industries, such as the boilermakers in shipbuilding and the textile printers in cotton. Close to them in earnings, although recruited from the ranks rather than through apprenticeship, came the elite of the railways workers, the engine drivers. These were the skilled workers who were most likely to display the characteristics of the 'labour aristocrat', cautious and defensive in politics and trade unionism, exclusive in social relationships. At the other extreme were skilled men who were paid less than the average for all manual workers, such as signalmen on the railways, weavers in the textile factories, and craftsmen whose trades had been undermined by technological change, like bootmakers and wheelwrights.

The typical Edwardian skilled worker stood between these groups. His earnings did not so much set him apart as allow him and his family to participate fully in working-class culture. He was, characteristically, either a miner, a textile worker, a building craftsman or an engineer. The miner was likely to have been the best paid, although he was not regarded as a craftsman, and the mining communities were socially egalitarian rather than exclusive. So to some extent were the textile districts, where the lower grades of workers were often women and teenagers from the families of skilled men. The building craftsman, although the worse paid and more vulnerable to unemployment, belonged to a traditional industry in which apprenticeship partly survived. He might represent the old craft culture, although bitter economic experience could give it a radical cast: as with Alice Richards's father, at the end of this book. The engineer, although now usually a factory worker, learnt his trade through apprenticeship, and was well paid and relatively secure. For him the attitudes of the 'labour aristocrat' could still make good sense.

We include here two children of Edwardian skilled workers both from the industrial regions: the first pointing towards the labour aristocrat, the second closer to the egalitarianism of the miner. We begin with the son of a craftsman in the engineering industry.

Frank Benson was brought up as one of a family of six, two boys and four girls, in the cotton town of Bolton. He was the second child. His father was an iron moulder in a textile machinery firm. 'He did that all his life. He came to Bolton [from a near-by village] to be apprenticed, as a moulder. It was a craft trade. He served an apprenticeship five years.' Frank's mother had been born in a suburb of Bolton itself, where her family had 'one of those small corner shops. Her stepfather and she used to help in it. She stayed at home and the rest of the family went out to work.'

As a boy, Frank had a precise picture of the local class structure:

> 'Well there was the wealthy class, the Chorley New Road people and the people that lived up Seymour Road, which was a residential area ... The local mill-owner, Colonel Hesketh, who was one of the important Bolton citizens, lived in a big house there. There were some other mill-owners, Mallinsons, who had mills and bleach works, and these were the aristocrats of Astley Bridge in those days. Particularly Colonel Hesketh. And the Ashworths, they were also cotton mill owners. These were the upper class as far as

we knew, we didn't know any nobility, they weren't titled people . . .

'Then there were the distinct professional classes – the doctors and the solicitors and the schoolmasters, who we thought were a class on their own . . .'

Frank Benson was brought up to touch the cap 'as a mark of respect' to such people. As regards the majority of the population, he felt no such need for deference.

'We thought ourselves as the respectable working class; we were a little bit above the labouring class who lived in the poorer districts of the town . . . Mostly artisans and craftsmen; cotton spinners would be included. The man in the cotton mill who was a sort of an employer in his own right. He was a spinner of a wheel gate and he employed two assistants, a side piecer and a little piecer, and he used to pay these from his own earnings, so he was a sort of employer you see. He was employed by the mill-owner and over him would be a mill manager; possibly what was termed an overlooker, overlooking the section of the mill in which his cotton spinning was done . . .

'They were the wealthy section of the working-class people in those days. Then there would be the fitters and the engineers. Father was in the foundry – he was a craftsman, a moulder. In the foundry there were different skilled crafts: moulders, pattern makers, fitters and one or two others, who had served their time at a particular trade. These were a class on their own, and would consider themselves somewhat distinct from the labouring classes, the people who used to do the fetching and carrying, and the assistants.

'They would all mix socially. There were respectable labourers who would mix in various church activities, who took part in the religious life of the church. You would mix with them. You wouldn't look down on them in any shape or form. The only people you'd look down on was the people who used to drink and neglect their family life.

These were the people you'd look down on ... We were called the respectable working class. And we were taught to make the best use of every halfpenny or penny that came into the house. My mother had that ingrained in her and we had it ingrained into us.'

One reason why the Bensons believed that in the last resort respectability was more important to social standing than income, was that they were not themselves invulnerable to poverty. There were times when Mr Benson was laid off 'because of shortage of orders and slack time', or trade disputes. He was once out of work for ten weeks during a strike. And even when he was working, 'when we were very young my father's wage wasn't an adequate one for three or four children'. It was only later, when the sisters started work in the cotton mills, that the family became more comfortable.

By the standards of the time, however, the Bensons lived well enough. Later they were able to move to a new house on a Co-operative estate, but when Frank was young they lived in a terrace house with two bedrooms above, and a sitting room, kitchen and washhouse below. It had a tiny front garden. Mrs Benson had no paid domestic help, but the children helped clean and cook, and Mr Benson also did a lot for his wife, looking after the children, washing up, making fires, mending footwear, and when Mrs Benson was ill taking over the cooking and cleaning. There was also a childless aunt who would come in when they had a new-born baby. The children were well enough clothed. For footwear they had weekday clogs and Sunday shoes. Their clothes were bought new once a year. 'We used to be fit out every May when it was Sunday School sermons.' At school they were among the better dressed children.

'You'd have some ragamuffin types, with parents who didn't care or who couldn't afford decent clothes, obviously bought their clothes at rummage sales or second-hand shops or pawn shops, and came to school untidy, especially round the necks. Some of the boys would wear a scarf and a nice clean celluloid collar which could be washed every day. If you wore a

> collar then you came from a good home. That was a real distinguishing mark.'

The Benson children were also adequately fed. They would be sent to school on a breakfast of porridge, or bread and half an egg. Tea was also a light meal. 'Mostly bread and butter and jam – or bread and margarine when things were bad. We had high tea on Sundays. That may be some boiled ham or a little bit of cold meat and salad, and jelly and maybe a tin of fruit, or a tin of salmon, which was quite a luxury.'

The main meal of the day was midday dinner, for which Mr Benson, who had gone out at six with a sandwich breakfast, would return to the family. By this hour he needed a substantial meal.

> 'He was a heavy worker. Heavy industry. He had to, it was a necessity that he should be fed, he was the breadwinner ... He used to run up Kay Street. There were two big foundries in Kay Street. I can remember all these chaps coming out with their black faces rushing up to catch special trams which were waiting for them at the top of Kay Street to bring them up to Astley Bridge and they would practically run into the house, sit down to a hot meal, just have a pull at the pipe for five minutes and then off back ...
>
> 'We'd have the cold meat on Monday. We'd have stew on Tuesday ... Wednesday was baking day and we had Lancashire potato pie ... On Thursday perhaps if the wages permitted we might have chops. Chops were a luxury. But I can remember the time when I've gone out, mother used to send me to the butcher's when we were really hard up, father was out of work, I'd go out with twopence and buy herbs and we'd just have soup made out of perhaps a bone and what we called pot herbs ...
>
> 'If the oven was heated, we'd have a rice pudding ... Maybe just a banana chopped up in milk. But we had a second course most dinners, unless times were bad.'

In spite of her husband's lack of time, Mrs Benson thus provided well-prepared cooking; and she also baked bread and cakes, and made jam, pickles and herb beer at home.

Meals at the Bensons' began with grace and continued with a strictness which was typical of many such families. 'We were taught to listen rather than talk.' The children did not confide their worries to their parents.

> 'We used to keep it to ourselves. I can't remember opening my heart to anybody, because we always had a guilty conscience about things we used to do ... I had a very good mother. But we were never spoiled ... There was very rigid discipline in the house. Mother would give us a religious talk in her own fashion. This was wrong and this was right and God wouldn't like us if we did this ... Any wrong doing was reported to father when he came home and if we did anything really wrong we would get thrashed for it. Petty pilfering in the house. Swearing ... What we call a deliberate punishment would be father. Mother would punish on impulse, you know, smacks.'

On Sundays, no games were allowed and the children were sent three times to the Church of England parish church. The children were taught that racecourses and theatres were 'dens of iniquity ... places for the devil'. Their reading was 'censored pretty well'. Comic papers such as the *Magnet* and the *Gem* were forbidden, although Frank would get second-hand copies and 'smuggle them into the house and read them in the privacy of my own bedroom'. But he was encouraged to join the new local Carnegie library 'and this was a real treasure to me ... Henty stories, adventure stories, school stories of the time. I was allowed to read them in the house, these were all right, because they were out of the public library.'

In the evenings, Mr and Mrs Benson would sometimes sit up reading the Bible together. On other nights Mrs Benson went out to the Co-operative Women's Guild, or 'to a Sunday School meeting or Sunday School concert in the evening, something like that. She would think that was a pleasant night out and a relief from domestic chores. She'd go by herself. She'd meet other people there, see her friends.'

Mr Benson was active in a number of fields: in his trade union, in the temperance movement, the Co-operative movement and the church. 'He'd come home from work, have his tea and get washed and probably three nights a week he'd be away somewhere to some sort of meeting.' On Sundays he was a local Anglican preacher, and would walk about the town to talk to various men's Bible classes. 'That was a crime to go on a tram on a Sunday.' He also did charity work at a mission in a slum district.

> 'He would help them wherever he could and my mother would. They used to think this was part of their Christian obligation to help people. My father would help to organize subscriptions for his own particular workmates who were down on their luck.'

His most prominent activity was for the Co-operative movement. He belonged to its education committee, and two or three nights weekly would take 'children's classes in industrial history or what he called the history and principles of the Co-operative movement'. Politically, Mr Benson was a rather old-fashioned Lib-Lab. 'My father had no room for the extreme socialist type of person – I think the association with atheists . . .' But he taught children not only 'about the Rochdale pioneers and the Christian Socialists and Kingsley', but also 'the story of Robert Owen and the Chartist movement'.

The Bensons had a full social life too, both with relatives and friends. Visiting couples were especially frequent for Sunday tea, but 'the door was always open for casual visitors. Mother would say, "have a cup of tea".' Or she would chat with her neighbours 'over the back yard wall'. When the family were together, parents and children would play games or sing at the piano. Christmas would be an especially gay day with presents such as dolls, toys, sweets, games and even once a watch. 'We always had a good Christmas dinner. A joint of pork or a fowl. In the afternoon Aunties and Uncles would come in for high tea and we'd have a party after tea and games and everybody would generally let their hair down, and have a jolly evening.' The Bensons were not invariably stern. In the summer, for Bolton holiday week, they could afford outings to the seaside too, and in some years a few nights in a lodging house.

Nevertheless, like many working-class boys Frank Benson got more of his fun outside of the house than in it. He would play with neighbours on a patch of ground by the house; or sometimes go boating, fishing with jam jars, walking on the moors, or cycling.

> 'We used to make our own outdoor sport. When the cricket season started we'd go round all the neighbours and collect pennies to buy cricket bat and ball and we'd form a local cricket team with neighbourhood boys of our own age, from the age of about ten onwards ... We used to build our wickets of bricks and stones ... We played various local other gangs of boys. And when the football season started we would do the same.'

The Bensons allowed Frank to play with any of the neighbours, but they did attempt to keep him away from rough boys in other districts. He was refused permission to join the Church Lads' Brigade, because his parents thought this 'rather rough for me'. He was also advised to keep away from 'the "Lamb brow" lot', beyond the Lamb Hotel in Seymour Road.

> 'It was a rather slummy area with a rough lot of lads. Big Catholic families very roughly brought up, some of them hadn't any footwear. We used to challenge them to our patch to play football or cricket and this would generally end in a quarrel with stone-throwing going on and this was terribly discouraged. Possibly for two reasons ... bad language or somebody's window being broken and this would mean we forfeited pocket money until the window was paid for. So that there was discouragement to associate with this group of boys. But it never prevented us because there was something of a challenge here.'

Similarly, as he grew into the age at which he began courting, although he was allowed to walk the local youth parade, 'mother kept an eye on your girl friends'.

These attempts to protect Frank Benson from the rougher aspects of local youth culture could hardly be effective when his leisure time was largely his own. He had plenty of opportunities for getting into mischief. He would range over the countryside as far as the Manchester Ship Canal, and sneak into Old Trafford ground without paying, to watch the cricket. They fought not only as neighbourhood gangs, but also 'used to gang up against the Wesleyans . . . We used to have running fights with the neighbouring school.' They indulged in minor vandalism. Despite his parents' respectability, Frank Benson was as afraid as the rest of the boys of the policemen.

> 'We used to make fun of the night watchman and that sort of thing and I remember once getting into real trouble with a policeman, was when we thought it great fun to turn his hut over, and he brought the local bobby on the job. And this involved calling at certain boys' houses. One of them was mine and the policeman knocked at the door, I had gone to bed, and I was brought downstairs and questioned by the policeman: was I in this gang that turned over the watchman's hut? And this was a terrible thing in our family. A policeman should knock at our door.'

In the event, however, the Bensons need not have been anxious for Frank. He was to end with a career which they wholeheartedly approved. He had started working before he went to school in the mornings. The spinners, who began work in the mill at six, had a half-hour break at eight, when they could be brought cooked breakfasts. 'My first job was carrying breakfasts up for two spinners in the cotton mill which earned me a penny from each of them . . . Then of course when I was going to school I took out papers': a daily round, and on Saturdays running the streets shouting 'football final'. His first full-time job on leaving school was as an ironmonger's errand boy, delivering on a hand-truck. 'A builder would ring up and say he wanted so many drain pipes or down spouts, nails or screws, nuts or bolts, and I would deliver these on a handcart, probably within any distance up to two miles from the town centre.' At the same time he was attending night school. 'I had this errand boy's job for a matter of ten months and then my father thought this was not quite the thing and he encouraged me to sit an exam for a job at the Co-op.' He succeeded, and became one of some forty boys on milk rounds. There was 'a lot of rough play about, especially when you was washing up when you came in'. Still, he had his feet on the ladder. 'It was a great thing to get on the Co-op. It was considered quite a good safe respectable job once you got on the Co-op.' And in due course, he was transferred to the grocery department, where he became an apprentice grocer, still continuing night school, to learn a trade of his own: a trade through which, unlike his father, he could rise to the managerial ranks.

Gwen Davies

The contrasts between the Bensons and our second skilled working-class family sprang principally from two sources. Firstly, Frank Benson was an elder child. Many parents were more relaxed with younger children, and as the first began to earn they had fewer economic difficulties. Secondly, the two families lived in very different contexts. The South Welsh mining and tinworks communities, besides the egalitarianism born of tough manual labour, had a peculiar intensity of religious and cultural life, recently reinforced by the socialist movement and the great religious revival of the 1900s. This helped to shape the story which follows.

Gwen Davies was born in Taibach, part of Port Talbot. She was the second youngest of a family of four boys and three girls, and the age span between the youngest and oldest was over twenty years. They were, by working-class standards, amply fed and well dressed, and after her first years they lived in a new house of their own, the end house of a terrace, with three bedrooms above, and a parlour, middle room, living room and scullery below.

Mr Davies was a tinworker:

'He was in the end a shearer. He was a rollerman in the first place, and then you'd go from the rollerman to the shearer and that was the highest peak in the tinworks at that time ... They wore little white aprons and they'd have a special little short skirt, when he was a roller man. I've watched them many times putting the sheets of tin in the rollers, and they had these big long tongs, and they'd throw them down, they'd bend them over, they had a special boot with nails in and this red hot sheet would come through from the furnace and they'd turn it over, then throw it back into the roller.'

As a result, although he was fond of looking after his children and kept the house in repair and would cook on alternate Sundays to allow his wife to get to chapel, Mr Davies was often too exhausted to do much after hours. Until he became a shearer, when he worked days only, he was employed for rotating eight-hour shifts, beginning at 6 a.m., 2 p.m. and 10 p.m. By the time that Gwen left school he was in his mid-fifties. 'It was really hard work in the tinworks then. I saw my father often having to sit out in the back garden, to get his voice when he came home. And he'd have to go to bed before he could eat his dinner.' Mrs Davies needed to cosset her husband:

'He wasn't a very strong man ... I can remember mother would go down at eleven o'clock to the works ... with a drop of lovely Welsh cowl cenin – leek soup ... I'm afraid she spoilt only the men, and the boys, my brothers. They seemed to be more pampered than the girls.'

There were still flashes in Mr Davies of the vivacious young man from Port Talbot, 'rather a dandy', who had first attracted his future wife at a singing festival. In the mornings, after he had lit the fire he would sometimes

'lightly whistle at the bottom of the stair, for us to come out of the bedroom, and we used to have in those days a basin of sop in the morning, see. It was made of bread, and that was sugared, with tea poured over it, and a lump of butter on the top and that was spread around, and then a piece of cheese with that. And he'd make different animals in the cheese, a cat or a rabbit or something, to amuse – he was very fond of the children.'

He enjoyed walks, and in winter skating, with his family. Occasionally he would go sea fishing in a rowing boat with his workmates, and very often he would take the children to look at the ships.

'He loved the sea. And he nearly ran away to sea when he was a boy – they caught him in time, on Miss Talbot's yacht in the Lynx. He loved the sea and he loved taking me down every Saturday afternoon to the docks which was full at that time of sailing ships, and he'd be describing the different ships to me and we'd go to the lock gates and we'd watch the pilots bringing in the ships . . . That was the thrill of my week, when my father would take me down to the docks.'

As he grew older, however, a more withdrawn side of Mr Davies came to dominate, no doubt partly through sheer tiredness. He was 'a very lovable person but very quiet. You couldn't discuss things with my father as you could with my mother. He was a very shy man. Not so conversational.' He was highly fastidious: a man who could not bear to kill a chicken, and who shunned any form of entertainment which might offend his religious views. When Mrs Davies first took the children to an opera he protested, 'You're taking the first step downhill. Now you're going to put the children on the road to destruction.' Although a convinced Liberal, he played no active part in politics, and he would not attend public houses. He sent one of the children to pay his subscription to the sickness benefit club upstairs in the Talbot Arms, while it was his wife who would go up for a jugful of beer to the Miners' Arms, even though the stout landlady, Gwen the Miner, 'was a very Godly woman . . .

and all the men would go there and discuss sermons'. Mr Davies was 'a home bird . . . My father was a Calvin and a puritan, all he lived for was his home, his family and his church . . . He couldn't see anything outside that.'

Mrs Davies was very different. Her spirit infused the household. 'My mother was what you would call a very deeply religious person, but a very happy witty person too. She loved everything great in the world – great musicians, great operas, great singers, great writers. Prolific reader.' She was sometimes known as 'Mary Davies y gantred', the singer; and before her marriage 'she was very popular in Carmarthen, and they would shout out, some of the crowd, a gang of boys who were very fond of my mother . . . "Well done, encore, Hopcyn Davies's blackbird" ',[2] as she sang in her black frock, white gloves, and black and white beaded collar. Hopcyn Davies, her father, was a Congregational deacon, and an engineer, a local figure of substance; so much so that when the tinworks went bankrupt, and some families were forced to emigrate, he lent the Davieses enough to keep afloat without recourse to poor relief, until eventually another firm bought the works, 'and we saw the first smoke for two years going up the stack'. Mrs Davies paid her father back in time. 'She'd rather give than receive.'

Mrs Davies combined enthusiasm with method. 'My mother was a great believer in good manners, organization, method. Method was a big word, she had that written up in the scullery, "Method". When she'd cook everything was back as she was using it, there was to be no mess on the tables, I never saw such a tidy person.' She was an enthusiast for home cooking, baking and so on. She had no regular paid help, and the children were all taught to help. She would even try to laugh their father out of his depressed state. At mealtimes, she encouraged talk. 'She liked to hear us discussing things,' the news, the sermon, local court cases. 'She would read the paper from beginning to end, and take it in like a blotting paper.' She was 'a wonderful person to share a worry with . . . very amusing, you'd never be bored with her'. She had high standards of behaviour, but she was not rigid and she preferred reasoning to physical discipline. 'She wasn't very keen on us having punishment. She liked awakening our conscience.' When argument at the family table grew too heated, she would simply raise a finger. A disobedient child would be sent to bed. 'The great boast she always made was she never saw one raise a hand in anger to the other.' The children were brought up 'to love each other' and also to believe that 'Parents are given us to guide us through life, just like the pilot of a ship.' And Mrs Davies phrased her own role characteristically: 'I'm a mother, I'm a Queen. I'd give my life for my children, my husband, but also I like to keep discipline and order in the family.'

They were a united family, 'very close and very wrapped up in each other', but at the same time very open to the world around them. 'Oh yes, we had a very happy home, full of life.' Both parents were enthusiastic Calvinistic Methodists, and religious activities were by no means confined to Sundays, when the children were not supposed to play games, and were taken to chapel even as infants in a shawl. Every night Mr Davies would read chapters from a family Bible. Grace was said both before and after meals. On Tuesday nights there was the Band of Hope, and on Wednesday nights the weekly church meeting. On two other nights there were regular prayer meetings, when a good verse chosen might lead to 'a wonderful warm fiery meeting'. Mr Davies would be overcome by emotion on some of these occasions: 'he was beautiful on prayer, he'd always weep, he was never good enough, and everybody else would weep'. On Thursday and Sunday evenings there was choir rehearsal. 'We had two hundred and fifty choir in our church at that time. Marvellous it was ... We'd perform the Messiah, the Elijah, Brahms Requiems, Rossini, Stabat Mater ...' Mr and Mrs Davies were active visitors of sick chapel members. And on Saturday nights some of the family might attend another near-by chapel service. But the climax was on Sundays, when the best clothes were brought out, 'clothes of respect', some specially made by Mrs Davies's dressmaker sisters: 'the whole brood of seven marching down from the church here dressed immaculately. She had a great pride in dressing herself and wc as a family.' And then, in the aftermath, 'Monday morning was a big day of brushing all the suits ... and fold them, put them by for the following Sunday.' With all this activity no wonder the children sometimes felt 'we'd no time to breathe, we were so occupied in our church'; or that they found their teenage heroes in the chapel. 'Today it's cricketers, footballers and boxers and what have you, but my heroes were ministers because I was hearing so much talk in the house, and we used to have such great preachers, giants of the pulpit, at that time.'

But plenty of energy apparently remained for secular social life. Mr Davies had several local relatives, and both parents had many chapel friends and neighbours. Although Mrs Davies relied on her Carmarthen sisters for an occasion such as a confinement, when she 'would pay them what they'd lose on the dressmaking to come down and look after her and the children', there was a considerable exchange of mutual help between neighbours. Mrs Davies was 'a marvellous woman with people in sickness ... You were one community.' Informal calling was frequent. 'They'd knock the door and walk in, they were that real friendly, but they'd knock at the door in case somebody was having a bath, you know, by the fire ... Every day there was somebody in and out. Oh, always a houseful, it was quite an open door for everybody. And very fond of music.' Callers were expected to join in the meal if the family were eating, as well as the music or talk. They would all sing round the piano, or perhaps listen to a solo performance by Gwen's brother Idris. 'If we had visitors his star turn was playing the Hallelujah chorus on the piano.' There were in fact two pianos in the house, and another brother could play the violin. Birthdays were big occasions, and also Hallowe'en: 'a whale of a time ducking apple night and the boys at the back pushing our heads under the water of course'. Best of all was Christmas: 'Oh a big tea, tarts, trifles, everything else and, all the crowd, the house was always packed. And then there was music in the front room, singing, hymns, carols – it was quite a day. And Boxing Day. We had two wonderful days ... It was always open door.'

There were other entertainments for the children: pet rabbits; collecting cigarette cards and pressed flowers; playing hockey and cricket in the near-by park; the usual street games; bicycling, and regular visits with their mother to the theatre, concerts, the cinema and to see friends. During the annual works closing week they went, along with many other families, to stay at Llandridnod Wells, where they took part in more music, and also recitations and mock legal trials. At other times they joined in a street outing up the valley, or to the beach:

> 'families would go there, we'd have a whale of a time. With baskets full of food . . . all the street go down, and they used to make then what they called small beer, herb beer that they'd make at home . . . and with you walking and shaking it would ferment, you see, the balm in it, and the corks would be flying all over the place . . . But there was always a fire lit and we'd undress before the fire and go into the sea . . . And years ago the mothers weren't as posh as they are now, all of them wouldn't have bathing costumes, they'd go in their nightdresses, and they would be floating in the sea you know, like a parachute.'

Taibach was an active, and in some senses a united community: against the zealous policeman, who was mocked in verse; as Welshmen against the English; and as Liberals against the Conservative party. But it was certainly not a classless society. Gwen Davies was cautioned against some playmates: 'My mother took objection to some, some were very, very rough.' She was also brought up to think, like a minority of superior working-class families, of craftsmen as middle class, while labourers were lower class. The upper class were local employers. Characteristically, these divisions were seen as depending more on education than occupation itself.

> 'There were those who were trying to educate the children, there were others who would stick in the same – if the father was a miner the boy had to be a miner, that type. Then there were the other type now like my parents, wanted to let us have a better place in the world than they had, wanted to educate us you see to get on a bit. Then there were the higher-class people who were moneyed people, who could afford to send their children away to boarding schools and

> college . . . Middle class I should think we were, you know, my mother wanted to give us a bit more than the ordinary people then. She liked us to rise above the ordinary.'

And Mrs Davies encouraged her children to like their teachers, and invite them home for pancake teas in the parlour. She would tell them, 'You'll never have too much education to please me.'

The connection between economic and social standing could not, however, be so easily separated.

> 'The elders of our church at that time were all of them either owners or bosses in the various works . . . And the West End and the Ffrwdwyllt works and the Dwffryn church were like one community. If you went to Dwffryn church you'd have a job in the Ffrwdwyllt works because [Edward Davies, the owner of the works] this Elder Deacon was so wrapped up in the church that you would always be sure of a job.'

The Elders were a formidable group, dressing for anniversaries in top hats and frock coats, and holding the power of excommunication. Although some working-class elders were now being elected, even the most respectable working-class families were expected to keep their place. There was an occasion when Mrs Edward Davies, who bought her anniversary clothes from an expensive dressmaker, and Mrs Davies (Gwen's mother), who chose hers from a fashion book to be made by her sister, appeared in almost the same dress. Mrs Edward Davies then

> 'went to the dressmakers, they were hauled over the coals, why had they made that frock for my mother like theirs. And they said they hadn't made it, that Mrs Davies had had it made by her sisters, and she had chosen it from the same book as they had, and that she had quite the same right to choose any frock she liked as they did. But anyway the disgust of those, now, that my mother – [wife of] a working man in the tinworks – should dress in the same style dress as they were. He was the owner of the works.'

But for the Davieses to be treated with snobbery was unusual. Locally they belonged to the elite. Their chapel was the most superior in the neighbourhood. 'They called the Methodists bigheads, because we were supposed to be so much more intellectual.' Their street was equally well known for its culture, nicknamed Piano Street. When Gwen Davies encountered rough children at school, she regarded them as from another world: blasphemous, 'terrible creatures', organized in sinister gangs, the Goitre gang and the Celluloid gang.

'They were the hooligans of the place, were terrible ... They thought you were a class above and they liked to have their revenge on you, coming in gangs and run after you and hammer you, and pelt stones. And coming home from school we were scared stiff of them ... They were from very poor homes you see, very poor, very dirty homes. They were children you wouldn't mix with. They weren't very sweet-smelling ... Oh it was heathenish, it was heathenish. Beyond.'

Gwen Davies's own ambition was to become a schoolteacher. Her father's hope was that she might marry a chapel minister. In the event, neither happened. The family had already decided to help her brother Idris set up his own business as an outfitter. 'He was the gentleman of the family, and always immaculate in dress.' Gwen was persuaded to leave school at fourteen and go to work for him.

'I felt very upset to tell you the truth, yes. My parents thought I'd do well in the business with Idris helping to build his business up, because I could speak Welsh or English and so many people would come down from the valleys to buy, you see, and you'd be surprised how keen they were on the Welsh ... My brother did the measuring of the suits and all that, but I did most of the serving, helped to dress the windows. My brother was very artistical, he won prizes for his window dressing. Plenty to do, look after the stocks, and I'd go to Cardiff to the warehouses to buy for him ... My mother and father kept us ... We were an expense. My parents never gained on one of us ...

'I loved it. I loved mixing with people. They all said I had patience in the business, my brother would be more irritable ... Some were real what we call "tabs" in those days; and there were the other sort that were very nice, very kind and considerate, wouldn't give you too much bother, but the tabs would – you could have a counter full of stuff, and they'd never be pleased, they'd go out without anything ... I used to like to have a little chat with the customers, talk football, cricket ... with the young men who'd come in to sit and have a little chat. It was a very homely shop, everybody liked coming in there.'

Gwen's leisure time as a shop assistant revolved still around the activities of the chapel, the choirs, and Welsh drama, and now also politics, which interested many of the young men. But perhaps surprisingly the man she was to marry, later a clerk, had come from England as the leading violinist in the orchestra at a local cinema.

'My brother had gone to lunch, and I alone was in the shop. He wanted a raincoat. And – talking and I fitted him up with a raincoat and – went to write the bill out. So I asked him for his name. And he was a bit of a tease, he said, "Jack Robinson". And I put – of course the name was Morley Whitelam – put the Jack Robinson down on the bill ... That's where I met him first ...'

Gwen Davies was thus to cross into the middle class through marriage. Her story again illustrates the web of connections across the borderline, as well as the active culture within the working class itself.

10 Working Class: the Semi-Skilled

Fred Mills

The semi-skilled were the central working class. They were essentially a class of servants and assistants: domestic servants, shop assistants, transport workers, machine-minders, craftsmen's mates, and the hired men on the land. Some, like upper servants, assistants in the better-class shops, or postmen, had jobs which were regarded as respectable and responsible, even if not very well paid. Horsemen could also take a certain pride in their work. Factory machine-minders and craftsmen's mates were little more than specialized labourers.

There were also variations in their typical ages. Farm and transport work were life-time occupations, but few parents were full-time domestic servants, shop assistants or semi-skilled factory hands. It was normally dropped at marriage, although some women returned part-time to it afterwards.

As service workers the semi-skilled were more evenly spread out across the country than the skilled. Indeed, our three families each stand at different points in the historic evolution of the British working class through industrialization and urbanization: Fred Mills is brought up in the southern countryside shaped by the agricultural revolution, Will Askham begins in a northern industrial village and moves to an industrial town, while Emmie Durham is a child of the city.

Rural society in southern and eastern Britain had at its head wealthy landowners like the Brandons, and at its base landless farm labourers. In East Anglia, with its large corn farms, the number of labourers to the average farm was highest of all. Fred Mills came from one of these labourers' families, in north-east Essex.

Fred Mills was one of twelve children. Their births had been spread over nearly twenty years, and the eldest son Arthur was born before his mother's marriage. Although Fred never knew more than seven children at home together, such a large family meant inevitable poverty on the wages of a farm labourer. 'We were so poor we was slightly on the rough side.' At school he was aware of the superiority not only of the farmers' daughters who came on bicycles, but of the children of craftsmen and the maltings workmen who were 'a little better off and of course they hadn't got so many children, no'. Even regularly paid men on the farms were in a better position than a labourer like his father: 'they might be being a cowman a seven day week and they was a bit better off like that weren't they?' He did not forget an occasion in the school playground when one girl objected to playing 'Kiss in the ring' with him, but enough of the others said, 'He's as good as what we are.' So Fred Mills was brought up to be deferential to any man: 'If a farmer was out there hold his horse or anything like that; always touch your cap to a schoolmaster ... I would call anybody "sir". At least a tramp as I would the King of England, don't make no difference to me.'

The Mills family were not without their pride. Mr Mills had been three years 'to sea as a youth. He was on a fishing smack.' Although he couldn't write, he could draw boats beautifully, and 'he could read the Bible and the Bible only, and he always read it out aloud'. When young he had been prominent at prayer meetings. 'He weren't no fool although he weren't educated, he weren't no fool. He'd say to me, you're dull of understanding, if he told me anything you know.' Mr Mills's low earnings were partly due to the fact that he suffered periodic gastric attacks. At these times, especially, Mrs Mills's relatives proved a standby. She had herself been in service, and 'she could spell a lot better than any one of us'. She had a sister who was the cook at a nearby house, and would save her earnings to buy clothes for the Mills children. Mrs Mills also had three brothers in a grocery business, who would send food parcels. Fred Mills remembered one of them refusing a tip from a traveller for holding his horse:

'The man offered my uncle a penny and me uncle wouldn't have it . . . Mr Maskell had already paid him for his job, he didn't want that penny, it was dishonest to take it. So that's the stock we come from.'

But help from relatives was not sufficient. In the worst times, before the eldest children were earning, the family was forced on to parish relief:

'had the old Relieving Officer round, so many loaves of bread and she had to have 'em all at once . . . so the bread got stale didn't it. They used to call this old gentleman who was the Relieving Officer "Old Dry Bread". If he allowed you to have anything he didn't allow you to have much on it. Of course and when he retired he got praised for looking after the business, being careful with what they'd got to issue out.'

Even at the best of times the children were partly dependent on charity. Fred would get bread and jam after school from a neighbour, with the warning, 'If you don't stop swearing I shan't give you no more.' They also begged from strangers: 'We used to run behind horse-drawn brakes and hansom cabs, four-wheeler things, and shout out "a copper".' For clothes, they went 'cadging, going round asking other people, if they've got any old clothes to give away'.

But even begging could not bring the Mills family more than a meagre sustenance. The boys wore no underclothing, and in summer went barefoot. They were underfed, with only tea and bread with perhaps home-made jam or lard for two meals, and the main meal at midday consisting of some form of batter or suet pudding. They could never afford a joint, and pieces of meat only once a week. Vegetables came from an allotment, but they did not normally keep hens or animals, and surprisingly did not go rabbiting. They never had milk to drink.

Like many rural labourers, Mr Mills had not stayed in the village where he was born, but moved three times. Each of their houses was small, with at most three bedrooms, a living room and a lean-to. Although friendly with neighbours, like many poor families they had not the resources to invite them in. The family did not play games together, or have singsongs. At Christmas the uncles might send oranges and nuts, but birthdays passed without presents or guests. On one birthday Fred 'went to bed and cried, I hadn't got no presents'. They read the Sunday paper, or school prize books, but they only saw the daily paper when the newsagent gave it to them to light fires. They never went away for a holiday. 'We used to play in the gutter, perhaps marbles, and bowling the hoops . . . Girls had wooden ones and the boys had iron.' There were other traditional games, such as foxes and hounds, and honeybee; and also cricket and football. Sometimes a travelling Punch and Judy would visit the schoolyard. There was the annual Sunday School outing. In summer they could go walking, and pick up apples. But for these English country children there was nothing equivalent to the story-telling, music and dancing which still flourished, as we saw in Peter Henry's story, both in family and community in the north.

Their parents had still less opportunity for recreation. Mrs Mills took in washing for money. 'She never had the time to play but she'd talk to me.' She did attend Baptist prayer meetings and mothers' meetings. Mr Mills no longer went to church, and rarely even to the pub. 'I don't think his money run to it.' Nor did he take much interest in politics. 'He used to vote mind you but I don't think he understood nothing much about it.' Elections were more fun for the boys:

> 'We used to have a rough band. We'd go out in the street with old tin cans knocking and making a aitch of a noise . . . We used to sing,
>
> Mrs Pankhurst
She's the first
And Mrs Lily with a nine-pound hammer in her hand
Breaking windows down the Strand
If you catch her
Lay her on a stretcher
Knock her on the Robert E. Lee.
>
> Hit her on the bottom that means I suppose. She tied herself to the railings didn't she?'

As was not uncommon among the poorest families in south-eastern England, Mr and Mrs Mills were not authoritarian as parents, nor rigid in their own household roles. Mr Mills 'used to be the first one up in the morning to light the fire and make toast before he went out at six o'clock in the morning'. He would mend shoes, make clothes for the children, wash up and even cook with some pride: 'He said, "a better pudden than your mother could make ain't it boy?" ' Both parents were affectionate and the children were rarely punished in any way. Fred never remembered any corporal punishment. Mealtimes, despite the large number of children, were very free and easy: there 'weren't all that rigmarole'. Religious observations, such as grace at meals, or play restrictions on Sundays, were not imposed. The children were left to pick up sexual attitudes for themselves, and allowed to go bathing in mixed groups without wearing any costumes. Even when one of Fred's older unmarried sisters had a child, although Mrs Mills may have been anxious 'I don't remember her particular showing it'. She certainly did not take this opportunity of explaining the facts of life:

> 'I had a sister, she had this baby what she said she had out of the mailcart, I realized soon after that. But I knew about sheep – and some other boy must have said something to me and I knew soon after this nephew of mine was born, yes. Wouldn't be about ten I don't reckon.'

For moral instruction it would seem that Mr and Mrs Mills relied on the children's schoolteachers. 'Well you really got that at school didn't we? My schoolmaster was ever so strict.' Nor did Fred's parents take much interest in what he learnt at school. Like the majority of working-class parents, they just let him find out for himself.

Although Fred was not a strong child, by the age of seven he was already earning by running errands, delivering eggs and bread, before and after school. At weekends he went to a near-by seaside town, where on a good day he could earn threepence for golf caddying. 'The summer months was the most profitable. 'Course sometimes if you went in the winter months you might go for nothing and get no job.' The boys would sit playing cards in the golf caddy house. Another job during the school holidays was helping a thatcher, standing on a man's shoulders to pull down the ropes, called 'yellums', so that the thatch did not blow loose. Fred could earn a shilling a week this way, and more if he used his money shrewdly.

> 'He'd say, "You're a toff, Fred" . . . He borrowed a shilling off me, and when he's got some money to pay me back, instead of giving me a shilling he gave me one and threepence . . . He was really a bit of an old toff himself . . . He was well educated, but he boozed you see.'

Fred Mills left school at the age of twelve. He was eventually to settle down for forty years as a bricklayer. But before this he went through a phase of shifting occupations, typical of an unskilled or semi-skilled worker in the early twentieth century.

Fred's first full-time job was on a farm, 'pulling the mangold' in the same field as his father. Another brother worked on that farm too. After three weeks, however, the farmer sacked him, perhaps because he suspected that the boy was under age. So he returned to seaside golf caddying, until the outbreak of war. Then in August 1914, when the local big house was taken over for billeting officers, he went to live in as a pantry boy and general servant. One of the officers after a few weeks took a liking to him, and 'asked me if I'd like a job as a page-boy in London'. Fred accepted, and was given his fare to South Kensington, and money for boots, a tie, and a livery suit and going-out suit from Harrods.

The officer's household consisted of a cook, parlourmaid, housemaid, gardener and a governess. There were three children, and the mistress, whom Fred thought meanly suspicious. 'I don't think she was at all nice . . . They were storing wine in the cupboard. She wouldn't let me put that wine in that cupboard myself. She wanted to check that all in herself.' There was a servants' room where they could rest, but Fred had nowhere adequate to sleep. He was given a camp bed, 'worse bed than what we've got at home', and had to keep all his possessions in a tiny tin box. His job was to answer the door, whistle for taxis, run errands, take the dog for afternoon walks, clean the front steps, door knob, hall and other brasses in the house, carry coal up from the basement, wash up, and serve the afternoon tea in a silver pot. For this he received five shillings a week.

There were pleasures in being in London on his half day. He dropped churchgoing and took up the music hall. But the job was spoilt by an unexpected entanglement. 'Shall I tell you the truth? Actually I fell in love with the cook. Well of course I weren't very happy. It's her fault, really, not mine.' He was only sixteen, she nineteen, and her fiancé had been killed in the war. She led him on: 'Well she did earlier on. Then she might have realized that I was only young and no job and no money ... Well I was upset for some months, yes. So I was glad to get home, so it didn't worry me getting the sack.' It was a relief when a sudden incident ended his London career:

> 'The cook had told me that this lady prior to marrying this officer was lower down in status. She's lower down and I was fool enough to write in my letter and tell my mother that. So what happened, when the front door bell rang, the parlourmaid said, "You go and answer the door" ... So when I'm gone she reads my letter and tells my mistress what I'd wrote home and told my mother that until she'd married she was lower down in being well off, and I reckon that's why I got the sack. But I got the sack, according to what she told me, for telling a lie, which one morning the housemaid was up late and she hadn't time to do her work, she said, do so-and-so for me Fred, and I didn't dust the hall. The missus asked me did I dust the hall, and I said, "Yes," and I hadn't.'

Back at home, Fred quickly found work potato picking. But that year his father died. 'They didn't take him to burial in a hearse, he went on a farm wagon. Well the same as what he worked all his life.' Meanwhile Fred bought a bicycle. 'If they wanted anything different, if they want a job in the building line's got to bike there to a different village or town. I biked miles.' For the moment he stayed in various farm jobs: pulling turnips, broadcasting seed, feeding cattle and pigs, carting, cleaning. After this he took labouring and cleaning work in an explosives factory; and became a sheeter's mate in a steel erecting gang. Then he set up on his own, selling bicycles. After fifteen months he went back to farm work. A mere chance placed him in his life's occupation:

> 'As I was on the way to Weeley I met a man born in Beaumont. He said, "I want a bricklayer's labourer at Beaumont, Fred." So I goes and packs up me job at Weeley, draws me money and forget me bucket what I pick the peas in, left them in the field, and when I got back a man said to me, he said, "Don't think you'll be any good to us, mate." "Well," I said, "you promised me a job and I've been and give the other job –" "All right, I'll give you a chance." And I worked till dinner, he say, "You'll do" . . . Even when I left him I couldn't raise a corner properly. No, he never put me to do that really. That's all line work. Well you could do that after half hour.'

Will Askham

As we move now to the north, to a smaller family whose father earned distinctly more, we find a less bare existence, even if below the level of Frank Benson's family. In the early twentieth century much of the industrial life of northern England remained, as it had begun, scattered in the countryside, in villages rather than towns, a mixture of old and new ways.

Will Askham was the youngest of two boys and four girls, all who survived of his parents' eleven children. His first years were spent in a quarry community near the head of one of the Pennine moor valleys in County Durham. His mother was Scottish. She had worked before marriage as a farmhand, and then 'in gentleman's service'. Mr Askham came from a Durham village further down the same valley. When Will was born he was already, like his wife, in his forties. He had begun in the quarry as a fireman, and then went on to the quarry railway line as a shunter. Later he was promoted to become a guard. But in all these jobs there was uncertainty of payment. 'When the quarries laid off through bad weather at any time, during the winter there were some times they were off for weeks, before they could get a job ... That's the reason why he came to shift.' Just before Will was ten years old, the whole family was to move to another small town, the railway junction to which the line from the quarry led, in search of more regular work.

It must have been a wrench to leave the quarry community. Mr Askham, who was a keen Liberal, had helped to start the railwaymen's union branch there at meetings in his house – secret, for fear of dismissal – and had become branch secretary. It was a place in which help was freely given, 'just when anyone was sick', and neighbours called frequently. The children played together freely, as they grew older cycling about the countryside or going for long walks on the fells. The Askhams had friends among the farm people as well as the quarrymen, and would sometimes invite 'those that lived on the fell' down to tea at weekends. The children would go up to help churn butter and chop turnips, or just wander through the woods. 'And when in wintertime the snow was sufficiently strong enough, there was a nice hill, and we used to take our sledges up and sledge down. The farmer he never interfere with you, no, no.' Mr Askham sometimes went to the pub; Mrs Askham to a chapel concert; the children to the travelling cinema, a horse-drawn four-wheeler which came up the valley. On the annual works trip by train for a day by the sea at Scarborough, the families would go as a whole. 'The friends of mother's was friends of dad's ... We congregated all together in the street where we lived, we were like one big family.'

The Askhams had relatives close by who 'lived practically up on the quarry face'. There was Will's grandfather, who must have been born in the 1820s or before, 'a very old man he looked to be with long white whiskers. And the last time I saw him, he was in the yard, he was sitting on a three-legged stool chopping sticks. Aye, chopping firesticks. And that's a long time ago.' His grandfather was held up as a pattern to him as a child: 'a nice quiet fellow'. There was also an aunt whom Mr Askham found particularly sympathetic.

'My father always used to say, "If you follow the Book, you won't go wrong." . . . An old aunt, she was an old lady, used to come and visit us often. She used to smoke a clay pipe, and shag tobacco. Me father used to sit at one side of the fireplace and me aunt at the other one, and they would sit and talk about the Bible. And every night before we went to bed she got the family Bible, she read a certain amount out of that Bible before we went to rest. Every night.

'Well I can tell you a story about it . . . We were little children, and me aunt came. And during the night-time, back end, if there was a moon she used to go out into the yard, and look at the moon, and prophesy what the world was going to be like tomorrow. And this particular night, it was a full moon. And she used to wear very thick-lensed spectacles, and they were thick, very thick; and a very broad, knitted hairnet, black, about half-inch square net.

'And this particular night she went into the yard, the yard door was shut, she went into the yard and was standing, looking at the moon – when the ticket lad came up with a ticket for me father. And me aunt was just standing. He took one look at her – and he off. He didn't leave no ticket. He off. He went up to the office, he said, he said, "I've –" he said, "I've seen the devil in Askham's yard." Aye, Aye. She frightened him.

'But – aye, she was grand. She would sit and play concertina. Aye, Aye. But she was always an agricultural worker. Aye, she was – real fine woman.'

The juxtaposition of traditional superstition and more recent religious enthusiasms was echoed in the musical occasions when the old lady would play for singers performing the latest music hall songs, and probably more traditional songs too. The immediate family were not very musical: none of them were good singers, though Will did learn the mouth organ. When alone, his parents would sit quietly, his mother knitting, his father perhaps reading his weekly *North Star* – 'He was a bit keen on the Parliament.' At best the children would play paper combs: 'Four or five of us sat around the fire tootling.' But when friends called, and there was an accompaniment, 'they would start a singsong. There used to be some fair decent singers among them. Aye, I've seen in our kitchen, I've seen about twelve, and a young fellow used to come, and he used to sing, "Grandfather's Clock".'

The Askhams were Primitive Methodists, strict in some respects, but far from sombre. 'All your toys, tops, balls and everything else, was put away on a Saturday evening and they were there until Monday.' They were sent to Sunday School in their best suits. As was now usual with working-class adults, Mrs Askham did not go to services, and her husband only occasionally.

> 'He used to go to the chapel, if there was any special visitor there, as a preacher. Or the Fiery Fishermen, that was well known – ooh, the chapel was packed when the Fiery Fishermen came. But they were good, oh they were nice chaps. There were four or five of them. They were good singers and they were good preachers. And they used to tell some very nice stories of the sea.'

At home, Will's parents insisted on discipline, but by the standards of the neighbourhood 'in a kindly manner . . . We were all brought up in a nice kindly atmosphere.' There was no great formality over meals, although grace was always said. The children could confide in their father. 'He would listen to you and then he would give you advice.' He scarcely ever punished them. Mrs Askham more often resorted to slapping, although more often 'it was just a matter of a gentle touch'. Neither needed the instrument which remained for all to see: 'On the mantelshelf, at the end, we had a cat o' nine tails hung on the end. And mother just need point at the cat o' nine tails and that was enough.' Mrs Askham was in practice an affectionate woman, 'a grand soul'. And both parents would entertain the children. She would dress up as an animal, or 'go out and have bit of a skip with us'. Their father would take them for walks. He would tell them ghost stories, of the haunted farm, where 'the servant girl at the farm, she made the beds on the morning and when they've gone at night for to get in they're all unmade. Going to the stables for to harness the horses for the day's work and when they've gone back they've been unharnessed.' He read the children stories too; or passages from the Bible.

Mrs Askham could not read; but one of the books in the house was hers, given her by a dying quarryman, whom she had nursed after he had been fatally injured by a blasting accident. 'And before he died he said to my mother, he says, "There's Bobby Burns on drawer's top there." He says, "It's yours."' But the Askhams had few other books. There was little margin of comfort in their material life. There were no family holidays away, no special celebrations at birthdays or Christmas. They had a decent five-room house in a terrace of railway cottages, but the housework was a struggle. Water had to be pumped up from a well. Mr Askham was on shifts, and although he helped a little he would do no cooking, so that his breakfast had to be prepared for starts in the small hours, or his dinners cooked late when he was on other shifts. Mrs Askham made her own bread and jam, and a variety of vegetables were grown in the garden. In good times they had bacon and bread for breakfast, and cheese and cakes for tea. For the midday dinner, liver, or rabbit pie or broth from 'a pluck and a sheep's head' were typical dishes. 'We had good meat three times a week. That was when me father was working of course. When the quarries were rough me father wasn't paid.' The children also had to be clothed, and the Askhams had high standards: new clothes at Easter, including kilts for the small boys.

By the time of their move, the eldest children were already earning, for 'some of the lassies' were day girls in service. Will had also begun work running errands and delivering tea on Saturdays. His parents made him save in a money box for his clothes.

Will's neighbours had mostly been working-class families in a similar situation, but he had grown up with the awareness of social hierarchy characteristic of country boys: a respect for the doctor, the clergy, even for 'the brethren' of the Primitive Methodist chapel, a feeling of distinction from 'rough' families who 'used to argufy and fight', and an admiration for the 'real toff', the lady or gentleman who 'used to acknowledge you, speak to you, and it didn't matter whether you were coming from work, black, or you were dressed up. You were still acknowledged.'

When the Askhams moved from the quarry to the railway junction, it was to a larger settlement, close enough to the countryside for Will to remain a keen walker:

> 'Oh aye, long ones . . . There was three of us. We left about half past nine and we walked to Durham, Durham to Langley Park and we stopped at Langley Park with an old friend, a widower . . . put us up for the night. And after breakfast we set off back again, and we came around by Broom Park, Spennymoor and Crowend, Canney Hill back down into town. That was a right good stretch.'

The town also had its own advantages for Will as he grew older. There was a larger group of young people there. He would chat with them in the street. 'If there was one of the lasses that was going an errand, we'll say, "Where are you going?" "Oh I'm going so-and-so. Are you coming?" "Aye, well – all right, I'll go with you." And – that was it.' He could join them at the music hall – or the station. 'There was always a lot of young people used to congregate at the station, to see the train come in on the Sunday night.'

The family's life was still centred upon the chapel and the railway. Indeed, Will followed his own father's career very closely on leaving school. After a brief job firing boilers at a colliery, and then a year as a day-servant to a spiritual herbalist, he started on the railway. He began in the shunting yard as an oiler lad, lubricating the wagons. Then he was promoted to shunter, and finally to guard. Each stage required a medical test, and the first a formal application and interview. In the shunting yard, however, the railway hierarchy did not impinge much, and although Will followed his father in becoming a union committee man and a banner carrier, it was the experience of solidarity rather than any hostility to his employers which inspired him. He regarded his company superior as 'a gentleman'. In his experience, 'the only interest that the officials had in view was to see the traffic flowing down the sidings . . . No, there was very very rarely any bother between men and their master.' In the shunting yard – as in the street – 'we were like one big family more than work . . . One of the happiest times of my life.' It was in this optimistic phase that Will Askham married a local girl. They married in church, came home for a small party, 'the wedding cake cut and the drink', and then, with a railway pass in his pocket, 'a landau came and we went to the station and in train then to Blackpool. Honeymoon at Blackpool.'

Emmie Durham

We move now into the city. Emmie Durham was an East Londoner, the daughter of a horse carter. Her childhood in part reflects the difficulties of maintaining some degree of family respectability on inadequate earnings, but also the relative anonymity which was possible – although certainly not inevitable – in the vast, shifting working-class districts in the conurbation, in contrast to the smaller, more personal neighbourhoods of the provinces. The family's own wanderings partly explain the very restricted contacts which they had with either neighbours or kin, despite their need for help, and their philosophy of giving it: 'My mother always shared with anyone, if she had it. And that's how she's taught us to do the same.' And their lack of local roots, as well as the absence of any large local middle class, accounts for Emmie's very vague perception of the local social structure, which she saw as entirely working class, 'all the same, bit rough'. As to other social classes, there 'may have been, but I don't know'. Unlike most Edwardian children, she knew nobody who was regarded as a 'real lady' or a 'real gentleman'.

Her mother's family came from Norfolk. Mrs Durham herself had grown up in Lambeth, in the days before free school education. 'That's why she couldn't read or write you see. I used to hold a pen in her hand to try and get her to write her name before she died. Cos she used to have to put a cross to everything.' But she brought up her children strictly. They were not to talk at meals, and 'we had to be quiet if she had anyone in there talking and that'. Although neither parent went to church, she sent her children to the parish Sunday School, and insisted on prayers at night and grace at meals: 'She'd always thank God for meals.' The children were made to bath twice weekly, an unusually high standard of cleanliness. Neither swearing nor card-playing was permitted. And if the children were disobedient, they 'used to get a hiding ... Father wouldn't touch us. My mother. I say she brought us up properly in the proper way. Behave ourself ... She was a bit obstinate at times – but she was a good woman ... He was much easier.'

Mr Durham, like his wife, had grown up in Lambeth, but he had moved early in his married life from South London to the new suburb of Walthamstow, and set up on his own as a coal carter. They 'had a nice house at Walthamstow, my father was his own governor in the coal business, my father had men working for him'. But he failed. 'He used to like a drop of drink, they used to rob him and he lost all his money like that.' He was reduced to mere casual work, carting coal or timber:

> 'a day here and a day there, when he could get it. He used to be out, oh two or three in the morning, queueing up for when they took on the men on the following morning, and perhaps the men in the front'd get a day's work and when his turn came he got nothing. And he'd wander around, see if he could get a bit of work, and he'd come home at twelve o'clock in the day with nothing. My mother would give him a bit of bread and cheese and a piece of Spanish onion to eat.'

For Mrs Durham it was a disastrous fall. One measure of the family's poverty was that from her mother's seventeen confinements, Emmie, who was the youngest, knew of only one brother and three sisters. Only the younger sister was still at home, and and as soon as she could leave school she started work in a rope factory. Even so they had little space. In one flat 'we had just the room to live in and one bedroom . . . There was a curtain in the middle. That's how we lived. But we were decent'. The Durhams moved between a number of tenements and houses, over several miles of East London: Mile End, West Ham, Limehouse and so on.

If a poor breadwinner, Mr Durham would atone by help about the house and with the children. He also earned a little extra by feeding other carters' horses on Sunday mornings, and using the pennies to buy food for his rabbits, which were kept not only as pets but for food in hard times. But the main burden fell on Mrs Durham. She had various means of earning – finding tenants for the landlord of the tenement, charring, or acting as a midwife – but the commonest was as a washerwoman.

> 'She used to take in washing. I've known her be up all night doing washing, up and down the board and hanging the washing up on all the pictures all round the room. She would say to me, "We are going to have different pictures tonight" – My mother used to stand me on a box near a tub, we used to have the wooden tubs to do the washing in then, and a scrubbing brush to scrub the washing, rub the soap on, and she used to let me do the tea towels and the handkerchiefs. She used to teach me. She said, "As you grow up you'll know how to do these things" . . . A shilling a dozen my mother used to get for that . . .
>
> 'We never starved, although it was very hard.'

The Durham family menus were certainly meagre: a breakfast of bread and dripping, a tea of bread and home-made jam (another sign of Mrs Durham's country background), and one good meal at midday – usually a stew, followed by pudding. They relied for meat on cheap pieces, and pork rind and bones. Very often Mrs Durham would go without. It was a struggle, too, to keep the family clothed. The only clothing and footwear bought was second-hand, and very often cut down. 'She always had the needle in her hands.'

There were bitter moments for all of them. At school Emmie would be regularly lined up to see if she was clean. 'We used to have inspection every morning and look at our boots or shoes what we were wearing. And should I make 'em a bit dirty . . . we got the cane.' Once she suffered a bad attack of food poisoning:

> 'And my father went over Bancroft Road, Board of Guardians over there, he went over there for the doctor. And it was like going before a judge and jury he said for a doctor. They asked him all the ins and outs, so anyway he got the doctor in the finish and the Relieving Officer says to my father, "Next time you come over put your new suit on." My father said, "If I had a new suit," he said, "I'd pawn it," he said, "and I'd pay for a doctor for my child, I wouldn't come to the likes of you." '

Probably the worst cost was that they were cut off from social life. The Durhams not only received no help from neighbours or relatives, but had very few callers: 'My mother never invited anybody.' Nor did they go out to visit others. Mr Durham would sometimes go for a stroll, but he rarely had the money for pleasures such as a drink or a bet. 'He'd like a drink if he had the money but very seldom.' Mrs Durham would sometimes join with neighbouring women friends on a Monday 'Mother's Day' celebration, a drink followed by dancing in the tenement courtyard, but this was almost her only occasion for enjoyment.

The family never went out for holidays, or to the theatre or music hall. They did not celebrate birthdays, or have singsongs, or play parlour games. They kept no more than two books, and took only a weekly paper. Mr and Mrs Durham took no part in either political or religious activities. They could not afford pocket money for Emmie, although she was permitted to earn farthings from neighbours for errands. And Emmie had to make her friends in the street or the park. As a child she would sometimes visit and help a neighbour upstairs who worked at home as a matchbox maker. But she never exchanged visits with other children. 'I never went in their places. My mother never had children in our place.' It seems likely that the effect of isolation, which must have been greater when Emmie was an infant in the flat, too young to be allowed out to play, was one reason why she was unusually late in learning to speak.

Emmie Durham left school at fourteen, but she was kept at home for another two years to help her mother with the washing work. Her father said, 'She's the last one and she'll stop at home and help you.' But Emmie wanted to go out to work, and when she was nearly sixteen her father allowed her to start. She began as a laundress. She was forced to leave the job because the steam affected her fingers, the flesh becoming all raw, sore, opening up. Emmie moved to a biscuit factory where she was employed 'putting cheese in these cheese biscuits, putting the tops on and putting them in the trays', and then to a brewery, where she was paid a considerably better wage for bottle-washing, sorting and labelling. There were dangers here too, from broken bottles at the bottom of the washing tank, as well as very long hours, and monotony. But with good pay, and the pleasures of 'larking about' as a group of young girls, Emmie settled down for some time at the brewery.

Although she was now earning, her parents – like others – expected her to be home promptly by ten o'clock. At the age of twenty, when she came in late, her mother 'got hold of my hair she has, pulled me in the road and half beat me. My mother. I was late.' But by this stage she had developed a social life of her own, particularly with one close girl friend, with whom she would go to the cinema. 'She'd sleep with me in my house one weekend and I'd go and sleep with her. She was a nice girl. She was the only true friend I – we was more like sisters you know.' But she was already being pursued by her future husband, who was to end this relatively pleasant stage of life. She had known him as a child – 'I could never get rid of him you know.' When, for example, she went with her girl friend to a fair,

> 'everywhere I went I'd look round, he'd be behind me. Yes. And then perhaps I'd go and queue up for the pictures, get an hour and a quarter for a penny, Charlie Chaplin's films, all silent films. And I'd queue up, and I'd forget all about him. He'd be behind me. He'd get to the pay box before me, put my penny down. And then I wouldn't talk to him, and we'd come out and I'd be with a girl friend and I used to say to 'em, "Before I go home I'm going to the fish shop," get a big piece and a ha'porth, lovely. I'd go in there, when it got to my turn . . . as I put my money down, someone'd put the money down before me, and I knew it was him behind, honest. Oh I had that ages, it seems I had to have him.'

He was a good-looking man, with elegance and spirit. In time Emmie found herself flattered by the assiduousness with which he attended her, waiting for her outside the brewery (to the interest of the other girls), and taking her for a walk, at the end of which 'he'd shake hands and kiss me'. Eventually she yielded, and the cycle of her life turned again to hardship and struggle. 'I fell in the cart with marrying him, but still, it's a gamble you have to take.'

11 The Poor

Richard Morgan

Seebohm Rowntree would probably have placed the Mills a little below his rigorous poverty line, but the Durhams a little above it. But there were others whose situation was much worse. The unskilled had still lower incomes. And there were also families in which the father had a better wage, but other difficulties, such as illness, death or family breakdown, brought far worse deprivations: like the Morgans.

Richard Morgan was fought over from birth. His mother was a Protestant girl from one of the Lancashire cotton towns who had moved into Manchester and, at the early age of eighteen, married a young Roman Catholic from Salford. There was nothing uncommon, by the 1900s, in a Catholic marrying a Protestant. Mr Morgan was a good earner, a seaman who was never short of work, and a handsome and likeable man. But he was too young to settle down when he married.

> 'Me father was one of the most handsome men in Salford . . . Women impulsively liked him. He was a happy-go-lucky soul. Never should have married of course, that class of man should never marry. Cos he was an adventurer by temperament. I loved him. I looked up to him. I thought he was everything . . .
>
> 'He'd throw his money away, and buy up apple carts. I remember him walking down the street . . . one Sunday afternoon, of course he'd had a few drinks and he was in a merry mood, and all the children come running, "Uncle

Johnnie, Uncle Johnnie" – he just walked up to this cart and took it off the chap and just tipped it over. And all the children dashed in there picking apples and pears, and the man was raving and me father, he put his hand in his pocket and pulled out – whether they'd be golden sovereigns I don't know but – a couple of pound – and the man was touching his cap . . .'

Mr Morgan never spent much time at home. When ashore, he had his own set of friends, whom he would see in pubs and clubs. And for long periods he was at sea, 'more or less away for years at a time. I haven't got much recollection of him.' Before Richard reached school age, his parents had definitely parted.

On both his father's and his mother's side, there were relatives willing to help him. If this was a case in which the extended family failed, it was certainly not for lack of interested kin. Mrs Morgan's mother lived near by, and would help her in confinements and sickness. There were other relatives whom she saw daily, 'next-door neighbours sort of thing'. There were many friends too who called, and would be offered tea. 'It was always open house, yes.' She had an ample five-room house, in which visitors could 'make music, sing, play the piano and sing'. The front room was kept for the bigger occasions, such as birthdays or christenings, when she entertained a considerable company, although for most of the week it was 'more like a mausoleum . . . The fire irons and all the brassware was always cleaned on a certain day and put away wrapped up in newspapers.'

Richard was his mother's oldest child, and the other two by her first marriage did not survive infancy. His own christening was the first occasion on which the two sides of his family struggled over his fate. His mother had agreed to a Roman Catholic marriage, but she had an elder sister who was 'a real bigot. And my father's mother was of the same criteria – she was a bigot. So between the two personalities there was a clash. And my mother was a very demure sort of person and this older sister of hers had her under her thumb.' So Richard was taken to a Protestant church and christened Richard Morgan.

> 'Well, the family hadn't broken down completely and me grandmother, which was me father's mother, came one day and asked could she take me out. Mother said "Yes". She took me out, and was hell-bent for St John's Catholic Cathedral. And took me in there and had me baptized again. Francis John.'

When Mrs Morgan eventually found herself deserted, she went to full-time work as a shop assistant in the centre of Manchester. She kept on the large house, although only she, and at times Richard, lived there. But Richard had no fixed home. For a while he was formally under his father's control, and went to live with his father's mother and was sent to a Roman Catholic school. Then he was taken back by his mother and sent to a Protestant school, and for a time lived with his mother's mother. 'I stayed with her till I was about six . . . I used to sleep in the same bed as grandma . . . I was sleeping with her the night she was found dead in the bed, following morning.' Sometimes he slept with an aunt, too.

Shuttled around in this confusing fashion, between various relatives and between attendance at Catholic and Protestant churches and schools, and disliking both kinds of school, Richard began to play truant. He found various jobs for different days, such as priming lamps for a neighbour, and at the market milking cattle and 'red raddling' – marking sheep with a red chalk. At first he was not missed at either school. But 'they eventually caught up with me'. At nine Richard was sent to a day industrial school, where he stayed until he left school at fourteen.

The industrial school day lasted from eight in the morning until half past five at night, lessons punctuated by regular parades and chores such as scrubbing. It was intended to be punitive.

> 'If you did anything seriously wrong like stealing or anything like that you got birched. That birch was like a besom

broom . . . At the apex it'd be twelve to fourteen inches wide and tapered down . . . Oh, it cut you . . . When I first went there I was very unhappy and I played truant. Anyway they got me and they took me and I was sentenced to five strokes of the birch. And the caretaker was a vicious old man called Paggin . . . He did the birching and he took a delight in everything.'

Richard's mother never punished him physically. She was 'the most affectionate woman I ever known. She wore her heart on her sleeve . . . She idolized me.' Nevertheless, she had completely failed to provide a proper basis for Richard's existence. She had allowed relatives to push her around so much that 'in the end I had no proper home'. Even when he was living with her, she could provide no regular meals because she was at work. He had to bathe in the public baths, or the canal, rather than at home. She could make him no clothes, and best buy something from the cheapest second-hand markets. They took no newspapers. She never played games with him. Richard was forced to make a life of his own.

In this he was at first helped by institutions, including the industrial school. The school provided him with three adequate meals a day. In the summer he was able to get a ticket, after searching interviews, for a mission camp holiday by the sea. On Sundays he went to the Ragged School, where the lantern slide show was something that he 'looked forward to every week'. He even relied on the Ragged School for the Christmas breakfast which was the reward of a year's regular attendance.

'We used to queue up at the morning and you was let in and you went through the door a paper bag was given you and in this paper bag was a meat pie, a mince pie and a ham sandwich. And then you all sat down . . . They serve you with tea. And then . . . you sang songs . . . And as each child came out through the door they'd be given a present. A little girl gets a doll. A boy'd get a wooden fire engine or a wooden train. Everybody got something.'

Richard Morgan kept a lasting respect for the kind of people who ran the Ragged School. 'The chapel was run by what we'd call intellectuals of the working-class people. People who did it from the goodness of their heart.'

He was also supported by the company of other boys. A group of them took over a cellar in the neighbourhood, and kept hens there, helping themselves to grain and maize from a big miller's by putting their hands through slits in the sacks. They went out at night catching birds with twigs of birdlime at the sewage farm, and the songbirds, linnets and larks and thrushes, they would sell to 'people in the street. Every house you went past had a singing bird.' They would congregate in the park to play football; or they would slip into the theatre. 'I used to go to the theatre but I never paid.'

But by the time he left school, Richard had lost the taste for company. What was left of his home life had collapsed, through the arrival in the house of another man. 'Her love for this man over-ruled her love for me. He pushed me out and she allowed him to . . . She was the only thing I had. And then this other man came into her life, and that was the end of my home life. I never had no more home life.' He was so unhappy that he would just disappear, sleeping out.

> 'I used to wait till eleven o'clock at night then walk down the canal in the pitch dark where other boys was frightened to death, wouldn't go, and I used to walk four or five miles, and there was a pavilion up near the colliery, and I had a secret way of getting in, and I used to go and sleep in there.'

At weekends he would go off on his own, walking long distances, and sleeping out in the woods. 'I was a loner.'

Before he left school Richard had already begun to earn, by picking iron off a local rubbish tip for a rag and bone merchant. His first full-time job was in a glassworks, assisting the skilled glassblowers: 'Twelve hours with a long rod with a bobbin – red-hot bottles on the end – like a fork effect, putting them in a "lear" – big oven with an open front. The flames was bit hot – they went slowly through to be tempered off.' Then he moved on to being a trolley boy. But on a boy's wages, and determined to keep away from home, how could he live? He could not afford to pay more than two nights a week, even for a Salvation Army shelter. He had seen enough of marriage to prevent any thoughts of attaching himself to anybody else. At the weekends he was desperate. 'I used to go from Friday evening till Monday morning and never had a drink, only water at the public taps, and no food.' How could he carry on? Richard Morgan eventually forced himself to make the choice between independence and destitution. He enlisted as a soldier.

Will Thorn

The childhood with which we end was that of an ex-soldier's son. The typical unskilled Edwardian was a labourer with no clear specialization, working casually and irregularly, by the hour. His best chances of work were in the big cities, on the streets, at the docks, or at the fringes of the life of luxury. For our last Edwardian we return, therefore, to London; and not to the level poverty of a solid working-class district, but to the sharper contrasts of the West End.

Will Thorn was the second eldest of eight children: six boys and two girls. His father was a general labourer, more out of work than in. He might get three months' digging, or a stretch as a porter, or even as a carman. But most of the time he was simply looking for work. He did look; but he would not take just any job. For example, he refused to go hopping: 'He wouldn't lower himself to do that.' He was a Londoner, who had started work as a butcher's roundsman, and met his future wife in this way. He then enlisted in the army, and was successful enough to become a sergeant major. 'He was a smart man, the old man was.' Out in India, he also got used to being waited on, having his boots cleaned and being shaved by the natives. But he was now a man in his forties without a trade. He never took to helping in the home. Depressed by failure, he preferred instead to keep 'out of the way. The pubs was open till twelve o'clock at night.' To his children, he was unsympathetic and strict, trying to force them into military habits such as cleaning the undersides of their boots. When angry with them he would 'knock the daylights out of you . . . He'd flay you with the belt or knock you – if he was shaving and you went by his elbow while he was shaving, you'd get a clump round the ear for that. We used to just dodge by him.'

Part of Mr Thorn's irritation was caused by the cramped conditions in which the family generally lived. They normally took two rooms, a single floor of an old house divided up, with different families on the three other floors, and a shared outside closet. The eight children would sleep in one bed, their parents in another bed in the kitchen. They were rarely in a house for a year.

> 'We had so many addresses, we couldn't pay the rent, we had to keep moving. And we come home from school and find your bits and pieces slung out on road, or passed over the wall to the next bloke to look after while the landlord come in, and he found nothing there.'

Local barrow firms even advertised: 'Keep moving, Humphreys will move you by moonlight.' But this very transience and hand-to-mouth poverty made it a community in which neighbours could do little to help each other. 'They was all busy looking after theirselves.' The Thorns had relatives, but these were also hard up, and if they came it was usually to borrow rather than lend. The family was forced to rely on its own resources.

This meant that Mrs Thorn had to take full-time work. She herself came, rather surprisingly, from a quite prosperous East Anglian gipsy background, and her parents, who had saved enough from a life of dealing in cattle, horses, oranges, pegs and so on, had retired to a country cottage, where they sometimes invited the children for a summer holiday. Mrs Thorn had been in service before marriage in a fashionable professional home, where she had been taught continental cooking styles. She now turned this skill to good use, working as a restaurant cook every day from before eight in the morning until eleven at night. She was a naturally sympathetic mother, who at weekends would encourage the children to talk at meals, 'have a laugh', tell how they had spent the day. But during the week they could see little of her. The infants were put in a nursery school for a penny a day; the others, from three upwards, were sent to school. The children were taught to do some housework, washing and sweeping and darning, but after school they were simply allowed 'to stop out till it was too cold and wet or . . . there was nobody out left to play with'. They put themselves to bed 'whatever time we come in'.

For the older children there was one vital task before bed: a long walk down to the restaurant to collect some fruits of their mother's labour. Mrs Thorn would smuggle food out of the restaurant by lowering a bag on a hook and string from an upper window: 'send it down full of grub for the next day's dinner'. Will was only once stopped by a policeman, who marched him back to the restaurant

> 'where the kitchen was up the top. And I whistled up and she looked down, she said, "What do you want?" I said to her, "The copper's nicked me." She said, "What the bloody hell does he want?" I said, "I suppose he wants some supper." So she came down, she brought him down a packet of sandwiches and a jug of cocoa. And then while he was getting that down, I nipped it.'

These perquisites provided the family's breakfast as well as tea the following day, supplemented by bought bread, potatoes or rice. At weekends they could normally afford to buy food for a good cooked meat meal. If they bought during the week it was cheap stale meat or stale bread. They also raided the yards where railway vans were being loaded. 'We used to get down there in groups and as they loaded the vans of bananas up so we used to knock a hand of bananas off.'

The sources of the family's clothes were similar: second-hand, 'on the railings, down the rag fair', or simply 'pulled' off a barrow. If relatively decent, they would be pawned. Will lost his temper when another member of a church choir, which he had joined for the pay, called him 'ragged arse'. He punched the fellow choirboy on the nose, and found himself expelled. But church remained a useful source of support. His parents never attended, but 'they used to send us to Sunday School on a Sunday, so they could get on the bed and enjoy themselves'. Will soon realized that churchgoers were 'only them that wanted something, went for what they could get. Mostly grub and old clothes. Or perhaps a promise of a day's work.' For regular attenders there were Christmas parcels; for the choir, seaside outings; for the Church Lads' Brigade, even a seaside holiday. Will, who became a drummer and bugler, 'enjoyed it . . . It was a bit of a giggle.' Attendance also gave opportunities for perks:

> 'You meet these old girls that stand in the porch at the church. "Good morning Mr So-and-so, good morning Charlie So-and-so. Glad to see you at church this morning. How's your mother? Is your father at work?" "No." "Well tell your mother to come round to me Wednesday or Thursday and I'll find her a day's work." Clean the bloody house out for two bob . . .'

A cook's wages, which were below those of an unskilled man, were certainly insufficient for a family of eight until the children began to earn. All too often they found themselves forced upon the mercies of the Relieving Officer, 'a nice bastard', who would put the children in a Poor Law school attached to the workhouse, and give the family a food ticket to tide them over until Mr Thorn found another job. Sometimes they were several weeks in the Poor Law school in a summer camp on the estate of a benevolent landowner who took them shooting: 'Show you how to shoot. And you could eat all the fruit there was laying on the ground. But you don't pick nothing off the trees.'

This was a lucky chance, but Will Thorn had to be shrewd enough to put himself in the way of such chances. There was little for him at home. There was no celebration of his birthday. Christmas he would spend singing in choirs for pennies and picking up food parcels. There could be no joining in family entertaining in a home so bare that 'when we had company, if we did, we was never allowed in. Because there wasn't enough chairs to sit on. Stay out in the street.' And in practice the Thorns had scarcely ever a caller: 'Couldn't afford to entertain them.' Nor could there be singsongs round a piano, parlour games, or the pleasure of reading. Will had to learn to pick up what fun he could outside the house. He went around with a group of boys. 'We all mucked in together . . . "Where are you going?" We moved about in gangs.' One evening they might be at the Wormwood Scrubs fair; another at the Metropolitan Music Hall in Edgware Road. 'You got three tickets, see, for a shilling. Perhaps there'd be nine of you going. When you get up the top, see, you used to work the attendant threepence and give him the other tickets, see, and he'd let you all in.' They would go bicycling: 'You might pinch a bike for a day and leave it the next day.' Or they would play pranks on suitable victims, such as the old man who came selling kindling logs,

> 'tarry logs, on a donkey barrow. And he used to have about nine logs in a bowl, and he'd take them downstairs to the ol' woman, fill her apron up. While he's gone down there we undone the traces of the donkey and as he come up the top of the steps he'd say, go on old girl, and then away'd go the donkey and up'd go the bloody lot. He run me all the way from Harrow Road to Gloucester Terrace, yes – with the whip.'

It is scarcely surprising that neither the Thorns nor any of their neighbours would let the boys play inside their homes. They were 'always frightened you'd pinch something'. But there was no lack of interest in the London streets. Another pleasure was to stand outside the police station on Saturday nights, when the drunks were taken in, listening to 'somebody hollering – was having a hiding'. In summer they also swam in the canal. They used the towpath for gambling over cigarette cards and playing pitch and toss, and the police would periodically notice their activities here. 'The copper used to send his helmet round for a collection. See? And he done it once too often, we slung his bloody helmet in the Cut . . . We just jumped in and swum the other side.'

So Will Thorn had to know his way around the world – and his own place in it. 'We lived with the rough.' Craftsmen, even if they recognized him: 'They ignored you. If they met you out, as much as they do to pass the time of day to you.' He had to know and acknowledge those who thought themselves superior, because too often he and his family depended on them. Even the shopkeepers, who might advance them food on tick, he learnt to call 'sir' – 'called everybody "Sir" who was anybody'.

He wanted to leave school long before he was fourteen. 'Hated the sight of it. I thought it was a waste of time, when I could be out earning money. When you're hungry you thought more about getting something to eat than you did about learning.' His brothers had the same attitude: one so much so that he was sent to a reformatory school.

> 'He played the wag too often. I hopped the wag too. I went fishing more than I went to school. The old man'd take you to school. While he's talking to the head master away I'd nip. I'd be gone. I'd stop away couple of nights and then turn up at home, get a bloody hiding, he'd take you back again. Get another hiding at school.'

But even if forced to stay at school, he was not short of devices for earning. 'You had to use your wits, you had to think to yourself, now what shall we do tonight to get a tanner?' On Sundays he could sing as often as four times in a choir. He could sell papers, or cut up hay as chaff for horses. On Saturdays he could sell biscuits outside a local grocer's. Or he could go out to Harrow Hill, to ride the chain horse which helped to pull carts up the hill. 'You saved up two shillings you see, and then you hired the horse, and they give you a bag of grub, and for that two bob you earned what you like. See? You could earn perhaps five shillings.' Another possibility was to minister to the thirst of the policemen on the beat by stealing a few bottles of beer and putting them on the canal wall, 'behind the trees there, and we would stand there and see 'em come and drink 'em and then we'd go and collect the money'. Perhaps his favourite source was cab ducking, helping the cabbies at the railway stations. 'You had to be quick on your feet,' or another boy might get there first. Will would

> 'hang about on the platform, and wait till the cabs are loaded up with the luggage, then you'd sit on behind and ride to where the cab stopped, see? And then you'd help the driver unpack the luggage and carry it in, he'd give you threepence, yes. And you do that two or three times a night and yu'd had a good night, you'd have a fish supper and all for twopence.'

Will Thorn was away from school to a full-time job at the earliest possible moment. 'I left school five minutes past four and I was at work in the pawn shop at five to five. I only went in there to try it, cos they said you get a good tea. I had a good tea in there. And showed me where the bed was, we pulled the bed out from under the counter. You sleep under the counter.' Will worked and slept there for over a year. When he had time off, he could borrow one of the pawned suits for the evening. 'My mate and I, we were the two best-dressed boys in the neighbourhood.' This was a new experience. And there was also entertainment in the job: the redeemers coming in 'half nigh pissed, Saturday night, they'd come in, boiling hot night Saturday night, some was eating fish and chips, some was eating tangerines, some had pease pudding and faggots. Cor blimey it was like Mother Kelly's doorstep in there.'

> 'I had several jobs after I left the pawn shop. I got a job as a porter in a block of flats. And I smacked the poor old head porter on the chin, because he wanted me to stop till ten o'clock at night, for no overtime . . . I wasn't there long enough. Used to get some good tips though, off the ladies that lived in the flats. You know just a couple of toms lived in the flats and if they didn't want to see anybody – "If Mr So-and-so calls this evening, tell him I'm out." Ladies of easy virtue. Perhaps they'd be enjoying themselves with a couple of blokes and one of their regulars'd call round. "Is Miss So-and-so in?" "No, she's out." "Oh,

all right, I'll leave my card, tell her I called." You get a shilling off of him. You get a shilling off her . . .

. . . I got a job at Whiteley's then. A van boy.'

It was to a job of this kind, although as an indoor packer in a different department store, that Will Thorn was eventually to settle. Meanwhile his brothers had begun to earn. As a result, the family began to enter a new phase. 'Things got better at home. There was more to eat. And mother still went to work see, she worked up till she died.' They moved into a four-room flat, and began to buy second-hand chairs, a sofa, even pictures, 'make the place look something like'. The Thorns were experiencing a phase in the life cycle of their family which approached even comfort; for the children, 'the first time we had room to breathe'. And even Mr Thorn was forced to change his ways a little. At seventeen or eighteen Will was prepared to administer his father some of his own medicine.

'I squared up to him and told him, "I'm going to have a showdown with you now. We've had enough of being knocked about just when you thought fit or when you'd had a drink." And he quietened down a bit then, cos my brother, he was older than me, and when he see me, he shaped up to him and all.

'And after that, he was a bit quieter.'

Part III
Instruments of Change

12 The Economy

No changes can be more far-reaching in their social effects than those in economic structure. The economy provides the work context in which most men spend most of their active hours; it supplies the resources upon which their standard of living is based; and it moulds many of their relationships within their own families and in the wider social structure. But as a conscious instrument of change, while undoubtedly critical, the economy is uncertain. We shall see that there are times, such as the First World War, when direct economic changes are brought about through the deliberate intentions of political government. But it is much more common, whatever political intentions may be, for these changes to occur in a more mysterious fashion. The late nineteenth and early twentieth century is generally recognized as an important turning-point in British economic history, when the British dominance of the world economy won in the early nineteenth century began to be steadily eroded. Why this should have been so is much more open to debate.

During the last hundred years, even while there has been little change in the distribution of income to different occupational classes, increasing national prosperity and wealth has allowed a steady increase in average working-class incomes. Real wages have risen regularly, decade by decade, including periods of high unemployment; indeed some of the most rapid gains have been made in periods of industrial depression, such as the late nineteenth century and the 1920s, because wages have fallen less rapidly than prices at these times.

But the years from 1900 to 1918 stand out as exceptional in two ways.

Firstly, real wages stopped rising. They were stagnant, or indeed slightly falling. Prices were rising, due chiefly to a change in the terms of international trade which made imports more expensive. Wages rose, but not enough to keep pace, a fact which accounts for much of the industrial bitterness of the time. The price rise affected all industrial countries, but Britain worst of all. This is the second point. Until 1900 British and American real wages had fluctuated at a similar level. Between 1900 and 1918 American incomes went decisively ahead of British, while German incomes began to catch up.

The British economy was clearly responding less effectively to the changing trade situation. This is not to say that it was at this stage a weak economy. The textile industries, which accounted for nearly half of Britain's exports, remained so strong that despite German, Italian, American and Japanese competition, Britain still held more than half the world's trade in cotton goods. British shipbuilding yards were similarly producing over half the world's new tonnage. Altogether the British share of world trade in manufactures in 1914 remained the largest of any country at 31 per cent. The reasons for disquiet lay not in the actual situation but in the trends. The British share of world trade was now steadily declining as the German share rose. Within a decade, Germany would be an industrial equal and the United States a formidable rival. Britain's hold on the textile market was a declining asset, for the significance of textiles in world trade was lessening. On the other hand, Germany and the United States were now ahead in their development of steel production, in the manufacture of machinery, and especially in the fast-growing electrical and chemical industries. The growth in British coal exports was simply providing fuel for the factories of rivals. It was apparent that, in the face of not only increasing protective tariffs but also the competition of American and German sales methods and standardized production, many British home manufacturers were being outclassed and outpriced. Indeed, but for the help of Indian manufactures produced on poverty wages, so cheap that they could overcome any tariff wall, the imperial balance of trade would already have been in difficulties.

The relative slowness of British industrial innovation in the early twentieth century was partly the price of early success. It was much easier to design factories or shipyards with rational layouts for mechanized mass production on large new sites in developing communities. British industry was locked into the scale of small family firms and the irregular tight sites surrounded by workmen's housing which had suited the early decades of the industrial revolution: the world of Frank Benson or – still – of Arnold Bennett's *Clayhanger*. At the same time, the very success of the former peripheries of the British world trade network meant that for the adventurous English-speaking entrepreneur or investor there were now better opportunities for fresh developments abroad, either in the white dominions of the Empire or in the United States. In the last years before 1914, British capital investment abroad actually exceeded investment at home, while the rate of outward English emigration was higher than in any other period. Thus at the very moment when creativity and capital were needed for industrial renewal at home, resources were being siphoned away.

The success of the Empire also helped to perpetuate another disadvantage. The English upper class had survived into the early twentieth century partly through its own adaptability, its willingness to earn money through urban development, mining and industry as well as through agriculture, and the absorption into its own ranks of the successful industrialist who chose to set himself up as a landed gentleman. At the same time the expanding system of public schools offered a training for the industrialist's sons in the gentlemanly style of life. It was an education which concentrated on the production of rulers and professional men, rather than businessmen or scientists. The Empire provided administrative and military careers for these public schoolboys. Relatively open social mobility thus simply led to the diversion of the sons of the most successful entrepreneurs into a non-productive imperial ruling class. It was clearly difficult to develop science-based industries while any promising heir to industrial influence was put in the classics stream.

Another economic handicap, according to some Edwardians, was the strength of British trade unionism, which raised wages, shortened hours, resisted innovations and even deliberately restricted output. But this argument appears less convincing when it is realized that the most strongly unionized industries, textiles, shipbuilding and coalmining, were exactly those whose export performance was best maintained before 1914. Indeed it is likely that British industry as a whole suffered more from the weakness of working-class bargaining power. The rapid advance of American real wages in the early twentieth century was not based on harder work, but on more mechanization. Already in the 1900s the average American manufacturing worker was assisted by twice as much mechanical horse-power as the British – a lead which has since widened. American manufacturers had mechanized more quickly than British industrialists principally because labour was in short supply and expensive. In the American labour force, moreover, skilled men predominated, partly because they could more easily afford to emigrate from Europe. Their high pay meant that they did not need additional income from their women working, so that American industrialists could not draw on cheap female labour; 22 per cent of the American manufacturing workforce was female, in contrast to 41 per cent in Britain. Nor, outside the plantation south and a few immigration centres, were there alternative supplies of cheap labour. American industrialists were thus forced towards the mechanized and standardized mass production which was to be the basis of twentieth-century industrial prosperity. British manufacturers, on the other hand, were supported both by an available pool of cheap casual labour and also by the largest group of skilled literate craftsmen in the world. This was the workforce which had made and grown with the industrial revolution. But once again, that early start was now a disadvantage. In the long run it was not an advantage that cheap factory labour delayed the introduction of machinery in industries such as shoe-making, screw-making, lockmaking or shovel-making; nor that British potteries could still afford to produce baths hand-made by craftsmen, or shipyards build cheaper ships than American or German yards without equipping their boilermakers with mechanical riveters or pneumatic drills.

It was the existence side by side of both a skilled workforce and a pool of underpaid cheap labour which accounted for the resistance of skilled men to new machinery: of compositors to linotype or engineers to turret lathes and borers. Innovation not only disrupted work patterns and sometimes eliminated processes which had given craftsmen pride and satisfaction, but threatened to reduce them to the relative insecurity and low pay of labourers. Only a situation of full employment and a general raising of working-class earnings to skilled levels could have reduced this need for self-defence.

The marked inequality of income within the working class also had the economic effect of delaying the advent of a mass consumption market and so of prolonging the economic viability of small-scale luxury trades. The rising real wages of the late nineteenth century had already made some impact on essential trades. The first multiple chains were established from the 1870s, nearly all in food: the Maypole Dairy Company, the Home and Colonial Stores, the International Tea Company, Eastmans the butchers, Lyons cheap tea shops and so on. After 1900 the number of branches in food chains was doubling in each decade, and the largest grocery chains already had over six hundred branches. There were already a few successful multiples also in footwear, men's clothing, haberdashery, hardware and the chemist's trades. The multiples adopted the successful example of the earlier Co-operative stores in combining the vertical integration of production, wholesaling and selling with a system of branch stores offering a standard range of products. But while the Co-operative strongholds had been confined to communities of highly paid skilled industrial workers, the general rise in incomes allowed the new chains to flourish on the basis of a general working-class market in the cities. So far, however, a mass market scarcely existed beyond food and a few other essentials. In the 1900s an average working-class family remained close to the subsistence level. When they moved, many families – like the Thorns – could put all their possessions on a single cart. Real wages had still a long way to rise before home production generally moved from luxury to mass production; and in the 1900s real wages were not even rising.

The stagnation of the overall situation should not, however, be exaggerated. Critical changes were in motion, such as the advances in social welfare, and the cumulative effect of universal education in almost eliminating illiteracy, which removed some of the major social distinctions between labourers and the best-paid manual workers. Similarly, if too slowly, the economy was responding to the new markets and techniques of the twentieth century. The annual reports of the factory inspectors invariably comment on the rapidly spreading use of electrical power, and the building of more spacious new factories lit by electricity. They reported the start of important new manufactures, such as artificial silk and plastics, gramophones and aeroplanes. In Lancashire cotton mills the new ring spindle was being introduced to some mills, while the first coal-cutting machines had appeared in the mines. Clothing factories were developing, while the boot trade had been successful in fighting off American imports through rapid mechanization. If watchmaking collapsed through not mechanizing, most of the Midland metal trades were slowly introducing factory methods, and the production of sewing machines and bicycles was developing fast, even if motor cars remained luxury craft products for the wealthy.

At the same time gradual shifts in the overall occupational structure were proceeding, which emerge clearly if we take a longer time perspective (Table 5). By this period the migration from agriculture was almost complete. Nor was the proportion in mining and industry to increase much during the next fifty years. On the other hand, the numbers in domestic and personal service were already falling significantly. So too, as the motor car began to replace the horse, were those in transport, a service occupation still largely dependent on the well-to-do. Meanwhile work in other services to the public, such as gas and electricity, was expanding. These public services in themselves, by making housework easier, made the transfer of housewives and servants to alternative work more possible – as did other technical developments of this period such as vacuum cleaners and man-made fibres. Employment in the shops and in leisure trades was also growing. There was thus a gradual general shift from personal service of the wealthy to mass service.

This was also reflected in the growth of public administration. The professional classes had not yet begun to increase significantly, but the expansion of clerical work was already considerable. Like shop work, it provided important new openings for working-class girls who would previously have entered domestic service. The largest clerical employer was still the government, followed by the city insurance houses, but the more progressive industrial firms were taking the step of appointing their first typist by 1910.

Table 5. Industrial distribution of workforce[1]

Percentage of occupied population, England, Wales and Scotland

	Agriculture, forestry and fishing	*Manufacture, mining and industry*	*Trade and transport*	*Domestic and personal*	*Public, professional and other*
1831	24·6	40·8	12·4	12·6	9·5
1851	21·7	42·9	15·8	13·0	6·7
1871	15·1	43·1	19·6	15·3	6·8
1911	8·3	46·4	21·5	13·9	9·9
1951	5·0	49·1	21·8	2·2	21·9

As a whole, manual occupations were slowly falling as a proportion of the workforce, although they still comprised 80 per cent of all occupations (Table 6). But more important, again looking at the long-term perspectives, was the gradual transformation of the character of manual work.

Mainly due to the introduction of new production methods, the proportion of skilled workers was slowly shrinking. The growing use in factories of semi-skilled and unskilled labour, especially by women, balanced the reduction of van boys, messenger boys and other male labouring work out of doors. These changes altered the typical experience of work itself. The work process became less varied. So did the social contacts which it provided.

Table 6. Occupational class distribution of workforce[2]

Percentage of occupied population, England, Wales and Scotland

	1911	*1921*	*1931*	*1951*
Professional	4·05	4·53	4·60	6·63
Employers, managers	10·14	10·46	10·36	10·50
Clerical and foremen	6·13	8·16	8·51	13·40
Skilled manual	30·56	28·83	26·72	24·95
Semiskilled manual	39·48	33·85	35·00	32·60
Unskilled manual	9·68	14·17	14·81	12·03
	100·00	100·00	100·00	100·00

As manufacture was concentrated in larger and more mechanized factories, and trade in multiple stores rather than family corner shops, the main satisfaction left in work was the company of other workers. Personal relationships with employers, and with customers, were declining within manufacture and trade, as well as directly through the shrinkage of personal service work. Of course the change was most obvious in the service occupations themselves. In return for loyalty, deference and long hours for low pay, personal service had offered not only security but also a sense of identification with a social superior. Although the growing public service occupations, such as the post office, police, railways and army, offered somewhat similar conditions, the loyalty which they required was corporate rather than personal; an identification with the function of the service and perhaps with the idea of social authority, rather than with a single master. So this too tended to make the experience of work – as well as the channels of social influence – less personal.

At the same time the most independent workers who were least tied to a single employer were slowly becoming fewer.

Self-employed craftsmen were already a small and shrinking group, a mere 6 per cent of all skilled men. The great age of the navvies, well-paid migrant construction labourers proud of their physical strength and their social independence, had passed with the peak of railway expansion. Although the miners had inherited some of their attitudes and their numbers were still growing, they were now also very close to their maximum. As the docks began to introduce more regular employment, some of the more demoralizing casual work in the cities began to disappear too. The full employment of the First World War, the new out-of-work benefits and the difficulties in moving introduced by shortage of housing would all help to pin down the migrant casual. In London by the 1920s, not only were council house tenants moving much less frequently, but the number of common lodging-house beds had fallen to half the 30,000 of the 1890s while even the 2,000 sleeping on the streets had almost disappeared. At the same time the use of public transport, chiefly to work, had more than trebled. There were far fewer men without a permanent home and a regular job. The pool of half-starved unskilled casual workers was drying up. But there were also fewer men with the pride of the London blacksmith's hammerman who 'said a man that stuck at a job all his life wasn't worth knowing. He believed in having a change . . . He did like his independence.'[3] At the same time, as machinery replaced a man's own dexterity and strength, one of the sources of working-class confidence in the face of middle-class claims to superiority was disappearing.

Lastly, as mechanized mass production gradually replaced the old craft workshops, the peculiar pride and satisfaction which accompanied some skilled work was often lost. One Edwardian Londoner, who was forced out of his trade in the 1900s through the competition of cheaper Swiss imports, remembers the attitude to work of the old watchmakers:

> 'My father had been a watchmaker, my grandfather had been a watchmaker as a master man, you see. The consequence was I had to be apprenticed and I had to serve seven years apprentice. I had to learn the parts by hand you see, like

they'd done . . . The first thing I had to do was to learn to use a lathe and what they used to call turns . . . to make the very fine things. Just bringing it down and making a cut in it. And to use all sorts of tools with skill and accuracy. And to be able to file a thing flat, so that it didn't come a round surface, it'd come dead flat . . . To work to very fine limits, to a tenth of a thousandth of an inch.

'Oh, yes, I liked the work. Oh yes, you see there was about half a dozen people sitting in a row on a bench in front of a long window, like it might be the side of a greenhouse so there was plenty of light on our benches you see. Well our bench where me father and I worked was eighteen inches . . . It was very interesting work once you got used to doing some of it, because you could see something for the work you put in. We were always trying to make something that was good. And if you could see some of the old-fashioned watches taken to pieces you'd find that the finish on the parts that were made was absolutely perfect and the modern machine-made article is not to be compared with it for the trouble that was taken to make 'em perfect. The shoulders where the pivots finished off were polished to a brilliant mirror polish and the edges were chamfered off, bevelled off. And a great deal of trouble was taken to make possible skilled work. Say for instance between where the pivot that was turned in the framework, what the wheels turned on that came up into the brass plates, and where the cogs started, that was sloped backwards so as to leave another square surface that could be polished like a mirror, you see, and the slope was polished. The thing had to be absolutely perfectly polished. Tremendous lot of hand work was done, absolutely inessential as far as the going of the watch was concerned, but it was an exhibition of skill on the part of the man who did the work . . . They did their best to turn out a masterpiece, you see. It had to be a masterpiece.'[4]

There were many others besides craftsmen whose feelings were intensely bound up in their work. To a miner, for example,

Coal, one of Edwardian Britain's principal exports, was got from the face by the miner's own dexterity and strength. Irregular and narrow seams were typical of the older pits and coal-cutting machines very rare.

Mass production of bicycles, based on an elaborate division of labour, allowed the introduction of women as semi-skilled workers, supervised by male craftsmen. This Coventry cycle factory thus anticipates First World War munitions production. The maze of power-belts was a frequent source of accidents.

The shrinking farm workforce was not generally helped by powered machinery, except for the thrashing of the corn harvest by travelling contract teams: steam thrashing tackle, made in Gainsborough, Lincolnshire, here seen at Old Newton, Suffolk.

A small town foundry which made the stoves on the left, as well as a range of other products. It did general and domestic repairs and was also a retail shop. This craft workshop, the family firm of Rumsby's of Bungay, Suffolk, is described in George Ewart Evans' *Where Beards Wag All*. The skills of patternmaking, moulding, casting and fitting were all needed for its small mixed business. In 1900 Harry Nathan Rumsby (*centre*) had taken over as manager from his father Nathan Rumsby (*foreground*) – 'a wonderful workman at the forge and bench'.

Domestic service, paid or unpaid, the principal occupation for women, had neither the advantages of mechanisation nor of recognition as a craft.

Drinking, the Edwardians' commonest leisure pursuit, was principally for men, but women and children also visited London pubs. Here the Whitechapel Road pavement becomes an outside room at a public house window.

Children setting off for a day's outing to the countryside from the densely populated East End of London; the neighbourhood fills the street.

The active social life of the city streets again shown by this Punch and Judy show in Trinity Square, Southwark.

Paul Martin (1864–1942) was one of the first photographers to exploit the new hand-held camera. He became a professional in 1904 and most of his undated photographs are more likely to come from the 1890s than the 1900s. Nevertheless, these scenes of ordinary people taken unawares vividly and uniquely convey the turn of the century holiday crowd: *above*, on Yarmouth beach; *below*, on August Bank Holiday 1898 at Hampstead.

Not all London homes had tap water in 1900, which accounted for some of the popularity of drinking fountains attached to horsetroughs. The girl in the background looks to come from a more prosperous home. Taken in Battersea by Paul Martin.

The wealth of London's West End attracted homeless tramps who slept out on the Embankment and park benches, in intervals between being moved on by the police; hence this man's attempt to sleep sitting.

Children and dogs of the well-to-do with their nursemaid – taking the air in Hyde Park, 1911.

West End parks saw regular parades of affluence on Sunday mornings after church: Rotten Row, Hyde Park, *c.* 1902.

Edwardians

The Ford home: Sidney stands in front of his mother on the right, with two neighbours.

Sidney Ford.

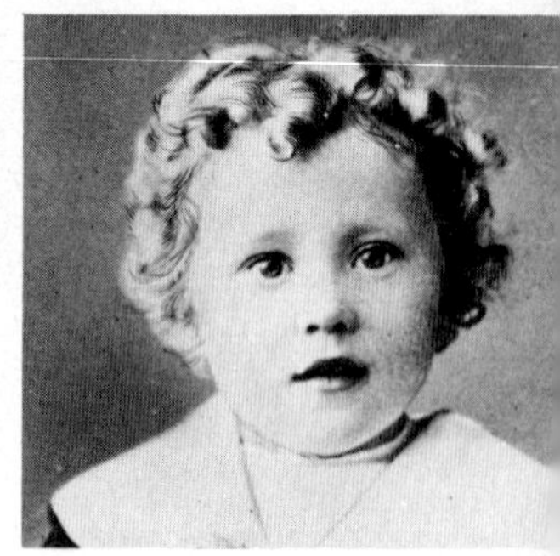

Gwen Davies as a teenager.

With her elder sister on Coronation Day 1902.

Peter Henry aged 16.

Fred Mills aged 20.

Grace with her father.

Grace Fulford's parents
during her infancy.

The Jarman family of Bury St Edmunds here portray a typical middle-class family dinner in their finely equipped dining room. A servant has brought the youngest child in for this occasion. The father was a photographer and art restorer.

A Shetland family sit around the fireplace in their crofter's cottage. The boy reads and the women spin; to the left and right are enclosed box beds, and fish split for smoking hang above.

The first pension (1908) originally titled 'Let's spend it Wisely'. Note the hairstyles: the Edwardian generations differed in taste, the younger men cutting their hair short while the old stuck to the longer hair fashionable in their own youth.

The regimentation which the poor feared: workhouse dinner at St Pancras 1900.

The typical shopkeeper was still an independent, with a large number of assistants. This London butcher of 1902 catered for working-class cash customers, reducing costs by cutting out loans on tick or middle-class customers on account. Like his rising rivals the chain stores, he believed in a full display of his wares on the street.

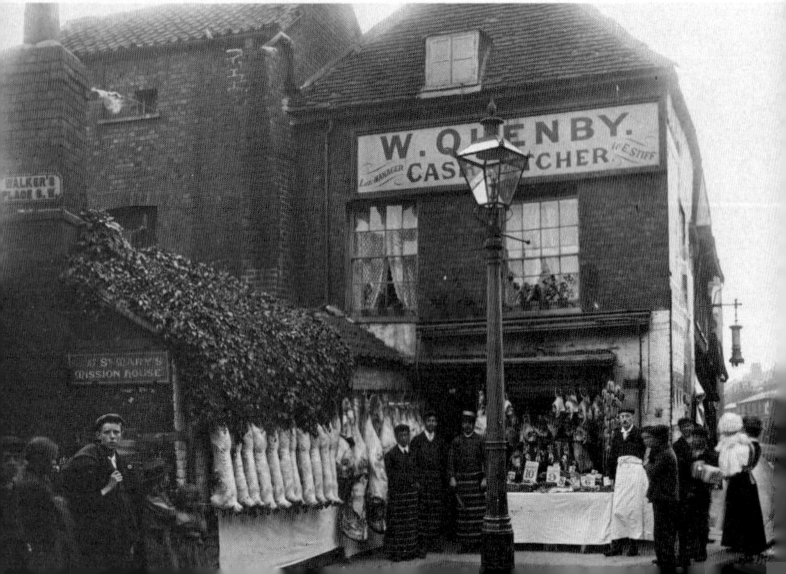

The heart of Perth, Scotland, a medium-sized town of the kind which for many Edwardians summed up urbanity: still little traffic to disturb the magnificent cast-iron street furniture or the mostly male spectators, some of whom are barefoot, watching the photographer.

The contrasting activity of Oxford Street, London: horse buses, private carriages and well-dressed shoppers.

With easy access to the city centre by railway, suburban Highgate offered the London commuter's family not only fresh air and trees, but amenities such as the public library up the hill on the left.

Riley's court, a slum in the centre of Leeds, cut through by the railway viaduct. Death rates in such districts were double those in the suburbs.

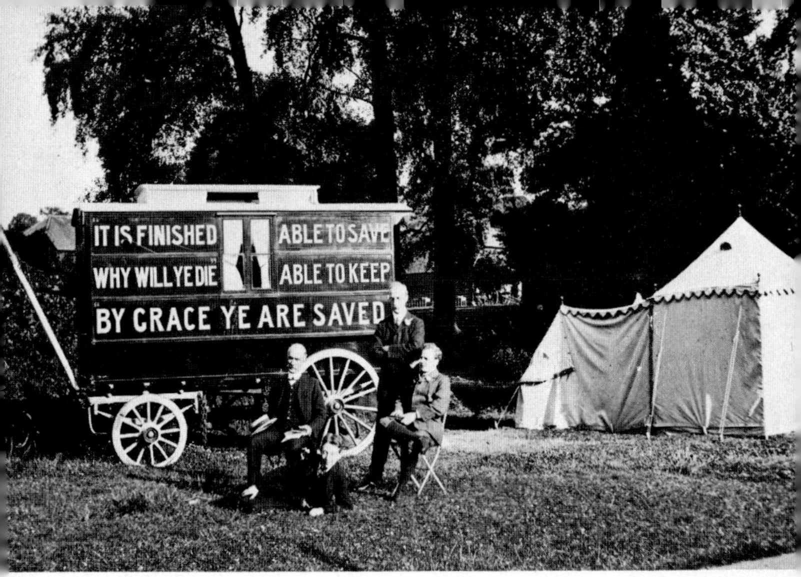

A travelling evangelists' camp at Shere, Surrey, in 1908, four years after the great Welsh religious revival.

A London school nurse conducting medical examinations in 1911. The new school health service revealed the extent of disease and vermin among children.

Militancy: Mary Phillips selling the *Suffragette*, October 1907

A Scottish policeman interrogates children who have taken food from the fields. In contrast to Paul Martin's photography (9, 10, 12) we have here a composed scene in the tradition of Victorian painting: its impact as much moral as visual.

showing the strength and courage necessary for work in the pit was a part of becoming a man. But craftsmen, as few other manual workers, will not uncommonly say that they 'loved' their work for its own sake. The ending of such pure pleasures was one of the prices to be paid in the slow march of economic progress. And like many of the consequences of economic change, fundamental though they were, it was not consciously chosen by most Edwardians, but stole upon them unawares.

13 Escape

Social Mobility and Crime

What chances, real or imaginery, had the individual Edwardian of escaping his social situation?

Real chances certainly did exist. Indeed it was individual moves for better housing or better work, attempts to nurture a business or to obtain better qualifications, which made up the general pattern of social change. And it was the desire for such self-improvement which demanded changes like the expansion of education. Information about social mobility itself is unfortunately very limited: it ignores women, focusing on work rather than social status, and on changes between fathers and sons rather than within a single life. But Edwardian men were constantly on the move for work: geographically, between industries, between grades – from unskilled labourer to semi-skilled transport worker, building artisan or small-scale trader. A publican's son starts as a sailor, get promoted to ship's officer, comes back to shore as a bus driver and ends as a property dealer. A farm labourer's son works in turn as farm labourer, soldier, skilled carpenter, self-employed carter and finally as unskilled roadman. How common were such careers?

We have better evidence of occupational movement between generations. Contrary to popular belief, chances of social mobility have not much improved during the past fifty or a hundred years. D. V. Glass's 1949 national study, *Social Mobility in Britain*, found surprisingly slight differences between those born in each decade, even before 1900. Half the children born into each of his seven occupational groups could expect to move out of it; half the professional group had fathers from a lower class; more than half of the unskilled had fallen from a better start. Most of these moves were just a short distance up or down the scale. This picture is supported by A. L. Bowley's surveys of five towns in 1915 and 1924, showing, for example, that under one in three labourers' sons remained unskilled, and half rose to the skilled class; while their daughters were still more successful.

Why was there not more change in a century of widening educational opportunity? Before 1914, it was easier for a man to set up on his own as a craftsman or small trader; and to achieve promotion at the works. Among businessmen, the former manual worker with only an elementary school education has been replaced by the grammar or public school man, who starts directly as a management trainee. Already by 1914, some employers were beginning to select and grade their employees on the basis of their school results. This affected women as well as men: their future held better chances in clerical work and teaching, but less hope of becoming a forewoman or opening a corner shop. Thus as education opened new paths, others were closed; and social destiny was being decided at an earlier age, when the effects of home background were inescapable. If the working-class child now has a chance to become a higher professional or a politician, he may well be less likely to become one of the rich.

The ordinary Edwardian, in short, had a reasonable hope of some social mobility, if slight; not much less than today, or indeed than his contemporaries in the superficially more democratic United States. This conclusion challenges complacent assumptions of social progress. It also helps to explain why more drastic change has not been demanded.

There was another real way out: crime. A small group of Edwardians lived by fraud and stealing. One successful Edwardian criminal, a professional pickpocket, was remembered by his grandson in the 1930s as

> 'an elderly and very distinguished-looking gentleman with a withered arm. He was always impeccably dressed: his suit had matching jacket and trousers for a start, which was a great rarity, and he wore a silk cravat with a diamond stick-pin . . ., gloves, a cane, grey spats, a homburg hat,

gentleman's boots . . . For a long time I thought he was someone special, a business man from the City perhaps.'[1]

Very little can be known about professional criminals in any period, for they are those who are caught least often. But there were probably not many of them. The police estimated that there were only 3,000 thieves and 400 receivers at large in the whole country. Professional prostitutes need to be added, but their number would be even more of a guess, especially as there was a fringe of mostly impoverished casuals who slipped in and out of prostitution.

There was of course no clear line separating the criminal from the ordinary population, any more than today. And again contrary to common belief, crime may have been as widespread in the early twentieth century as today. Statistics of crimes 'known to the police' were kept deliberately low then to suggest police efficiency. The number of persons actually prosecuted was as high in the 1900s as in the 1950s, while the murder rate has remained remarkably steady and exceptionally low by international standards, and assaults have fallen markedly. Most middle-class crime, then as now, consisted of frauds which escaped notice. Many shopkeepers, for example, deliberately taught assistants to give short weight. The truth is that accurate estimates of the extent of crime, past or present, are quite impossible. We can only know with any certainty about those who have been caught and convicted.

Convicted Edwardian juveniles, as now, had mostly committed some form of theft, and vandalism was already a social problem. But a third of them, unlike today, were simply prosecuted for obstruction or other street offences. Most were fined, although a few were put on probation, sent to an industrial school or whipped. Convicted adults usually received a short prison sentence – under a fortnight – even for a minor offence. A third of the typical prisoners admitted were thus drunks, and a quarter had simply been begging, sleeping out, loitering and so on. But nine out of ten serious (indictable) offences – as today – were against property rather than persons. Most prisoners were clearly to a large extent victims of their social situation. They started from small, crowded homes, often with a rough mother or drunken father; truanted from school to earn money, and were often illiterate; learnt no trade. Two-thirds were unskilled labourers, often unmarried, living in transient lodgings. Prostitutes were commonly former servants who had been seduced by an employer. Crime may have provided a few professionals with a means of self-improvement, but the typical Edwardian prisoner was simply a social failure at the bottom of an unequal society.

Crime was also a protest of the desperate, however ineffective, which reminded Edwardians of the imperfections of their society. It drove some to demand stricter law enforcement, others to combat the sources of crime. Sometimes the two attitudes converged. Later school leaving, school meals and health inspection, and the probation service, were not just humane gestures in an empty context. They were also attacks upon a slum street culture which Edwardians found threatening.

Leisure and drink

For those who could neither work nor break their way out, there were various other routes of escape. There were, for example, minorities who broke the typical Edwardian pattern of sexual restraint: the clandestine liaisons at some country house parties; and the prostitutes soliciting in city centre streets like the Haymarket in London, who paraded the sexual underworld for all to see. This underworld already included a few facilities for experimentation with drugs. Lady Dorothy Mills's novel, *The Laughter of Fools*, gives one account of a demi-monde of Soho nightclubs with black dance bands, opium dens and free-love parties during the First World War. It had some connections, through the avant-garde arts world, with the left-wing intelligentsia of the Fabian Society and the newly-formed socialist societies at the universities. This radical Bohemia found its most characteristic voice in the journal *New Age*. Its influence can also be felt in Shaw's plays and Wells's novels, and the painting of Sickert and Wyndham Lewis. It looked forward, not just to inter-war Bloomsbury, but to the much more widespread experimental culture of the present.

Similar influences inspired the search of some of the early settlers of the first garden cities, founded in the 1900s at Letchworth and Welwyn, for a more congenial type of community. And more generally, the millions of Edwardians who sought a better life through emigrating abroad need to be remembered. So must the surprisingly extensive influence – and achievements – of the fine arts and literature at this time. Edwardian novelists ranged from Bennett, Forster and Lawrence to Marie Corelli, while older classics like Dickens remained widely popular. Large crowds annually packed the art establishment show at the Royal Academy. Music was still more popular. Elgar's latest compositions were performed at northern choral festivals. Vaughan Williams's music combined the choral tradition with the influence of newly-collected folksong. The English musical revival was rediscovering its own roots. Edwardians whistled in the streets. Some two thousand songs could still be collected from a single parish in north-east Scotland. Miners joined colliery bands, and fishermen in the days before radio would

> 'sing to pass the time away when you're on deck. When you stood in the wheelhouse, you – if you didn't sing a little song you'd be a-meditating about something, thinking about home, boy, yes, used to sing a little song. And break the monotony you see, and that took all your thoughts away from everything, all troubles.'[2]

Music or literature helped to ease the monotony of many Edwardian lives.

For the majority, however, certainly the most popular means of escape for men, and possibly for women too, was drink. Every Edwardian adult consumed, on average, six pints of beer every week. It may have accounted for as much as a sixth of overall working-class family income. Alcoholic consumption was to halve between 1910 and 1930 and its decline, already begun, was thus a critical social change.

With public houses open all day and until midnight in London, drunkards were commonplace. The police brought over 4,500 prosecutions for drunkenness every week. Social workers identified drink as a principal source of poverty. The Edinburgh Charity Organisation Society went so far as to categorize half the families of 1,400 poor school children investigated as drunken, printing lurid descriptions of fights between parents with the mother's 'hair down, her face one mess of blood ... the man cursing at her ... the children white and sobbing'.[3] But if such scenes were without doubt all too common, the importance of drink as a cause of poverty was exaggerated by most observers. Significantly, neither Booth nor Rowntree put a figure to it. Two government studies, both of relatively demoralized groups in cities with high drunkenness rates, found that of London unskilled men in the workhouses only 13 per cent were drunken, while there was evidence of drunkenness in only 10 per cent of Aberdeen families who lost a child under two years old.[4] It seems unlikely that Edwardian working-class families with a regularly drunk parent could have been as many as 5 per cent overall, and only a minority would have been violent.

The true role of drinking in Edwardian Britain was much more humdrum. Beer was the basis of leisure. It took the place which is now more often filled by cigarettes and television. Children would fetch jugs from the pubs for tired parents to relax at home at the end of the day. At funerals and weddings, at harvest, at the initiation of apprentices, at ordinary work breaks, a glass of beer would be exchanged.

Inside the home, the only herald of the mass entertainment of the future was the newspaper. The English read them more than any other nation. *Lloyds Weekly News* reached a million copies in the 1890s, and so for a brief moment in the Boer War did the *Daily Mail*. But even so, daily papers were reaching less than a fifth of the adult population in 1910. Most homes just took Sundays. 'The most cheerful among my patients and their friends,' observed a district nurse, 'have been confirmed newspaper-readers.'[5] But a paper once a week was a poor substitute for a nightly glass of beer. Nor were other forms of reading normal. The public libraries lent less than two books a head a year – a sixth of recent figures. In Middlesbrough Lady Bell estimated that only a quarter of families there read both books and papers. There were some great readers, of science, religion and politics as well as novels; but they were a small group. Commoner hobbies among men were gardening, or keeping pets. At weekends families made their own amusements – chatting with callers, a sing-song or perhaps cards. A drink helped them on.

Although entertainment outside the home was more varied, almost everywhere drinking in a public house was the most readily and continuously available. In villages there was little else, even if the countryside itself provided relief for townsmen – walking, fishing and bicycling were especially common recreations. Among sports, cricket, bowls and tennis attracted large numbers of players to their grounds, but the most popular was football. It was played in every street. It was also the leading spectator sport, attracting weekly crowds of over 20,000 in the large towns. With the young it had become a cult. 'No subject arouses their enthusiasm like football. Nothing is so hotly discussed or so accurately known.'[6] Players had become personal heroes. 'A most amazing knowledge is betrayed of the personal appearance, character, and moral weakness of each individual player.'[7] Interest was also stimulated by the spread of the coupon system of betting, which although locally organized had made considerable headway in the north. Anxious social reformers claimed that football made up half the national expenditure on gambling. Certainly betting had become a well-organized business, especially at horse race meetings. At the Doncaster races in 1901, for example, 30,000 telegrams were sent out by the special telegraphists provided by the Post Office. But in fact the Edwardian population spent about twenty times as much money on beer as on gambling.

Race meetings also provided a traditional attraction for excursions, even among the relatively poor. Ordinary town working-class families also sometimes made day outings to the seaside on Bank Holidays, and in the north, where factories closed for a whole 'wakes week' in most districts, a week in a seaside boarding house was becoming common. The Victoria pier, the tower and the great wheel at Blackpool date from the 1890s. The seaside carnival, like the travelling fairs, with their steam roundabouts and cake-walks, their cinema and Punch and Judy shows, provided important breaks in the weekly routine, and drinking was one of their intrinsic pleasures.

In most towns the serious-minded could join a natural history society, a debating society, a choir or a band. Dancing was a popular pleasure, but for the working classes there were few places to dance between the street – outside a pub or around a street organ – and the scandalous dancing saloon. Another possibility was the cinema which was spreading very rapidly. By 1917 there were 4,500 cinemas open, and since none was licensed they provided a definite alternative to the public house. But its audience was largely youthful, including many children. Music halls were fewer, and cost a little more, but were more representative of ordinary Edwardian taste for a night out: best clothes were worn, the jokes were sexier and drinks were served. For all the alternatives, concluded a representative study of one city, 'it still remains true that the public house is the centre of social intercourse among working men in Norwich'.[8]

In the public house, a drinker found both comfort and company. He escaped into a world which was benign, rather than vicious. For a slum-dweller, the neighbourhood bar had some of the attractions of a respectable home. 'The whole scene is comfortable, quiet, and orderly,' wrote Charles Booth. 'Actual drunkenness is very much the exception.' A few drinkers would sit chatting quietly. 'Behind the bar will be a decent middle-aged woman, something above her customers in class, very neatly dressed, respecting herself and respected by them.'[9] Customers would normally be known and sometimes have their own seat. Besides drink they would find warmth, cheerful lighting, newspapers to read and food to eat – quite often free on the counter. Bargains could be struck with bookmakers, foremen treated in the hope of future work, pay divided among work groups and a portion of it saved up in a slate club. Public houses provided rooms in which trade union branches and clubs could meet, and they organized sports teams and outings. The larger pubs were ingeniously designed to attract all kinds of customer into their sets of divided bars, dazzling with gas lamps, gilt lettering and engraved glass at the street corners. Above all, the pubs were the only places for relaxation outside the home almost always close by and open free. In Edwardian Britain there was one public house for every three hundred people. Not even the churches could afford so ubiquitous a refuge.

Religion

The relationship of the churches with the material world was certainly complex. If their intrinsic purposes were spiritual, the characteristics of different denominations, their successes and failures, reflected the society to which they ministered. They also helped to mould it. Religion could provide a force for general change. It could also inspire individual Edwardians to a self-discipline which through hard work, temperance and thrift could lead to success. But where the churches provided chiefly consolation, like the public house they offered an alternative rather than a stimulus to change.

In the early twentieth century Sunday church-going was already a minority habit. In 1851 the national religious census had found 40 per cent of the population attending at least one church service. Local surveys now suggested just over 25 per cent overall: only 20 per cent in the large cities and industrial towns, 30 per cent or more in the countryside, as high as 50 per cent in resorts. The churches secured the attendance of most children at Sunday Schools, but fewer men than women, fewer townsmen than countrymen. In their competition with the pubs they appeared to be losing. On a single Sunday in the iron and steel town of Middlesbrough, for example, four times as many people of all ages were counted entering the public houses as the churches.[10]

These figures should be treated with caution. Most Edwardians believed, if imprecisely, in a Christian God; and also in luck, and very likely in ghosts. They taught their children to pray. The majority still had some formal religious attachment.

In Scotland three-quarters had a church connection, while in England the established church still baptized more than two-thirds of all infants.

The Church of England was in general the most successful in appealing to a wide range of social classes. It is true that it could nowhere claim a hold as complete as that of the chapel in the homogeneous Welsh mining communities or the ultra-Calvinistic 'Wee Frees' in many Scottish crofting townships. Nor had its slum clergy the authority of the Roman Catholic priests among the colonies of Irish poor. Religious strength here came partly from a central role in the culture of a national minority group. The Church of England was an 'established' rather than a national church and it was clearly identified with the interests of the comfortable and powerful classes. Its parish clergy preached a creed of social respect and social duty, of loyalty and obedience. Landowners and employers attended because they believed that the church was a buttress to the social structure:

> '"I must go to church and read the lessons. They expect me."
>
> '"Are you a Christian?" asked the Italian Countess, with sudden interest.
>
> '"No," said Alexander, "I'm not. But I believe in keeping up the old institutions."'[11]

And in smaller communities, where the patronage of the well-to-do offered both employment and aid in distress, many of the working classes also attended church; some because they genuinely believed in its message, others because the farmer or the mistress sent them.

In the cities employers usually lived in another district, and could not keep track of a man's Sunday habits. The parish churches instead tended to provide general social services. Regular attenders from the poorer classes were rewarded with gifts of clothing, boots, blankets, coal and winter soup and teas. A well-organized London parish such as St Dunstan's, Stepney, was staffed by six clergy, nine paid scripture readers and lady visitors, and over a hundred voluntary workers. It offered clubs for men and for boys and girls, a gymnasium, women's meetings, sewing classes, a library, a band and a savings society. In winter there were dances, concerts, plays and a pantomime; in summer, excursions, cricket and a flower show. 'It seems to be regarded as part of the duty of the Church to supply decent amusements,' commented Booth.[12]

In the long run neither patronage nor entertainment proved capable of holding church attendance. 'You can buy a congregation, but it melts away as soon as the payments cease.' Independent working men who liked a drink or bet felt that 'in honesty, they must hold themselves aloof'.[13] They were also increasingly willing to criticize the hypocrisies of those who did attend. As Will Crooks observed, '"Let them practise what they preach" is now heard on every side. "They talk of how Christ bade us care for the poor and the sick, yet outside the pulpit and pew they are above this sort of thing".'[14] By the 1900s in London, 'the quiet poor, if they attend any religious service, are more or less bribed', while the majority of the working class, apart from family rituals – funerals, weddings, baptisms and churchings – regarded the church with 'simply utter indifference'.[15]

Nonconformity fell in the end to the same indifference, despite its distinct appeal. The chapels almost openly vied with the pubs and music halls in their architectural floridity, bright lettering and warmth within, the hearty singing and the stewards ready to welcome strangers at the door. Each denomination tended to concentrate on a particular social level, from the well-to-do Congregationalists and Wesleyans to the lower-middle-class Baptists and respectable working-class Primitive Methodists; and individual chapels also varied, depending on their location. Here was a supportive community – especially for newcomers to a district:

> 'For a vast number of respectable, intelligent, fairly prosperous families the chapel is the *only* social centre; its meetings the only approach to amusement, its friendships the chief

road to desirable marriage, and often the chief source of prosperity in business.'[16]

In the 1900s the Nonconformists, with their stress on participation and lay government, slightly outdistanced the Anglicans in their combined numbers of active members. But changes were taking place which struck at their foundations too. Their ultimate strength had lain in the decisiveness with which they rejected the material for the spiritual world. The chapels were now not only organizing clubs and condoning worldly pleasures such as football, novel-reading and even dancing, but their doctrines had been reinterpreted in a more comfortable direction. Instead of an authoritarian God punishing evil-doers with hell-fire, the emphasis was upon the humanity of Christ and the fatherhood of God, upon fellowship and service rather than faith and obedience. The fervour essential to recruitment was thus being undercut. In the early 1900s a group of Cornish Methodists was overheard in a railway carriage

> 'discussing the decrease in the number of converts and the decline of revivals during the last few years. One of them, a stout, elderly person, said he did not take so pessimistic a view ... "All I have got to do is to preach my Judgement-Day sermon to set them howling." The others were silent for a little, and then one said, "Do you think it wise to say much about everlasting punishment at the present juncture?" No one replied to the question, and after an uncomfortable interval they changed the subject'.[17]

It is difficult not to feel that in giving way to the current the churches destroyed much of their own power to resist. By the First World War they were even yielding at their strongest point and source, their hold on the young. The mushrooming, from 1908, of the Scouting movement, which had over 200,000 members by 1920, confronted the Sunday Schools with an alternative secular moral education and entertainment: camp craft, nature observation, peace between classes and – despite its militaristic guise – between nations, and an undenominational God. But there may have been very little the churches could have done to prevent the growth of secularism in a century of growing urban anonymity, rising material comfort, state-provided social security, mass entertainment in the home, education and rationalism.

What were the consequences of this change? For the indifferent majority it would, perhaps, be chiefly important in encouraging a less doctrinal and more tolerant morality in family and personal relationships: the kind of working-class morality which was already discernible in the humour of the music halls and the advice columns of the popular press. In this sense the decline of the churches, like the decline of the pubs, was simply part of the shift to a more home-centred society.

The same could not be said of those whose faith was more intense. The strength which religion could still show in the industrial Britain of the early twentieth century should not be underestimated. In the great religious revival of 1904–5 in Wales, led by a young ex-coalminer, Evan Roberts, there were many scenes of emotional intensity approaching medieval ecstasy. The less privileged groups in the population, young people and women, seized control of chapel meetings; and while crowds stood outside in the streets swaying backwards and forwards 'as if they were half mad', inside the chapels, so crowded that there was not even standing room, men and women prayed hour by hour for the unconverted, bursting at each conversion into a familiar hymn such as 'Happy day, when Jesus washed my sins away'. Some were moved to physical ecstasy: 'prostrations, contortions, paroxysms'. Young women lay on the pew floors wailing and praying. To professional ministers these aspects of the revival could prove distasteful. 'It gradually deteriorated into an orgy of singing and praying, like a pagan feast.' But they could not deny the dramatic increase in chapel membership and the halving of drunkenness convictions in the revival years; or the astonishing spirit of communal welcome which it opened to social untouchables: 'The more notorious a man has been as a gambler, the warmer would be his welcome in the homes of the people and into the Church and Society. They were, in many instances, fed, clothed and lodged free of charge for weeks and months altogether.'[18]

Here was a true cry of the oppressed soul, which echoed in the world from which it sprang. We have seen how it infused the family life of Gwen Davies; and how the Bensons and Fords too combined missionary and social work. We can go further. If the tension between religious ideals and the class society which the churches served often gave a reason for dropping church attendance, it drove others to try to change that society. A small group of Anglican clergy became socialists, and there was a much wider and older connection between Nonconformity, political radicalism and the labour movement. Many Primitive Methodist chapels, for example, had been the cells which provided leaders for trade union branches among the miners and farm labourers. While this link was much less significant by the 1900s, the political influence of religion was certainly not exhausted. There were connections between the general reanimation of Nonconformity in the 1900s and the Liberal political triumph of 1906, between the subsequent Anglican resurgence and the Conservative recovery of 1910, between the Welsh religious revival and the radical Welsh socialism which sprang up in its wake. Especially in the north, many of the founders of the new Labour party, such as Keir Hardie and Arthur Henderson, spoke a language which came as much from the chapels as from the hustings. In his first campaign at Blackburn in 1900, as if in a revivalist mission, Philip Snowden called on the voters to

> 'help us to take the children out of these foetid hovels into the pure air of God's own plain. Come with us and call to the man with the muckrake, and tell him to lift his eyes from the earth and to grasp the heavenly crown above his head. Come with us and help us to remove poverty, sin, and suffering, and to bring hope, and health, and joy, and brotherhood to every child of our Common Father' (Loud Cheers).[19]

Six years later he won victory. There can be no doubt that the force that carried him and other radicals and socialists into the Edwardian Parliament was partly religious. And it is also likely that the slow decline of religion, and its replacement by channels of influence such as the mass media, which discouraged vigorous ideological debate, helped to reduce the chances of politics bringing about any fundamental social change in twentieth-century Britain.

14 Solidarity

We turn now to consider, in this chapter and the next, the collective actions which were open to those Edwardians who wished to change their social situation. They were of two kinds, immediate and long-term. The first was collective resistance to some kind of social relationship, which although perhaps legal, seemed a manifest injustice. The second was an attempt, through politics, to change the law itself. Although the two kinds of action seem clearly distinct, they were in fact closely related. For the working-class Edwardian, politics certainly now seemed to offer the best hope of bringing change through collective pressure. But it was the latest stage in an evolution which had seen many phases: peasant rebellion, eighteenth-century food riots, Luddite machine-breaking, and trade union action, which for decades had also been illegal. The vote itself had been secured partly through the threat of force. The two kinds of action thus represent a historical continuity. They shared, moreover, the impact of a class consciousness which was moulded through collective experience, and they also shared the language and moral values through which this consciousness was expressed.

Both kinds of action rested on some degree of force, and in the case of collective resistance, particularly in view of the uncertain state of trade union law, this force was not always legal. Politics depended upon the ultimate sanction of force in implementing the law. This is true, however, of all modern societies, and what is much more critical is the limitation, through convention and practice, of the forms and justifications of collective resistance, and of the violence of both legal and illegal force. In these respects – remembering our exclusion of Ireland from this account – Edwardian Britain was exceptional.

By comparison with most societies in a wide perspective over time, early twentieth-century Britain stands out as unusually democratic. Its government was responsible to a parliamentary assembly elected, as we shall see, by quite a wide class of voters. Most local government was now elective too. In national if not always in local government, bribery, corruption and venial forms of patronage had been effectively eliminated by the late nineteenth century. Church and military were clearly subordinate to the civil authority. The civil power certainly rested partly on the ultimate sanction of force by either the police or the army. But neither was at all formidable by modern standards. Most of the army was stationed in India and other remote parts of the Empire, distanced by the weeks at sea from any possibility of meddling at home. Those troops stationed in Britain were used on a few critical occasions to help maintain order during strikes, when the local police had proved too few and sometimes also too easily provoked to violence against the strikers. There were clashes of this kind during the South Wales mine strike of 1910–11, where the county police were commanded by a Captain Lindsay, whose main previous experience was as an army commander in Egypt. Unlike most officers, he seems to have believed the same strong hand appropriate in Britain as with natives elsewhere, and was even prepared to lend his men to the colliery managers for the purposes of enforcing wage deductions claimed against the men as damages from another, earlier strike. The intervention of the army to enforce order in this case, with strict Home Office instructions to be tolerant of minor friction, almost certainly prevented the eruption of mass violence.

Troops were also brought in during the 1911 Salford seamen's strike (which was to end in victory for the men) more obviously to the advantage of the employers, for their role was partly to protect blackleg workers who were unloading food, but also because the police had again lost control; and at Liverpool and Llanelly again in 1911 there were clashes with troops resulting in deaths.

In general, however, troops were very rarely used to maintain authority in early twentieth-century Britain. The policeman's baton was thus the commonest instrument used to enforce the law; and incidents even of this kind were unusual. Civil authority normally operated within a common balance of consent. Policemen functioned as local watchmen, patrolling regular beats on foot. If they cuffed footballing children with their capes or twisted the arms of drunks, they knew that they would not be the less liked by respectable householders. They showed some respect for the roughest streets by normally keeping away from them. A good many accepted small bribes for tolerating street betting and were glad to quaff the pint of beer left on the wall by a publican. But this was as much as was normally said against them. By the standards of the late twentieth-century world the Edwardian police were a restrained force. They were also highly localized, so that it was easy enough for anybody who clashed with them to slip the attentions of the civil authority by moving. Even a fingerprint system for known criminals was not started before 1901. Edwardian citizens were not documented. It was not even necessary to produce a birth certificate when age was legally critical, as in starting full-time work, joining the army or marriage, although misstatement of age on these occasions was known to be common. In so far as Edwardian Britain, despite its manifest social inequalities, was law-abiding, this was due much more to common acceptance than to constraint. Conversely, those Edwardians who wished for social change rarely thought of physical force as a convincing means.

This helps to explain why collective resistance was usually seen as a means of adjustment rather than of fundamental social change. There was normally a notion of restitution which provided a moral justification for the action even when illegal, and generally the more obvious the illegality, the more prominent the justification. This moral justification is perhaps most striking in our first example. This is itself significant, for we shall move with historical development, from land seizure through to trade unionism, and from local to national solidarity. We begin, briefly, with the countryside.

Outbreaks of land seizure were not uncommon in certain parts of early twentieth-century Britain. They took place in a specific social situation in which landlords were regarded as outsiders by the local community. The landlords of the crofting townships in western Scotland, unlike English squires, rarely lived near their tenants, and this no doubt partly explains the scant respect with which they were treated when interests clashed. As small subsistence farmers the crofters were a socially homogeneous group, and since the late nineteenth century they had enjoyed legally protected tenancies of their land. But there was too little land in the townships to meet the population growth that continued in many districts into the twentieth century. Many would-be crofters were forced to squat on their parents' land, or the common grazing, or even in wooden shacks on the foreshore. On several occasions during the Edwardian period a band of these landless young men invaded a large farm, divided it into holdings for themselves, brought in stock and dug the ground for potatoes. Usually they received the moral backing of the neighbouring townships in this action. It was frequently argued that they were recapturing land used by crofting families in the perhaps distant past. The best-known instance of a successful land seizure was the capture of the island of Vatersay which, after the imprisonment of the leading raiders and their release because of public outcry, had to be officially bought by the Congested Districts Board to set up a new crofting community in 1909. It represented a type of collective action which in some respects looked back to an ancient tradition of communal migration. But equally it carried some of the lessons learnt from kin who had set up new townships in Canada and other parts of the empire, and it could also be said to anticipate the collective squatting of homeless town dwellers today.

Much more widespread in the Edwardian countryside than land seizure was the collective disregarding of certain of the property rights of landlords. The poaching of rabbits and game continued throughout Britain and was generally regarded as a justifiable if risky activity. It was certainly not seen as an ordinary form of theft. Wild life was considered, like wild fruit and hedgerow firewood, as a natural heritage which belonged more properly to the community than to landlords. Indeed in parts of Scotland and Wales, where sporting English landlords were disliked as absentee foreigners, poaching sometimes became deliberately provocative. An official report of 1913 deplored the continuance of organized raids on Welsh landlords' fishing grounds:

> 'Receiving the open support of some of the inhabitants, and the passive toleration of the remainder . . . this mischievous practice has always been difficult to deal with. Serious riots, involving bloodshed, have only too frequently resulted from endeavours to prevent it. Arming themselves with spears, . . . and sometimes blackening their faces to avoid recognition, these "Rebecca-ites", as they style themselves, muster along the river banks in large gangs, sometimes fifty or sixty strong. Their progress along the river is marked by the flare of torches, which serve the double purpose of ostentating their presence and of indicating the fish lying in the water.'[1]

This kind of collective deviance did not disappear with the move into the towns, even if it was rarely so openly defiant. In many work situations minor theft was widely condoned and almost a tradition. Brewery workers tapped free beer from the warehouse barrels, dockers picked up spillings, miners enjoyed free coal. The poorest working-class children, as we have seen with Will Thorn, relied on theft for some of their food and clothing. And it was in the same spirit that large parties of poor Londoners, setting out on their annual holidays to pick hops in Kent, combined to make the excursion financially viable.

> 'From London, two shillings it was, the fare, from London Bridge to Maidstone. And six out of ten never paid . . . they'd be all under the seats . . . all hid underneath. We evaded, after a certain age . . . Well then when we get to Maidstone, the barrier'd be there with the ticket collector . . . And then there'd be a hue and cry, "Oh where's my mum, my mum's got my ticket, she's gone up there," and we'd go through. He couldn't stop us, because while he was trying to stop one he'd lose about fifty.'

Once settled in at their camp, they did not confine their interests to the hops.

> 'You'd see the potatotes growing, and you went in between, and you dug up a lot and put the stalks back in the ground and you covered up. Went out in the middle and took a big cabbage or you took a swede . . . Well [the farmer] might miss one now and then, but we was artful as well as them. We didn't take it right in sight of the roadway so if he rode along on his horse he could see it. We took it out in the middle of the field. I looked over with a stick, a little piece of stick with a bit of paper on it, or a twig, and we knew that, we'd stick that in, and of a night-time we'd go along when everything was asleep and we'd fetch that. And we went to the town, we went to Faversham . . . Fruit, yes, we took that in the daytime . . . They couldn't watch everything . . . We'd pinch the fruit and sell it to somebody. You couldn't eat it all, what you took.'[2]

With urbanization and industrialization, however, much more sophisticated forms of collective resistance than this had developed. A particularly effective development, for example, was the rent strike, which secured its first major success in the passing of the Rent Restriction Act during the First World War, after large numbers of working-class women in Glasgow had refused rent, resisted eviction and staged a mass protest outside the local sheriff's office. The campaign, it is important to note, was for fair rents, and not for free housing: for justice rather than for change.

The essential object of trade unionism, which was by far the most extensive and best organized of all working-class institutions and our most important concern here, was similarly defensive: fair wages and fair work conditions. Unions were certainly formed on the assumption of a conflict of interest between employers and workmen. But their aim was to mediate this conflict rather than to fan it, to seek agreements rather than impose total victory. Although, as we shall see it, attitudes changed significantly towards the end of our period, for most of it trade unions had no wish to take over the industrial system and run it themselves. Their object was to secure a fair share, and no more, of the earnings of capitalism for their members. Their notion of a fair share was a traditional and hierarchical one. It is no accident that since the 1900s the differential earnings of British workmen, the mostly highly unionized working class in the world, have remained uncannily constant. Paradoxically, the most important long-term gain which the unions can claim to have brought is a fringe benefit, the shortening of working hours. By the 1900s hours had already fallen significantly, so that a fifty-five-hour week was standard, and the minority of occupations in which a seventy-hour week was common, such as shopkeeping and transport, were mostly ill-organized. But the reduction of hours also depended partly upon the legal protection of women and children under the Factory Acts, and in 1908 the miners used industrial action to force political legislation imposing an eight-hour day on all coal owners. Although with a politically divided membership it was tactful for trade unions to appear non-political, they had to work within an accepted political and legal framework. And when that framework was challenged as it was by the Taff Vale decision with its threat to their funds, the unions were quick to join their own political organization, the new Labour party; a development which made still less likely any major non-parliamentary political action on their part.

There were also personal reasons why trade union leaders were seldom consistently aggressive. Even the founders of new unions tended to become bureaucrats living off their members' dues and anxious to avoid the financial dangers of unnecessary conflicts: 'the ample waistcoats and gold watch chains, accompanied by fat cigars, which are to be seen at the Trades Union Congress and other meetings'.[3] Just as the radical politician was often mellowed by absorption into London society, so the trade union leader sooner or later felt himself more at home with colleagues in Congress than among dissatisfied branch members.

There were some once radical trade unionists whose change of views went further than this. Sidney and Beatrice Webb recorded a vivid account of the effect which promotion could have on the rank-and-file enthusiast.

> 'As Branch Secretary, working at his trade, our friend, though superior in energy and ability to the rank and file of his members, remained in close touch with their feelings and desires. His promotion to a salaried office brings him wider knowledge and larger ideas. To the ordinary Trade Unionist the claim of the workman is that of Justice. He believes, almost as a matter of principle, that in any dispute the capitalist is in the wrong and the workman in the right. But when, as a District Delegate, it becomes his business to be perpetually investigating the exact circumstances of the men's quarrels, negotiating with employers, and arranging compromises, he begins more and more to recognize that there is something to be urged on the other side ... There is also an unconscious bias at work. Whilst the points at issue no longer affect his own earnings or conditions of employment, any disputes between his members and their employers increase his work and add to his worry. The former vivid sense of the privations and subjection of the artisan's life gradually fades from his mind; and he begins more and more to regard all complaints as perverse and unreasonable.
>
> 'With this intellectual change may come a more invidious transformation. Nowadays the salaried officer of a great Union is courted and flattered by the middle class. He is asked to dine with them, and will admire their well-appointed houses, their fine carpets, the ease and luxury of their lives. Possibly, too, his wife begins to be dissatisfied. She will point out how So-and-so, who served his apprenticeship in the same shop, is now well-off ... whilst he is receiving £2 or £4 a week without any chance of increase. And so the remarks of his wife and her relations, the workings of his own mind, the increase of years, a growing desire to be settled in life and to see the future clear before him and his children, and perhaps also a little envy of his middle-class friends, all begin insidiously, silently, un-

known even to himself, to work a change in his views of life. He goes to live in a little villa in a lower middle-class suburb. The move leads to his dropping his workmen friends; and his wife changes her acquaintances. With the habits of his new neighbours he insensibly adopts more and more of their ideas. Gradually he finds himself at issue with his members, who no longer agree to his proposals with the old alacrity. All this comes about by degrees, neither party understanding the cause. He attributes the breach to the influences of a clique of malcontents, or perhaps to the wild views held by the younger generation. They think him proud and "stuck-up", overcautious, and even apathetic in trade affairs. His manner to his members, and particularly to the unemployed who call for donation, undergoes a change. He begins to look down upon them all as "common workmen"; but the unemployed he scorns as men who have made a failure of their lives; and his scorn is probably undisguised. This arouses hatred ... So gradually he loses the sympathy and support of those upon whom his position depends. At last the climax comes. A great strike threatens to involve the Society in desperate war ... He finds himself in small sympathy with the men's demands, and eventually arranges a compromise on terms distasteful to a large section of his members ... At his next appearance before a general meeting cries of "treachery" and "bribery" are raised ... Secure in the consciousness of freedom from outward taint, he faces the meeting boldly, throws the accusation back in their faces, and for the moment carries his point. But his position now becomes rapidly unbearable. On all sides he finds suspicion deepening into hatred. The members, it is true, re-elect him to his post; but they elect at the same time an Executive Committee pledged to oppose him in every way ... Harassed on all sides, distrusted and thwarted by his Executive Committee, at length he loses heart. He looks out for some opening of escape, and finally accepting a small appointment, lays down his Secretaryship with heartfelt relief and disappears for ever from the Trade Union world.'[4]

There were certainly such occasions when the members of a union rebelled against their leaders. The Durham miners struck against the new hours, which enforced night-work, negotiated in 1910. In 1910 the engineers forcibly ejected the autocratic full-time executive from their union offices. But these were rare incidents. Most members were content to leave union business to their officials. They worked too long hours to wish to spend much leisure time attending branch meetings; or if they did so, it was as much for the pleasure of a drink among a few friends. Except in the crisis of a strike there was no mass participation in union activity.

In the early 1900s the trade unions were in any case in a relatively weak position. Effective industrial action was usually only possible in boom years of full employment, but these were lean years. Trade unionism covered only a small minority of the working class, even if larger than in any other country: membership was only 15 per cent of the total occupied workforce. The new unions which had first successfully organized the unskilled in the 1890s, the Dockers and the Gasworkers, were struggling for survival with a shrunken membership. Unionism was otherwise largely confined to the better-paid working class: the miners, shipbuilders, cotton workers, printers and engineers. Over half the miners were union members, in contrast to one in eight transport workers or builders, and one in twenty women workers. Until 1910 in most of Britain trade unionism remained typically an instrument for the protection of the strong in the working class, not so inaptly symbolized by gold watch chains. Members called each other 'gentlemen' and tried to enforce ineffective craft regulations for apprenticeship with special advantages for their own sons. When deprived of the power of choosing and paying their own less skilled assistants they protested bitterly. If they struck, it was for the privileges of an elite.

It was only in a few special places, most notably the cotton towns and the mining districts, that trade unionism already sprang from the working-class community as a whole. Organization here was helped by the concentration of work in a few places, good earnings which enabled most families to pay dues, and a hierarchy at work based on sex and age rather than admission to a craft. There was thus a range of grades of worker in most families. The good earnings in addition reduced movement out of the district and so made for stability in local leadership. Social pressures were consequently much stronger than in the shifting, relatively anonymous working-class quarters of the big cities. A blackleg could expect to find himself cold-shouldered in the shops, women and children following him in a taunting crowd, and his housefront clearly chalked 'scab' to attract window smashers. When the miners struck in South Wales in 1910, the whole community rose like an army on the morning of battle:

> 'Shortly after 5 am on the morning of November 7th, Noah Rees, secretary of the Cambrian Lodge, together with W. H. Mainwaring and "a trumpeter" went through the streets, and roused the miners and their families. The repeated sound of the cornet or bugle was immediately effective: and in a matter of minutes hundreds were out-of-doors and forming up in processions towards the colliery nearest to their homes. Half-a-mile from Pandy, at 5.30 in the morning, men, women and children were coming to Clydach Vale to put out the fires at Cambrian Colliery . . . "We drew the fire before breakfast in the Cambrian Colliery. There were pickets in every lane. Never had there been such picketing before."[5]

The great South Wales strike of 1910–11, however, like the rebellions of the Durham miners and the engineers against their executives in the same years, was itself a sign of an important change in the atmosphere and aims of trade union action. The achievement of trade unionism up to this date must not be minimized. More than any other form of collective action, it had ensured in a society of continual change and increasing wealth that the working class gained its portion. It not only secured the slowly rising real earnings which were the basis of an improving general standard of life, but added its pressure to the demands for shorter working hours, better housing and better education. All this was of fundamental importance to twentieth-century Britain. But it now began to seem that trade unionism might push much further. The next fifteen years were to see a new fierceness, and also a new idealism, appearing in industrial conflict, which culminated in the bitter strikes of the post-war period and the General Strike of 1926.

The four years up to the First World War, the first stage in this new phase, bore many resemblances to the last great leap forward of trade unionism at the end of the 1880s. The revival of the economy had brought a situation of rising employment favourable to trade union activity. A general 'labour unrest' was again symbolized by a much publicized successful strike by the London dockers. Total union membership by 1914 had increased, by a third, to reach 20 per cent of the occupied workforce, and this time, moreover, the wave of unrest was sufficiently sustained to give a permanent and secure foundation to unionism for women and for the unskilled – and even to give it a foothold among clerical workers.

On the other hand there were also significant differences in atmosphere. In 1889 the dockers had won partly through a widespread public sympathy for their plight, and had emphasized their own 'respectability' in their campaign. But the strikes of 1910–14 were fought with troops standing by to enforce order. When the dock owners brought a shipload of blacklegs up the Thames in 1911, a tactic which had helped to defeat the London dockers in 1900, they were forbidden by the Home Office to discharge their strikebreakers for fear of violence. Troops were actually used in Liverpool, Salford, South Wales and elsewhere. Nor did Ben Tillett, the London dock-workers' leader, minimize the basic struggle which underlay these tense wage battles. In 1912 the dockers' union hold was again broken, after a counter-attack by the owners and an unsuccessful call for a general docks and shipping strike: a defeat which Tillett in his union report concluded was due to 'a lack of class loyalty and class-conscience . . . Revolutionary political agitation is essential'.[6] And revolutionary political agitation, which would have probably meant electoral socialism in 1889, to the younger leaders was as likely to imply syndicalism and the revolutionary general strike.

The call for a general docks and shipping strike, even if unsuccessful, was itself symptomatic of a new sense of class solidarity in the trade union movement. Its failure in fact led to the founding in 1914 of the formidable Triple Alliance of mining, railway and transport unions for mutual support in strike action, which was to play such a critical role in the post-First World War industrial struggle. Both the miners and the railwaymen had shown themselves capable of successful strike action on a national scale. The national strike of 800,000 miners in 1912, the largest strike yet seen in Britain, was indeed of such immediate impact that the government was forced to concede a national legal minimum wage for mineworkers. The Act was rushed through Parliament within days. Immediate government intervention in search of a settlement was also produced by the first national railway strike in 1911. A widening solidarity could also be sensed at other levels of the labour movement. There were times, as at Salford and at Bermondsey in 1911, when the rash of strikes among the unskilled reached such dimensions that they took on something of the character of a mass community protest. Some of the craft unions were affected too, most notably on the railways, and in the building and engineering industries. It was the solidarity produced by the first national railway strike which led to negotiations between the General Workers' Union and the more exclusive Amalgamated Society of Railway Servants; and although the Railway Servants at first rejected the notion that 'every Tom, Jack and Harry that works upon the railway, irrespective of his position' should be able to join the union, it was on very much this basis that the National Union of Railwaymen was eventually formed.[7]

Industrial unionism appeared among the building craftsmen too, and in the 'all grades' movements of the engineers. Both felt threatened by the introduction of new industrial methods, which had undercut so many once privileged skilled occupations in the past. Innovation in the building industry was in practice rather slower, but the engineers were already feeling the impact of work-study methods and the advanced division of labour, reducing them step by step from superior craftsmen to semi-skilled mechanics. The strong tendency to replace time wages by piecework pay added to these insecurities. In self-defence they turned to the organization of the industry as a whole. One factor in the new trade unionism was thus the impact of long-term change in the industrial and occupational structure. It was this new mood which drove the engineers to repudiate their own over-conservative executive, and took the London building workers into the prolonged strike and lock-out of 1914, which was only ended by the outbreak of war.

The First World War brought only a brief respite for employers. Far from ending industrial conflict, the war carried it forward to a new level. Its four years of full employment enabled the unions to make the greatest advance in membership in their entire history, doubling their national strength to reach a record 40 per cent of the workforce. The need to protect real wages against quickening inflation meant that by 1917, after two relatively quiet years, as many days were being lost through strikes in the key engineering industries as in 1910 or 1913. At the same time, the most militant trade unionists were now making increasingly challenging demands. The engineers' anxieties and radicalism grew especially as their factories faced the main brunt of the demand for military munitions, so that these once exclusive craftsmen were confronted not merely by an accelerated introduction of the new work methods, but their replacement by a mass influx of barely trained women. This was the situation in which Lloyd George found himself jeered by mass meetings of workers; in which thousands of Glasgow and Sheffield factory workers defied wartime legislation by striking; and in which shop stewards, the leaders of the engineers' movement, were able to advance from arguments about pay and demarcation to demanding control by workers of employment and dismissal, training, promotion and supervision. Nor were they alone in this. With its greatly increased numbers the trade union movement could now speak with justifiable confidence. The miners, now its recognized vanguard, resolved at their 1918 conference in favour of 'joint control and administration by the workmen and the State' of the mines. 'We have the brains among the miners to work the mines.'[8]

They were to fail in their aim for the moment, not so much because they lost confidence in themselves but because they were still exceptional in their attitudes. The rest of the working classes soon shrank back after the war to a more traditional passiveness once the women had been sent away from the workshops, especially when unemployment returned to pre-war levels. While the scale of national strike conflict mounted to its culmination in the General Strike, and the core of the movement remained very strong, much of the new membership of the war years slipped away. It is too easy to forget, faced by the more dramatic industrial solidarity of the Clydeside, that many of the unions which had swollen in the war took a much more prosaic view of their role. The Workers' Union, for example, was by 1918 the second largest of all trade unions, and had expanded with particular success among unskilled and semi-skilled workers, including women. But it provided no education in new ideals to a membership which was apathetic, prepared to leave control of policy to professional officers whose philosophy was scarcely distinguishable from that of conservative businessmen. Its organizers were officially advised at conferences that their primary task should be 'making calculations for the purpose of selling supplies of labour by bulk', and that in negotiating with employers they should make demands 'on a pure business basis and talk matters over as though we were selling bicycles'.[9]

In short, those elements which had long made trade unionism a primarily defensive form of collective action had certainly not disappeared. In retrospect they seem as significant as the new militancy. But contemporaries, rightly, were less concerned with the organizers of the Workers' Union than with the new voices of the miners and the engineers, or with Ben Tillett stirring his massed 'comrades' on Tower Hill. For as we shall see, it was such voices, expressing the mood of labour unrest, the new class solidarity, that mattered in the political crisis of Edwardian Britain.

15 Politics

For the overwhelming majority of Edwardians, politics offered the most obvious means of collective action for social change. Even during the crisis of the pre-war years, although physical force was increasingly advocated, very few rejected parliamentary politics. It was the belief that electoral victory offered a real hope of social transformation which sustained that significant minority of Edwardians for whom politics was a faith: the chapel members with a social conscience who were 'confirmed in Liberal principles', the former Liberals and Conservatives who were 'converted' to socialism, and also those men and women who offered their own suffering in the cause of votes for women. We began this book by asking whether there had been rewards from their political faith. In a wider sense, we shall find the answer in our concluding chapters. Political action, perhaps most clearly of all our instruments of change, provided an essential indirect thrust behind changing class relationships, the rising living standards of the working classes, and even changes within the family. Political influence on the social attitudes and work of an individual family could also be diffuse. Among our Edwardians, we could point to the Bensons: and especially the Richardses, one of the two families with whom we shall conclude. Here, however, we have a more limited task. What were the direct rewards of politics? The answer, we shall discover, will be unspectacular. Was this because the political system was less favourable to change than Edwardians believed? Was politics, perhaps, better designed to control social change than to generate it; a means of collective action commonly as defensive as trade unionism, for all its formidable potential?

We shall begin with the voters. The Edwardian franchise was well short of full democracy. Under a third of all adults were registered voters, as opposed to over 95 per cent today. The electors consisted of men who were heads of households, some who were lodgers, and owners of property and graduates. The extension of the right to vote, at the end of our period in 1918, to all adult men and some adult women (those over thirty with a small property qualification), with the reduction at the same time of residence qualifications and plural voting rights, was in itself a significant political achievement. The pre-1918 franchise nevertheless offered two advantages to reformers which have since disappeared. Women, who were denied the parliamentary vote although many were already local electors, have ironically since proved on balance to support Conservatism, despite a strong contribution to other parties. On the other hand, Members were still sent to Westminster from the whole of Ireland, in numbers which had not been reduced in proportion with the post-famine loss of population, and they normally supported radical social measures.

But if the inclusion of the Irish and the exclusion of women brought advantages, in other ways the Edwardian electoral system was weighted against the radical. There was a heavy bias in favour of wealth and education. In theory a single London property-owner might have been eligible to vote in thirty-seven constituencies. A working-class lodger, by contrast, would probably not be registered at all, for he was obliged to make a special request for a vote, and if his request was challenged and he had to appear in court it would cost him a day's earnings. The working class was also disadvantaged by the requirement of a year's residence in a constituency before registration. In the cities, where housing was easy to find and transport was still too expensive for many workmen, families often moved as the men changed (or lost) jobs. It was quite common for a third of the households in a working-class district to move during a year. Middle-class families were much more stable; they normally owned their houses and changed jobs infrequently.

Election costs were limited by law, so that election work had to be carried out largely by volunteers, as today. But the average cost of fighting an election was nearly £1,000, ten times a skilled man's average annual wage. Electioneering was already highly professionalized, with teams of canvassers, motor cars, the organization of postal voting, the transfer of volunteers to marginal seats, and mass advertising through leaflets and hoardings. It is true that in an age without radio and television public speaking by candidates themselves was still vital, and a man only had to be a good speaker to attract an audience. Outdoor political speaking, indeed, provided regular weekend entertainment in the towns, even for the apolitical. One London ex-soldier, a regular drunk,

> 'used to go Sunday to listen to the speakers down at the arches at St Pancras, that's where he used to take me brother, but I don't think he knew anything about politics. He was a royalist... I got the King and Queen tattooed on me chest in the Southampton Road there. That's how patriotic I was and I even done me share didn't I?'[1]

It was not an age in which an ordinary man's opinions could yet be drowned by the noise of the mass media. At general elections it was rather the hecklers and throwers of flour bags, fish and other missiles who could have the last word against the leading politicians. Although the typical meeting was not disorderly, disturbances were common, and provided one rough guide to swings of popular opinion.

Both the distribution of the vote itself and the expense and professionalization of election campaigning thus placed the working classes at a serious disadvantage. On the other hand, they could make their voices heard, and despite the inequalities of the franchise they did hold the majority of the votes. How did the parties try to win them?

Although the newly-formed Labour party offered Edwardians in roughly one in every six constituencies the chance of casting a straight class vote, the effective choice in most elections lay between the Conservative and Liberal parties. And despite a distinct fear, growing at this time, that politics might become too open a class struggle, the character of each party in practice assumed the existence of class interests and class conflict.

The Conservatives, who were in power from 1895 until 1905, based their electoral strength on the middle-class vote. Although there was still an important Liberal minority in the middle classes, the stage had been reached when a Yorkshire small businessman who was a Liberal town councillor could be regarded as indiscreet for so acting against his own natural interests: 'People used to tell him that as a business man he had no business to be so outright a Liberal.'[2] But the middle-class vote was insufficient to win victory alone. In addition the Conservatives secured between one-third and a half of the working-class vote. It was a working-class vote which asserted the essential unity rather than antagonism of class interests. Hence the Conservatives were significantly least successful in those regions where the middle-class presence was weakest: the north, Scotland and Wales.

There were, however, areas of active working-class Conservatism to be found in Lancashire. It was fed by the hostility felt for the large enclaves of Irish Catholics who supported the Liberals. Here, in contrast to their methods anywhere else, local Conservative parties were organized on a dual basis, with democratic federations based on the Conservative Working Men's Clubs alongside the usual exclusive party Constitutionalist Associations. Similarly, although with less active working-class participation, the Conservatives were able to profit from the fears brought by the waves of Jewish immigration into east London in the late nineteenth and early twentieth centuries. In general the Conservatives were able to present themselves as the party of patriotism, of true Protestant Englishmen, of Church and Empire. They perhaps exaggerated the extent to which the working classes also shared similar feelings. The jingo mobs of the Boer War, who after the celebrations of the relief of Mafeking smashed the windows of various Liberal anti-war shopkeepers, seem to have been most often led by middle-class men such as clerks, even if those arrested were generally working-class drunks. But the Conservative party leaders were able to sweep back to power in the 1900 election, fought during the Boer War, by appealing to the country 'not as Conservatives, not as politicians, but as Englishmen, to induce men to register votes in favour of that policy for which our gallant soldiers had fought, and for which the hills and plains of South Africa had been dyed red with their blood'.[3]

But there was another reason for the success of the Conservatives in 1900, apart from their appeal to the instincts of communal self-defence: war had brought a rare spell of full employment. Economic interest, even if short-term, was in fact a normal and essential factor in the Conservative working-class vote. There have been attempts in recent comment to separate working-class Conservatives into those whose attitudes are traditional, who vote for authority out of deferential respect, and those who are pragmatic, calculating their self-interest, but in practice the two attitudes were intertwined. We might attempt to contrast two working-class Conservative voters. The first, a bricklayer's labourer in well-to-do Oxford, 'accepted the idea that those in a position of education were the authority and the people to govern. They knew best.'[4] The second, a straw-hat maker who went against the Liberal current in Luton, 'always said there was plenty of work about when the Conservatives was in'.[5] But each of them was sufficiently traditional to send his children to church, although the Luton man did not himself attend; each was unpragmatic enough to have had too large a family; and very likely each worked for Conservative employers.

More interesting are the different forms which pragmatism took at different levels of the working classes. Among well-paid skilled men, the Conservatives were especially those with their eyes on a lower middle-class standard of living. They tended to stay with a firm for life, sometimes being promoted to the position of foremen. They had small families and were quite often Nonconformists. Political loyalty to Conservatism certainly paid the skilled Liverpool man who had 'been made a foreman shipwright in the Dock Board and he thought if he incurred their displeasure by giving any other than a Conservative opinion on a thing it might have clapped on him'.[6]

At the other extreme, among the unskilled, there were happy-go-lucky fathers of large families who could not be bothered with political discussion at all: 'The only views they got ... all as they wanted was enough money as they could get a drink.

And then I think the rest of their pleasure was getting kids ... It was drink and then come in – and bed. That was it. That's where the big families came in.'[7] This Staffordshire labourer was a typical Edwardian 'don't know', who probably voted Conservative in the same spirit as the Liverpool carter who certainly did: 'He never seemed to bother about anything in any line like that. Just as long as dad had his smoke and a job to go to he was happy.'[8] Conservatism of this kind might be described as pragmatic apathy. But among the casual, irregularly employed, the true pragmatism was surely political adaptability, like that of an Essex farmworker: 'My father was a Liberal one year and Conservative the next, depending on whom he worked for.'[9]

There were more generally substantial benefits offered to the working-class voter by the Conservatives in addition to work itself. The party had long supported a series of paternalistic social policies, such as factory inspection, the restriction of working hours for women and children, and slum clearance. In its years of office before 1905 it introduced important legislation for workmen's accident compensation and municipal housing; started the first national scheme of relief work for the unemployed in depressed years – in practice helping the casual unskilled rather than the 'deserving' regular workers for whom it was intended; and accepted the principle of old age pensions. Equally important, the party itself provided a considerable amount of charitable social welfare. A critical argument for supporting a wealthy parliamentary candidate was his greater ability to send donations to soup kitchens, coal and clothing clubs, sports clubs and churches. It was not surprising that in a West Country textile town, where the Conservative mill-owners provided work and houses, food tickets and other charity through the chapels, and also sat as magistrates, the most assiduously deferential cap-raisers were the secret Liberals: 'They kept it to theirself. Yes, they kept quiet, yes, you had to keep quiet in those days, yes.'[10] It was equally important, in those very few constituencies where electors still expected to be treated with beer or a shilling, that the politically cynical pragmatist should conceal any allegiance. 'Whichever side gets in, they don't do nort,' complained a Devon fisherman to a canvasser:

> 'Hanged if I blame ol' Charlie Whimble for saying anybody can have his vote, which way they like for five shillings. He'll never get five shill'orth out of it no other way, never, so long as he lives . . . nuther one of the sides is worth voting for, an' if you don't vote, then that don't make nothing no better. You can do nort.'[11]

It was not at this time only the politically cynical who had to keep their views to themselves. Some of the Conservative voting of the Edwardian working class was a response to more direct social pressure. In the countryside, especially, it was the letter rather than the spirit of the secret ballot which was observed. At the 1910 General Election there were landowners who not merely stood with their agent and loyal farmers in the school yard outside the polling booth, but had contrived that 'one of the checkers at the door was a carpenter employed on the estate, and seated at the table in the booth was Sir D. Broughton's chief clerk, Mr Cope'.[12] It was in response to intimidation of this kind that the Edwardian countryman had developed the reticence and the deviousness towards the well-to-do for which he was notorious. The drivers of Conservative motor cars taking electors to the polls never really knew whose side they were helping. Even an East Anglian farmer could be fooled by the wry humour of one of his labourers:

> ' "Well, Joesy," he say, "You mind where you go," he said, "you'll vote the same as I do." '
>
> He said, "I shall do the same as you do, I shall vote for meself, sir, and that's what you're going to do." That old man was a blue and uncle was a Liberal, but he little thought that uncle was going to vote Liberal.'[13]

The farm labourer's assumption that a vote for himself was a vote for the Liberals is an appropriate sentiment with which to turn, now, to consider the second effective choice open to most

Edwardian electors: the Liberal party. For the greatest strength of the Liberal party in these years lay precisely in the extent to which it had established itself as the natural voice of working-class interests. The labourer who simply 'thought it was the working men's party' was a representative Liberal voter of the 1900s. How reasonable was this view?

The Liberal party had a traditional reputation of supporting the causes of the underprivileged through its identification with the defence of Nonconformity and the granting of Irish Home Rule. Both these issues were still alive in the 1900s, although active middle-class Nonconformist Liberal activity was only a temporary revival, due to the Conservative government's provision of public rate support for church schools in the Education Acts of 1902–3. But the political realignment of the late nineteenth century, which had made the Conservatives increasingly the party of industrial businessmen as well as of landlords, was still more important in identifying their rivals as the party of the people, and the Edwardian Conservatives played into the Liberals' hands. Firstly, the Conservatives did not attempt to reverse the judicial Taff Vale decision of 1903 which laid all trade unions open to the payment of damages to employers for strike action, and thus threw the infant Labour party into the arms of the Liberals. A secret electoral pact between the two was forged in that year. Secondly, they allowed the Conservative peers in the House of Lords to take the extraordinary step of vetoing the 1909 budget, so that the 1910 elections were fought on the issue of Peers versus People. In a political controversy of this sort, the Liberals could not merely rally working-class voters, but drew on a wider basis of social support than was ever normally to be available to the future Labour party. At the same time they succeeded in reinforcing their appeal by offering a range of immediate social reforms, which were the fruits of a new social radicalism in the party, publicly personified by figures like Lloyd George and Churchill, but strongly influenced by less well-known writers such as Charles Masterman.

A struggling Lancashire newsagent summed up the social basis of the party's electoral success well enough in his view that Liberalism 'was more for the working man and the tradesman.

They used to reckon the Conservatives were the highbrow and the rich men.'[14] With its strongholds in the Celtic north and west, and in the industrial north, rather than London and the south where middle-class influence was stronger, Liberalism provided a reverse mirror to Conservatism. Similarly, within the middle classes Liberal support tended to come from Nonconformists rather than Anglicans. Among the working classes, there were variations between trades which paralleled the general differences between regions:

> 'Men on railways, the goods side and drivers and firemen not brought into touch with the public are Radicals, but passenger guards and porters who are also underpaid but with funds augmented by tips and the patronage of the rich, are Conservatives.'[15]

In general it was the ordinary, solid working-class constituencies, rather than the slums, that the Liberals could rely upon. Thus while among skilled workers the socially ambitious were often drawn to Conservatism, with the very poor the self-improving father of a small family was more likely to be a radical, or a socialist. The slums, one Liberal electioneer wrote, were

> 'usually the stronghold of the Conservatives . . . but if you find an oasis in this desert – a dwelling with white curtains, a bright door knocker and flowers in the window – you have found a Radical who has not lost hope and wants to get on . . .'[16]

The Liberals were fortunate in the issues which the Conservatives presented to them in these years: the church school issue which revived Nonconformist political fervour, the rejection of the budget by the peers, and also the delay in the granting of Home Rule which kept the Irish members at Westminster. These issues, together with the Liberal social programme and the secret electoral pact with Labour, gave Liberalism a new – and as it turned out, a last – flowering as the 'progressive' party of social reform. For the moment, the Labour party was reduced to a trade union interest group in Parliament, greatly outnumbered by both Conservative and Liberal manufacturers. In by-elections after 1910 it ceased to make significant progress. The secret pact had, moreover, not merely greatly helped the Liberal recovery in working-class constituencies, but favoured the election of trade unionists where straight socialists might have otherwise succeeded. For the time being, it appeared irrelevant that Labour had immense potential advantages in its ability to secure the financial support of trade unions and to maintain local grass-roots political activity, especially in the vast one-class poorer districts of the cities; although here, since the old radical working men's clubs had largely abandoned active political work for Liberals, Liberal councillors were increasingly rare and many of the Liberal Associations were already moribund. It was also possible to ignore the steady progress of socialist support within the trade unions, which was bringing the remaining trade unionist Liberal seats, such as the Midland mining constituencies, step by step into the Labour party; a socialist advance which was also a factor in the pre-war outburst of trade union militancy, the long-term political effects of which had yet to be seen. The socialist groups both within and outside the Labour party, small in number even if the seed of their ideas was now widely influential among the younger generation, could simply be scoffed at as 'atheists' while the immediate policies which they had proposed were put into effect. The socialists had advocated, at first to derision, labour exchanges, free school doctors, free school feeding, free secondary and university education, subsidized housing and help for the unemployed. The first three of their demands were now to be met, and gestures towards the others were also made.

The Liberal social programme did not stop here. Lloyd George introduced, for the tiny working-class minority who survived to the age of seventy, a pension of £13 a year, means-tested and also character-tested, excluding those on poor relief as well as former criminals. This was an important step; even if as critical in establishing state acceptance of a sub-subsistence standard of living for the 'deserving' aged as of their right to state advance. His controversial budget of 1909 was again a much smaller advance towards egalitarianism than the fuss which it engendered would suggest. Asquith's budget of 1907 had already helped the salaried and professional middle classes by distinguishing between earned and unearned income and reducing tax on earned incomes. The working classes received no benefit being below the tax threshold, so that redistribution was simply within the upper and middle classes. Lloyd George pushed a little further. Income tax was now raised from the standard 5 per cent to a maximum of 8 per cent for the largest unearned incomes, and maximum death duty rates to 15 per cent. Drink taxes were also increased. A very small revenue was also to be derived from landowners through the taxation of leasehold property, undeveloped land and unearned increments. The more significant but again marginal increases of graduated taxation in the 1914 budget rightly attracted slight attention.

Lloyd George's most striking social measures before 1914 were his introduction of two schemes of National Insurance in 1911–13. Health Insurance provided workers (but not their families) with medical attention from a national system of panel doctors. Unemployment Insurance organized unemployment pay in certain trades. Although there were state and employers' contributions in each case, it is equally striking that under each scheme workers were now legally forced to be thrifty. The schemes, moreover, helped those best able to help themselves. For sick women, children and old people, and for the typical unemployed casual worker, poor relief remained the only available assistance.

Lloyd George's social policies were thus not of a kind likely to eradicate the drastic inequalities of Edwardian society. Their aim was well characterized by his colleague Churchill, who himself introduced the national system of labour exchanges, and also the Trade Boards Act of 1909, which enabled the setting of minimum wages in some of the worst sweated industries such as tailoring. Certainly Churchill, son of a great country house, could be moved by poverty. While fighting a Manchester by-election he walked from his base at the Midland Hotel into the slums. 'Fancy,' he said, 'living in one of these streets – never seeing anything beautiful – never eating anything savoury – *never saying anything clever*.'[17] But he accepted such cultural disabilities as ineradicable. The most that could be done, as he put it at Dundee in 1908, was to provide a safety net: 'We want to draw a line below which we will not allow persons to live and labour, yet above which they may compete with all the strength of their manhood.'[18]

In his essential respect for a competitive free enterprise system Churchill was typical of the Liberal leaders. Even Lloyd George, for all his demagogic speeches against landlords, his friendly references to socialism, his lifelong Welsh dislike of the establishment symbolism of titles and established church, never intended to secure more than some overdue concession to an increasingly restless industrial working class. His dramatic strike interventions had the aim of knocking sense into both industrialists and unions, each side obstinate.

There were, in short, significant social advances achieved through the Edwardian Liberal governments, but they in no sense approached the social transformation that their radical supporters called for. They are more easily understood as a modest readjustment to meet rising working-class expectations in a society of generally increasing wealth. Politically they also represented an attempt to answer the growing strength of the labour movement. But could the Liberals have gone further than this? There are two reasons for doubt, one springing from their own party, the other from the nature of the political system itself.

The Liberal party did not merely depend upon working-class votes. It also needed the financial support of the small minority of well-to-do Liberals. In many districts their contributions were essential to keep up its electoral organization. The Liberals won electoral support from the trade unions, but unlike the Labour party they never secured union financial backing. And, as the *Manchester Guardian* put it, 'What would be the state of the Liberal Party chest if it depended on the voluntary subscriptions of the rank and file?'[19] The party could not afford policies so radical that they alienated its wealthy backers. It therefore trod a dangerously narrow path. The desperate, almost open sale of future peerages by Liberal party organizers was one measure of its difficulties.

There was, however, another more fundamental reason why the political system in the early twentieth century was less favourable to social change than might have been thought. Edwardian politics is better understood as a system less for fostering change than for maintaining stability, with the aid of periodic but slight adjustments, while at the same time providing, through elections, for the regular venting of exasperation. The franchise as we have seen was biased in favour of the well-to-do. So was the selection of candidates by the Liberal and Conservative parties, neither normally in public. Even in the most radical Edwardian Parliament, elected by the Liberal landslide of 1906, a sixth of the Members were Old Etonians and a third had been to Oxford or Cambridge. A fifth were landowners; nearly two-fifths active businessmen; and nearly half involved in finance or insurance. A mere tenth were working-class, mostly trade unionists. The average age of Members was almost fifty. In the choice of government ministers a further conservative bias was introduced. Representation of the House of Lords was necessary, and indeed in the thirty years before 1916 peers and their descendants comprised half of all cabinet ministers. The Liberal cabinet of 1906 was unusual in cutting aristocratic participation to a third, and introducing one working man. But one should not imagine that the Liberal leaders, if middle-class in origin, came of humble backgrounds. Campbell-Bannerman for example, Prime Minister in 1906, was the son of a Glasgow businessman, considerably wealthier than most landowners, and like a typical upper-class gentleman he spent his summers in a Scottish castle and wintered at Marienbad. When they got to power, ministers were usually old. Even the Conservative *National Review* attacked the 1900 cabinet as 'an assemblage of sexagenarians, most of whom have little knowledge or conception of the problems to be solved, who are bound by the shibboleths of a bygone era . . . It is not the kind of body to reorganize the nation.'[20]

And if the cabinet could be persuaded to vigorous action, there stood above them, as Lloyd George was to discover, the opinion of the House of Lords and the King. In being prepared to defy, even to bait, the Lords, Lloyd George was exceptional. No doubt his Welsh resistance to incorporation into London upper-class society fortified him. The London season coincided with the summer session of Parliament, integrating the social and political systems, and providing a further influence towards the politics of consensus. Society in fact provided a mirror to the political system:

> 'Society in England is a national institution ... [with] a central meeting ground in London during the season ... Its members have an extraordinarily wide acquaintance with one another from one end of the land to the other. They are connected by marriage, by early association at the public schools and at Oxford or Cambridge, and they are brought constantly together by entertainments in the capital, and visits at country houses. Such a constitution gives to society great solidity and great influence, without the narrowness and rigidity that attends a purely hereditary caste.'[21]

It was a system that had proved through the nineteenth century that, by adapting to and through social change, force could be avoided in politics. But in the years before 1914 there were signs that the consensus upon which the system rested might be breaking. This was the Edwardian crisis which we shall examine in the next chapter. The Conservatives incited, first the Lords' veto of the 1909 budget, and then civil war and army mutiny in Ireland. The new trade union militancy had brought talk of a General Strike. And suffragettes demanded the vote with civil disobedience and destruction.

Underlying this eruption of force was exasperation with the failure of the political system in general, and the Liberal governments in particular, to provide sufficiently decisive solutions to the social problems of the period. Part of the background to the crisis was in fact the steadily widening influence of those movements which the Liberals had attempted to disregard: feminism and socialism. We must be sure not to repeat their mistake.

Families like the Richardses, with their refusal to recognize class distinction, their open help for the unfortunate, and their instinctive respect for the independence of women as well as men, were setting new social standards. And in the early socialist branches there was a fervour and energy rare in politics. 'We were all in good jobs, all very enthusiastic, and convinced our mission was to revolutionize the world,' George Lansbury recalled of the Bow and Bromley Social Democrats in East London. 'Our branch meetings were like revivalist gatherings. We opened with a song and closed with one, and often read together some extracts from economic and historical writings.'[22] The branches organized study-classes, debates, concerts, Socialist Sunday Schools and – above all – outdoor propaganda meetings. A dedicated socialist might speak at six different outdoor meetings on a single Sunday, walking from stump to stump to help keep the message going. 'The bond of unity which held us together and never failed was our faith that, out of the seeming hopelessness and despair which a society based on riches and poverty creates, a nobler, more enduring civilization would be built. We were enthusiasts because we were certain of victory.'[23] It would have paid the politicians to give them more attention.

Equally, because its source was in the failure to solve social problems through parliamentary politics, the Edwardian crisis provides confirmation for a reduced assessment of the direct fruits of political activity in these years. There was a certain flexibility in the social system, and it was none the less real for being small. Lloyd George's Old Age Pensions for example, minimal though they were, did suffice to transform the last years of some old people, like the poorest of the cottagers in Flora Thompson's *Lark Rise*:

> 'They were relieved of anxiety. They were suddenly rich. Independent for life! At first when they went down to the Post Office to draw it, tears of gratitude would run down the cheeks of some, and they would say as they picked up their money, "God bless that Lord George! (for they could not believe one so powerful and munificent could be a plain 'Mr') and God bless *you*, miss!"'[24]

But such crumbs from the rich man's table were small steps towards radical social change, let alone the nobler civilization of which Lansbury and his friends dreamt. When compared with the political thunder heard at elections, the rainfall proved slight. It is easy enough to understand the point of view of the man on the building site who refused to be moved by the socialist speeches of a fellow plasterer:

> 'There ain't no use in the likes of us trubblin' our 'eds or quarrelling about politics. It don't make a dam bit of difference who you votes for or who gets in. They're hall the same: workin' the horicle for their own benefit. You can talk till you're black in the face, but you won't never be able to alter it.'[25]

16 The Edwardian Crisis

For five years from 1909 there were not a few perceptive Edwardians who believed that Britain faced a social and political crisis of exceptional severity: a crisis which might finally be settled through civil violence rather than through parliamentary politics. It was created by the convergence of a series of inflamed disputes, each challenging the legal framework of Edwardian society: feminism, the budget veto by the House of Lords, the revolt of labour and the threat of civil war in Ireland. Lloyd George, speaking in the City of London in July 1914, said that the coincidence of renewed labour unrest with an outbreak of fighting in Ireland would create a critical situation, 'the gravest with which any government has had to deal for centuries'. The first Russian Revolution had already occurred. There were other European countries in which similar upheavals seemed likely – and indeed did follow the First World War. But for the outbreak of war in August 1914, might Britain have followed a similar path? How serious was the Edwardian crisis?

The simplest answer is, of course, that there was no early twentieth-century British revolution, and the majority of Edwardians never thought one likely. One of the most persuasive accounts of the crisis is George Dangerfield's *Strange Death of Liberal England*, and Dangerfield himself was a child of these years. But his own recollections suggested no awareness of approaching catastrophe. Nor did a more representative Edwardian like the West End luxury hatter Fred Willis: 'When my Lord came in to have his hat ironed on those spring mornings in the springtime of this century I firmly believed that kind of life was to continue for ever. Catastrophes might and did happen elsewhere ...'[1] Charles Masterman, the suburban radical politician, wrote cogently enough of his fears of 'The Multitude', the working classes whom he watched as they coalesced into the city crowd:

> 'There is a note of menace in it . . . possibilities of violence in its waywardness . . . It will cheer the police which is scattering it like chaff and spray, mock openly at those who have come with set purposes, idle and sprawl on a summer afternoon at Hyde Park or an autumn evening in Parliament Square. But one feels that the smile might turn suddenly into a fierce snarl of savagery . . .'[2]

But Charles Booth, who knew the London working classes far more intimately than Masterman, did not sense such pent-up savagery. We can see the same contrast in painting, between the faceless city crowd of Wyndham Lewis's burning abstract chords, and the more cautious, but again more representative reality which Sickert found in the quiet poverty of Camden Town.[3] The Edwardian crisis was not greeted by millenarian enthusiasm in revolutionary multitudes. Nor did it substantially affect the general trend of social violence in Britain which, measured for example by the frequency of common assault, continued downwards. This was true even of the critical general elections of 1910, which saw few disturbances by comparison with earlier elections. It was much more those in authority who felt the Edwardian crisis. For them it was a moment of truth, in a rough, if transitional, passage.

Feminism

Of all the challenges to authority before 1914, it was possibly feminism which most often made a direct and personal impact. Consider the 'lofty theorist' portrayed by Olive Schreiner, standing 'before the drawing-room fire in spotless shirt-front and perfectly fitting clothes', holding forth about women as divine child-bearers, yet all the while expecting his tea to be made and his boots cleaned by some woman acting as an 'elderly house drudge'.[4] The entry of feminism might have shattered the humbug of this domestic fantasy. Or take the two educated young men caught by Virginia Woolf discussing the nature of woman in *The Voyage Out*:

> ' "Women interest me," said Hewet, who, sitting on the bed with his chin resting on his knees, paid no attention to the undressing of Mr Hirst.
>
> ' "They're so stupid," said Hirst. "You're sitting on my pyjamas."
>
> ' "I suppose they *are* stupid?" Hewet wondered.
>
> ' "There can't be two opinions about that . . ." '[5]

For these men again, an encounter with an argumentative feminist could have been profoundly disturbing. Yet it was to just such encounters that thousands of respectable Edwardian men had to adapt. And what they had to witness outside their homes was still more surprising. Mass rallies of women, as many as a quarter of a million in London parks, assembled to demand the right to vote and sit for Parliament. At one demonstration in Parliament Square in 1910 over a hundred women were arrested in clashes with the police, and many injured. The code of chivalry was still further strained when Lady Constance Lytton, disguised as a seamstress, was arrested at a demonstration in Liverpool, and permanently paralysed as a result of forcible feeding in prison. Other well-to-do women had already begun to refuse to pay taxes without representation. After the narrow failure of a suffrage bill in 1912, civil disobedience became increasingly widespread. Suffragettes were prepared to break windows, slash pictures, poison golf greens, set fire to public buildings, tie themselves to railings and hunger-strike out of prison. There was no sign, in the last months before the outbreak of the First World War, that anything less than the concession of the vote could end the women's rebellion.

Nor was the vote all that women were now demanding. There was talk, very occasionally accompanied by actual experiment, about new forms of marriage; communes, trial marriage, and, especially interestingly, the introduction into conventional marriage of the same 'freedom of bargaining to the best advantage, permitted as a matter of course to every other worker' – including the payment of a wage for housework.[6] The most advanced new marriage manuals, such as Maud Braby's *Modern Marriage and How to Bear It*, could be found not only advocating 'marriage on approval' and wild oats for women, but the treatment of infidelity in marriage also 'in a philosophical spirit', as well as the deliberate fostering of male friendships for married women. The husband should be packed off to his club to enable the wife to 'go out on her own account and do a little dinner and theatre with a discreet admirer'.[7] Husbands, by contrast, were being asked to take their own marital roles more seriously. There were suggestions that men ought to be present at childbirth. And when they were at work, as employers they ought to drop 'the habit of judging a woman entirely by externals' and instead take notice of 'steady work and strict attendance to business'.[8]

There were some Edwardians for whom these developments seemed portents of entire catastrophe. The distinguished doctor, Sir Almroth Wright, author of *The Unexpurgated Case against Woman Suffrage*, argued that both empire and civil order would disintegrate if not held together by the physical force of men. Mentally, on the other hand, women were again inferior, irresponsive to evidence, lacking in proportion, accepting the congenial as true, incapable, indeed, 'of framing anything that could pass muster as a great generalization'.

> 'Has woman advanced? . . . If to move about more freely, to read more freely, to speak out her mind more freely, and to have emancipated herself from traditional beliefs – and, I would add, traditional ethics – is to have advanced, woman has indubitably advanced.
>
> 'But the educated native too has advanced in all these respects; and he also tells us that he is pulling up level with the white man.'

To argue for equality was an absurdity in either case. Even belief in equal pay was a sign of 'mental disorder'. To contemplate the fulfilment of the feminist campaign was unspeakable:

women on every committee, every governing board, every bench, every Parliament – 'until we shall have everywhere one vast cock-and-hen show'.[9] If the end result was less disastrous to the social order than Sir Almroth predicted, it was not merely because his characterization of womankind was misguided.

The feminist campaign was never as threatening as he imagined. It was unable to draw on a sufficiently wide basis for its recruitment. The commonly found argument that feminism was caused by the rise of paid employment for women outside the household is misleading. A more immediately critical development was the increasing tendency during the nineteenth century for middle-class men to work away from their homes, often as a result of the family's migration to a suburban house, while at the same time the well-to-do wife, amply assisted by servants, was now tending to have fewer children, and yet was barred by convention from working. The potential recruits, and organizers, for feminism were often among those who could 'in early middle age be found sitting alone in an empty house'. Olive Schreiner cites the marital experience of the wife of a leading barrister:

> 'My husband is always increasingly absorbed in his legal duties, of which I understand nothing, and which so do not interest me. My children are all growing up and at school. I have servants enough to attend to my house. When he comes home in the evening, if I try to amuse him by telling him of the things I have been doing during the day, of the bazaars I am working for, the shopping I have done, the visits I have paid, he is bored. He is anxious to get away to his study, his books, and his men friends, and I am left utterly alone. If it were not for the society of women and other men with whom I have more in common, I could not bear my life. When we first met as boy and girl, and fell in love, we danced and rode together and seemed to have everything in common; now we have nothing.'[10]

The separation of work from the home had rigidified the roles of husbands and wives and aggravated the tendencies of men to stereotype women as emotional – and perhaps romantic – but incapable. It resulted, especially in the middle classes, in alienated wives; just as the same process of economic transition in the shift of work from the home to the factory at the other end of the social scale often produced alienated workers. It was in this middle-class discontent, rather than among working-class women, that the core of the feminist movement was formed.

Working-class participation in the women's movement on the other hand, wherever it was significant, does appear to have been directly related to the growth of paid factory work for women. There was strong support for the suffragette campaign from an early stage in the textile districts, and one of the movement's full-time workers was a Lancashire textile worker, Annie Kenney. By 1914 important support had also been organized by Sylvia Pankhurst in her East London Federation. Conversely many leading feminists played a part in the development of women's trade unionism.

Some of the elements thus existed for a united campaign. Besides joining the demand for the vote – which was borne forward on the same groundswell of political ideas as the extension of the vote to all working-class men – the feminists were agreed on the need to reform the marriage laws. The Women's Co-operative Guild gave important evidence to the Royal Commission on Divorce of 1909. The East London Federation was also to develop, during the war years, a more ambitious programme for the benefit of working-class women, including a children's play centre and clinic for working mothers, a co-operative toy-making factory offering equal pay and a campaign to improve the wages and conditions of home workers. But this programme was exceptional, and it came too late to change the general character of the feminist movement. Although the feminists received some strong support from within the labour movement, there remained many working-class men who believed that the aim of trade unionism should be to restrict or exclude women workers, rather than to secure them equal conditions. The miners for example were still asking in 1911, against continued protests from the women themselves, for the legal prohibition of women's work on the pit brow. Working-class women similarly were by no means innate feminists. Even East London factory workers could not have been thoroughly won to the cause without a prolonged campaign. Many observers noticed, for example, that factory girls tended to evaluate work places less on criteria such as the wages offered or skills required, and more by social factors such as the appearance of fellow workers. Thus, 'an order that no hair curlers may be worn in the factory has a marked effect in raising the social standing of its workers among their fellows'.[11] Women were as likely to carry home attitudes into their work life as trade attitudes into the home. And if this was true of city factory girls, the feminists were still further from changing the views of millions of working-class wives, overburdened with child care, who considered politics a luxury suitable only for men who had the time to think, and resented lecturing from women who had never had to struggle: 'I reckon they suffragettes wants half-a-dozen kids like this yer squad o' mine. That'd steady 'em.'[12]

Some of the suffragettes were eventually driven into a more thorough attempt to organize working-class support by their failure to win the vote from the Liberal government. Others drew a different tactical conclusion. It was this failure which also explains the transformation of their respectable campaign for parliamentary rights into a thoroughly militant agitation. These were the years in which some of the movement's leaders began to call for a whole-hearted onslaught on male domination. Christabel Pankhurst, for example, accused three-quarters of all men of venereal disease, and called for the abandonment of all physical relationships 'between the spiritually developed women of this new day and men who in thought and conduct with regard to sex matters are their inferiors'.[13] Frightened male observers found particularly 'disgusting examples' of the new 'accursed spirit of sex antagonism' in the training of women militants in hand-to-hand combat, and how to wind policemen.[14] But the irony is that the militant struggle for the vote at the same time reduced the long-term threat of feminism to the social order. It concentrated the movement's aims on the male-dominated world of politics, rather than on the home, where a transformation would have been much more profound in its impact. This was why, once they were given recognition by the male political establishment on the suspension of civil disobedience at the outbreak of war, its most militant leaders were so easily absorbed. In this they followed the same path as many successful trade unionists and socialists, losing contact with the real needs of their followers. The feminists had failed to give sufficient weight to a broad social programme, including marriage reform, birth control and support for working mothers, for which the winning of the vote would have been a means rather than the central issue. Despite its apparent triumph in the 1918 franchise, this is the essential reason for the failure of Edwardian feminism to end 'the custom of regarding one half of the race as sent into the world to excite desire in the other half', and to win a future in which it could no longer be said of the destiny of children: 'Boys are to be happy in themselves; the girls are to make others happy.'[15]

The particular aim of the suffrage movement also explains why the violence which accompanied it constituted a temporary nuisance rather than a serious threat to parliamentary politics. The suffragettes were challenging Parliament simply in order to gain their own right to participate in its processes. It was above all sheer frustration with the Liberal resistance to their case which drove so many respectable well-to-do women to civil disobedience. Their violence, moreover, either consisted of symbolic vandalism or was self-inflicted, like the most famous episode of their entire campaign, the suicide of Emily Davison, who threw herself under the horses at the Derby of 1913. Such events made the newspaper headlines, and they were intended to, but they scarcely interrupted the normal social order.

The inability of Edwardian governments to grant women the vote did itself indicate the weakness of the political system when a fundamental change had become necessary. Politicians had exhausted the arguments against women's suffrage before 1914 and most were glad enough to concede it when the war work of women provided a dignified opportunity. Liberals, committed to social progress, could not oppose votes for women without embarrassment. Conservatives, who were already aware from local election results that women tended to support them, and knew that their own women volunteers found the anti-suffrage case increasingly unacceptable, were equally glad.

When it came in 1918 the concession of women's suffrage thus brought little immediate change. Certainly it laid the ground upon which a more dignified civic position for women could be built. But a Bolton engineer was not much moved by that. As his son remembered:

> 'Me mother had a vote . . . and he said to her he said, "Now I want you come with me and vote." So she went to Oxford Road School voting, and he said, "If you vote you'll get two glasses of brandy at Liberal Club after." So he took her up voting and me mother were deaf and . . . he were going with her into stall like and a bobby what were there called old Bobby Brooks, knew me father very well, lived round there, and he said, "Nay," he said, "Jack, thou can't go and show her." He said, "She'll only have put what I tell her" . . . She got her two brandies. She'd do what me dad told her. Me dad were number one at our house.'[16]

It was a change of real significance; and yet, when it had come, the system stood remarkably little altered. In one respect, at least, the Edwardian crisis had seemed a more serious threat to political authority than it proved to be.

The revolt of the upper classes and Ulster

The civil disobedience of feminists was not the only rebellion of the respectable classes in the early twentieth century. These years saw an unusual series of such outbreaks. Some looked back to the mid-nineteenth-century dissenting resistance to tithes and church rates, and some anticipate the radical civil disobedience of the 1960s, but other aspects of this phase of Edwardian unrest were unique in British history. It begins with old-fashioned dissent: the Nonconformist campaign of refusal to pay local government rates, after the 1902–3 Education Acts had enabled these to be used in support of church schools. The earliest militant feminist civil disobedience followed. Later on women, but this time Conservative women, were again involved in resistance, to the 1911 insurance schemes. A Servants' Tax Registers Defence League was formed, and the Dowager Lady Desart chaired a huge meeting of women in the Albert Hall who chanted in turn, 'Taffy was a Welshman, Taffy was a thief', and 'We won't pay!' The servant-employing public was even encouraged by *The Times* not to observe the Act. And although this particular campaign proved evanescent, it indicated how far unrest had gripped even the conservative well-to-do by 1911.

The revolt of the upper classes proper began with the astonishing decision of the House of Lords to veto the 1909 budget in protest at the unspectacular taxation of landowners which it anticipated. Their clearly unconstitutional action, which had no precedent for over 250 years, yet was carried by an overwhelming majority of peers, can hardly be explained by the feuding within the Conservative leadership. Even the incitement on the one side of Lloyd George, and on the other of the *Daily Mail* and *The Times*, both papers now mouthpieces of the new master of mass sensationalism, Lord Northcliffe, could hardly in themselves have provoked such political suicide. But there was an underlying reason for the protest from the Lords backbenches. Despite the creation of a number of industrial peerages, and the general interpenetration of the landowning, professional and business classes, the hereditary aristocracy still over-represented the older form of English wealth, the land. Landowners had been hard hit by the agricultural depression. With the advent of the 1906 government, the aristocracy no longer had a majority in the cabinet. Now a radical chancellor proposed to tax their inherited wealth. Already in retreat, they felt their whole order at stake. And in a sense they were right, for although the 1909 budget brought Britain little nearer to economic equality, the struggle to pass it did ensure the political recognition, through the curtailment of the House of Lords veto, of the fact that power in Britain ultimately lay with the industrial and urban rather than the rural classes.

In rejecting the budget, the House of Lords provided the issue upon which the social radicals in the Liberal party could rally the working-class vote in the 1910 elections. They also ensured months of campaigning in which the class nature of politics was exceptionally emphasized by government leaders. Already in July 1909 Lloyd George was making his famous Limehouse speech to a packed, responsive audience of East Londoners, jeering at dukes and landowners as men whose unearned rentals came not from business, but blackmail – 'a piece of insolence which no intelligent man would tolerate'. Four months later at Newcastle Lloyd George warned the Lords:

> 'Let them realize what they are doing. They are forcing a Revolution, and they will get it. The Lords may decree a revolution, but the people will direct it. If they begin, issues will be raised that they little dream of . . .
>
> 'Who made ten thousand people owners of the soil, and the rest of us trespassers in the land of our birth? . . . Where did the table of that law come from? Whose finger inscribed it?'[17]

Churchill too was deliberately raising the threat of class war. At Leicester in September 1909 he declared:

> 'We are at the cross-ways. If we stand on in the old happy-go-lucky way, the richer classes ever growing in wealth and in number, and ever declining in responsibility, the very poor remaining plunged or plunging even deeper into helpless, hopeless misery, then I think there is nothing before us but savage strife between class and class.'[18]

Like other social radicals such as Masterman, Churchill's fear of open class war was a real one. Yet such speeches seemed to make its outbreak more likely. It was to be two more years, including two general elections, before the Lords issue was settled. Was it surprising, and entirely incredible, when *The Times* declared of the militant labour unrest of 1911 that 'this spirit has been distinctly fostered by the conspicuous incitements to class hatred uttered by the Chancellor of the Exchequer in his electioneering campaigns'? Lloyd George's real purpose was undoubtedly different. It is significant that his fiercest attacks were directed to peers and landlords rather than to businessmen. His real aim was to bring the modifications, significant but not drastic, in the social and political system which he believed were necessary to avert a class war. But to achieve this he needed both to keep the support of the working classes and to frighten the wealthy and employing classes into concessions. His revolutionary class oratory was therefore essential to his purpose. It both stoked the Edwardian crisis and eased its solution. It made the transitional passage also a rough one.

The revolt of the conservative classes was not settled even by their defeat in the second general election of 1910. The backbenchers of the Lords fought the curtailment of their veto to the end, despite the King's promise to swamp them with specially created Liberal peers. In the summer of 1911 a 'no surrender' movement was led by Lord Willoughby de Broke, a peer with more hunting than political experience, joined by the ancient ex-Lord Chancellor, the Earl of Halsbury. They failed narrowly, largely due to the last-minute intervention of Balfour, Conservative leader in the Commons. But Balfour paid for his moderation. In the autumn he was ousted from the party leadership. His successor was to introduce a new dimension to the Conservative rebellion. He was Bonar Law, the harsh self-conscious son of an Ulster manse.

We shall consider Ulster only briefly, for Ireland has not been part of our subject in this book. It is clear enough, however, that by the summer of 1914 Ireland was close to civil war, and equally that a good deal of the responsibility for this situation lay with the Conservatives. The 1906 Liberal government had not needed Irish parliamentary support and had not introduced a Home Rule bill. Disappointment fostered the rise in the Irish countryside of Sinn Fein, a radical nationalist movement which drew on the long tradition of agrarian violence in Ireland. At the same time a socialist-led trade union movement had sprung up in the towns, beginning with the Belfast dock strike of 1907. Urban conditions were still worse in Dublin, where recorded mortality rates were higher than in any other European city, and the series of industrial disputes culminated in the famous strike of 1913.

Despite considerable support from British trade unionists, including a shipload of food, the strike failed; and after their defeat the urban militants turned their energies also to the nationalist cause. Meanwhile in 1911, the Liberal government, now depending upon the Irish representatives for their majority in Parliament, had agreed to introduce legislation for Home Rule.

There was at once a revival of the Ulster resistance which had sprung up against the 1886 Home Rule bill. The Orange Lodges and Unionist Clubs declared in conference that they would not submit, and chose to lead them Sir Edward Carson, the sombre, fanatical Protestant Dublin lawyer, previously best known as the prosecutor of Oscar Wilde. During 1912 he formed the Ulster Volunteers, a private army which imported arms and ammunition, was commanded by the ex-India frontier General Sir George Richardson, and within a year was 100,000 strong. At the same time the Ulster Covenant was launched with a ceremonial signing. Within weeks a quarter of a million signatories had declared themselves 'convinced in our consciences' that Home Rule would be 'subversive of civil and religious freedom', and pledged 'throughout this our time of threatened calamity to stand by one another ... in using all means which may be found necessary to defeat the present conspiracy to set up a Home Rule Parliament in Ireland'. Carson then formed his provisional government.

These developments, which in most contexts would have been denounced as treason, were widely supported by Conservative politicians in Britain. F. E. Smith declared to a meeting at Lincoln that if Home Rule came 'with Ulster undoubtedly in arms ... I tell you that Ulster will not stand alone.' Another MP, Colonel Hickman, announced that 'personally they have all my sympathies' and 'when the time comes if there is any fighting to be done – I am going to be in it'.[19] But the most remarkable speech came from the Conservative leader himself. At Blenheim Palace in July 1912 Bonar Law told a vast Conservative meeting that the Liberal government was simply 'a revolutionary committee which seized by fraud upon despotic power' and that their opposition should no longer be bound by normal political conventions. 'I said the other day in the House of Commons and I repeat here that there are things stronger than Parliamentary majorities.' If Home Rule was imposed upon Ulstermen,

> 'they would be justified in resisting by all means in their power, including force. I said so then, and I say now, with a full sense of the responsibility which attaches to my position, that if the attempt be made under present conditions I can imagine no length of resistance to which Ulster will go in which I shall not be ready to support them.'[20]

Were these inflammatory declarations mere bluff for party political ends? Private correspondence of these years suggests not. Viscount Esher, one of the King's private advisers, thought Carson's methods 'the right and above board ones. Those who hate Home Rule sufficiently should be ready to risk their skins.' He told Curzon, ex-Viceroy of India, that Carson should 'be encouraged to provoke a contest at an early date'. And Curzon also thought that the problem must 'solve itself in battle on the soil of Ireland'.[21] In any case, by the summer of 1914 the threat of civil war, even if born in the unreal atmosphere of the Lords rebellion, had gone beyond the control of party politics. The Irish nationalists had launched their own Irish volunteers, in answer to the Ulstermen, and soon equal to them in numbers. A strikers' defence organization had also been formed, the Citizen Army. The Liberal government now prohibited the import of arms, but the opposing private armies were already formed. Then, at the end of November 1913, in a speech at Dublin, Bonar Law took a further fatal step. He appealed to the British army stationed in Ireland not to fight if they were ordered to impose Home Rule; to desert, as had the army of King James II. There was no civil war then. 'Why? Because his own army refused to fight for him.'[22] And in March 1914 his call was answered by the Curragh mutiny. When the decision had been made to prepare for the British army to move to Ulster, a large body of officers, including the entire staff of some brigades, made it known that they preferred to accept dismissal if ordered north. But they were not dismissed. The Liberal government was thus left disarmed and helpless. Preparations for civil war continued. A month later the Ulster Volunteers successfully smuggled in 30,000 rifles and three million rounds of ammunition at Larne. In July the King himself made a desperate last attempt to find a solution through an all-party conference at Buckingham Palace. It failed. Two days later the Irish nationalists replied with their own gun-running. This time the army intervened. They were stoned by the crowds and fired in retaliation, killing three and injuring thirty-eight. 'The country is now confronted,' *The Times* pronounced, 'with one of the greatest crises in the history of the British race.'[23] Civil war within the United Kingdom appeared inevitable.

Almost certainly it was. Civil war in Ireland was postponed by the First World War, but it broke out afterwards. It was to cost hundreds of lives, leave thousands homeless, and end with more than ten thousand Irishmen in internment camps. There is little reason for believing that the outcome would have been substantially different but for the World War. The crux of the problem, the refusal of Ulster to join an independent Ireland, and of the Irish nationalists to accept the partition of Ireland, was no more soluble then than later.

There is, however, a second lesson from the post-war sequel. The Irish crisis again coincided with serious industrial unrest. But the Irish rebellion did not ignite a revolution in Britain. Nor would this have been likely earlier. Lloyd George, in warning of this possibility, was confusing two very different movements. Certainly it was a bitter disappointment to the Liberals, after all that they had suffered in their support of Home Rule, to realize that its granting would not end political violence in Ireland. But Ireland had never been peaceful for long. Nor on the other hand had its violence previously been translated into British politics. There were two reasons for this. One was the latent hostility of the British working class to the Irish as Roman Catholics and as cheap immigrant labour. A civil war in Ireland would have alienated, or divided, the British labour movement, rather than uniting it in alliance with nationalism.

Secondly the nationalists, like the Ulstermen, drew on a social support which was essentially conservative rather than radical. This was less true in the mid nineteenth century, but by 1914 the Conservative land purchase acts, even if they had failed to kill Home Rule by kindness, had converted the Irish into a nation of small freeholders. These thrifty Catholic farmers, as independence was to show, provided a barren ground for social revolutionaries.

The labour unrest

The outbreak of war led in Britain itself to the ending of the rebellion of the conservative classes. By 1915 their political leaders were back in office as part of a coalition government, and had no further need to operate outside the law. They were not able to unmake the Irish confrontation, but in Britain conservative violence was relegated to lower levels, such as the breaking up of pacifist meetings and wartime strikes with rowdies organized by the seamen's union leader, Captain Edward Tupper: 'I admit the sailors' fists weren't gentle,' he boasted.[24] But the mention of unions and strikes brings us back to the third, and perhaps the most serious, element in the pre-war crisis: the labour unrest.

We have already seen the transformation of the trade union movement during the Edwardian period. In 1900 the main force for militancy in British trade unions appeared to be the unskilled workers, and their organization was indubitably weak. By 1918 not merely had the unions of the unskilled revived, and the movement as a whole carried forward to unprecedented strength, but the miners, who were moderate Liberals in 1900, and the engineers, formerly cautious craftsmen, were now its militant vanguard. Much of this change had already happened by 1914. Most critical, it seemed, was the increasing violence and scale of industrial action, and the fostering of this by trade unionists influenced by syndicalism, with its doctrine of the revolutionary general strike. It was after a speech to strikers by the syndicalist Tom Mann in Liverpool in August 1911 that a crowd stoned troops and attacked prison vans after arrests had been made. The troops opened fire and killed two people. Tom Mann was himself imprisoned for issuing his 'Don't Shoot' appeal to soldiers. In another incident at Llanelly there were more deaths resulting from an attack on a train. During the railway strike troops were standing by to overawe disorder in more than thirty places. But the unrest seemed unending. At one point there were eighteen separate disputes in Lancashire alone. It also seemed international, not only in its syndicalist and socialist doctrines, but also in the waves of strikes which affected France and other countries at the same time. At the beginning of 1912 *The Times* warned that 'the public must be prepared for a conflict between Labour and Capital, or between employers and employed, upon a scale as has never occurred before'.[25] And indeed 1912 was the year, not only of Lord Devonport's successful counter-attack on the London dockers, but also when a group of South Welsh miners launched their demand for workers' control in *The Miners' Next Step*, and the miners as a national body were able to force the Prime Minister, reduced to tears, to rush minimum wage legislation through Parliament. Well might the exiled Lenin write, in an anonymous article in *Pravda*: 'Since the miners' strike the British proletariat *is no longer the same*. The workers have learned to fight. They have come to see the *path* that will lead them to victory . . . In Britain a change has taken place in the balance of social forces.'[26] And if 1913, with the failure of the great Dublin strike, marked less of an advance for labour, it seemed possible that, but for the outbreak of war, the autumn of 1914 might have brought a decisive battle. There were strikes threatened on the Scottish coalfields and also the railways. The founding of the Triple Alliance, which covered over a million unionized workers, would bind each to the support of the other. A general strike in 1914 might, moreover, have drawn uncomfortable inspiration from the Irish crisis. J. H. Thomas, the railwaymen's leader, threatened the House of Commons in March that if the wage negotiations then in progress failed and a strike seemed likely to break out in November, the lesson he might draw from Ulster was 'to go to the railwaymen, tell them that I believe the railway companies are going to resist their demands, that in order to prepare for the worst they must organize their forces; and that the half million capital in the union should be used to provide arms and ammunition for them'.[27]

In a general struggle – though not in the use of violence – the unions could have counted on the backing of George Lansbury's *Daily Herald*, then an unusually radical daily newspaper, which had itself originated as a printers' strike sheet in 1911. It provided a voice for labour in answer to Northcliffe. It also symbolized the new solidarity of the labour movement. Its impact can be seen, indeed, engraved in a new obscure monument, which witnesses how widespread that solidarity had become: the free school built 'to be a centre of Rural Democracy' by the labourers of a Norfolk village, in protest at the dismissal in March 1914 of their schoolteachers, who had been active trade union supporters. The foundation stone of the Burston Strike School was laid in 1917 by George Lansbury, and its façade is cut with the names of socialist and trade union branches from all over the country who subscribed to it. They range from pacifist groups to workers in torpedo yards. Foremost among them are the railwaymen and the miners.

In some respects the advent of the war further radicalized the trade union movement, as well as strengthening it. The use of leaving certificates as a form of industrial conscription especially fostered hostility to both employers and the state. 'Workmen resented the idea that they were tied and, as they sometimes put it, virtually in a state of slavery.'[28] The accelerated reorganization of engineering factories with division of labour in order to produce munitions greatly increased the fear of skilled engineers for the standing of their craft. The strongest opposition to the Munitions Act came from Clydeside. Here, according to a report of December 1915,

> 'You find resistance to the Act, and a determination to cripple and crab it, exalted into a principle of belief, and tenaciously held and publicly preached by workmen who judged by conventional standards, are honest, industrious operatives, are elders of the Kirk and have their boys fighting at the Front.'[29]

There were moments when industrial unrest became very widespread and even a political strike against the war seemed possible. But as before the war, the revolutionary strike never in fact materialized. The war, while heightening tensions, also made a decisive struggle in certain ways less likely. It interrupted for at least two years the pre-war momentum of general industrial conflict. It removed a high proportion of active younger workers to the armed forces. Above all it meant that any widespread industrial unrest was vulnerable to its own success, for the military danger which it could cause. When faced by angry crowds of wounded soldiers, the engineering rank and file were not prepared to force a decisive strike against the war. Only defeat in the war itself could have produced a really revolutionary situation.

Short of the absolute failure of the government and the collapse of social authority, the labour unrest thus remained during wartime a limited threat. And in peacetime also, to be really threatening the industrial struggle would have had to converge upon a political crisis in which concession was no longer possible. Although the House of Lords veto issue could possibly have created such a confrontation, in fact such a situation was never approached. Before the war the government never indeed faced more than a specifically industrial challenge. Its considerable reserves of strength did not need to be tested. Lloyd George's policy of combining concession with coercion was far from being exhausted. Lenin himself recognized how as a 'master of political cunning, a popular orator, able to make any kind of speech, even r-r-revolutionary speeches before Labour audiences, capable of securing fairly considerable sops for the obedient workers, in the shape of social reforms (insurance, etc.), Lloyd George serves the bourgeoisie splendidly'.[30] In bringing Britain through the period of adjustment which he had himself partly provoked, Lloyd George had not yet lost his touch. And the full coercive power of the troops was not needed.

Lloyd George alone could not, of course, have brought this about. The true explanation lies principally in the nature of the labour unrest: in the character of the changed balance of social forces which brought it about. Recognition of this change brought panic in some quarters. The panic was real enough, but essentially ill-founded. George Askwith, the government's professional conciliator, provides a telling insight into both sides of the labour unrest in his account of the Hull dock strike of 1911. He was called in by the employers, who were helpless at the sudden outburst. 'Fires, looting, riots had started at once. They were thoroughly surprised and could not understand the cause.' After hours of negotiation between the two sides, Askwith thought he had reached a settlement. It was announced to a 15,000-strong meeting of dockers. It was now Askwith's turn to be surprised:

> 'An angry roar of "No!" rang out; and "Let's fire the docks!" from outskirts where men ran off ... I hastily told them to keep quiet, and to their credit they did ... There was dead silence ... As clearly as I could I said the meeting was adjourned; the employers and their representatives were going to continue to negotiate. They must go home. With two constables in front, we walked through that crowd back to the hotel in perfect peace.'

But Askwith entered the hotel to find a scene of turmoil in the hall.

> 'I heard a town councillor remark that he had been in Paris during the Commune and had never seen anything like this: the women were worse than anything he had ever seen, and he had not known there were such people in Hull – women with hair streaming and half nude, reeling through the streets, smashing and destroying. "Then you ought to have known," said an angry employer ...
>
> 'What was the real cause of the refusal to accept an agreed settlement? I told the leaders of the men very plainly they must find out ... [and] speak to them on the value of negotiation in preference to force ... The rest of the day was spent in interviews with merchants anxious to get their goods cleared, and insisting that the military should come

in and that goods ought to be unloaded at any cost. Some Bradford consignees were urging delivery of fresh eggs – Bradford had no eggs. The Hull merchants concerned admitted the eggs came from the Baltic, and had been collected over a period of several weeks or months. I suggested Bradford might wait for its "fresh" eggs a few days longer . . .'[31]

It took Askwith three days to reach an acceptable settlement.

The Hull strike was one of the most serious outbreaks of the labour unrest. Its course was significant: a sudden uprising, met by panic among the well-to-do, but in the mass of the workers by no more than firmness in negotiable demands. It is important, too, to remember that in these years far more disputes were settled without strikes; and also that there have always been periodic skirmishes during industrial conflict. They normally pass unnoticed unless given press publicity. There is a wide gap between such skirmishes and the revolutionary general strike.

The Edwardian labour unrest undoubtedly represented a heightening of working-class consciousness such as had not been seen in Britain since the end of Chartism. Besides the immediate halt in real wages, there were deeper reasons for the growing class solidarity: the increasing residential segregation of the cities, the tendency of work to concentrate in larger units, the division of labour and the competition of clerical occupations which both undermined the former exclusiveness of the craftsmen. The working class was now separately organized in not only the trade unions, but also the Labour party. Its culture also appeared increasingly separate and homogeneous with the waning of religious influence; focused upon the public house, the music hall and the cinema. Working-class literacy was now general and schooling normally on a common local basis. The rising standard of life ensured that the Co-operative societies were now imitated by food and clothing chains which were beginning to standardize consumption patterns. All this was a change. The cloth cap, by 1914 a ubiquitous working (as opposed to leisure) headgear, symbolized this new consolidation.

Here then was a working class which was more united and more formidable. Better education and a rising standard of life made it better organized, more confident. They also brought rising expectations; expectations which were further fostered by the return of migrants from the more democratic colonial societies of Canada and Australia. As Askwith put it in 1913, 'There is a spirit abroad of unrest, of movement, a spirit and desire of improvement, of alteration.'[32]

But improvement itself brought more of a stake in the existing social fabric. For trade unionists, for example, the institutionalization of a social welfare bureaucracy created hundreds of new official job opportunities. Some of them were deliberately given as rewards to labour leaders who continued to support the Liberals. For union members, recognition by employers was frequently accompanied by mutual agreements to institutionalize conciliation and arbitration procedures, and thus for the general acceptance of existing wage structures. The industrial growth which brought rising wages had at the same time reduced the numbers of independent labourers. Increased possessions created their own perspectives; and education now offered better chances to working-class parents for their children. It was in this context that the gains and recognitions which Edwardian governments offered to the working classes as a whole were taken. There was sufficient concession to the new labour strength to contain the expectations of most working-class families within the existing social order.

The new organized strength of labour thus led to negotiation, rather than mounting confrontation. A revolutionary situation was not approached because it required a combination of structural stresses on the working classes – stresses which certainly existed – with an inflexible response, and ultimately collapse, by authority. The historical experience of neither side predisposed it towards such a course. The ideology of the governing class was not exhausted by the hysteria of the upstart Northcliffe or the paranoia of Hull merchants. The Conservative leaders could draw on a long tradition of social paternalism, and the Liberals of democratic radicalism. More recently, younger generations of public schoolboys and university graduates had been impelled towards sympathy with working-class aspirations through residence in the settlements planted in poor districts since the 1880s, with the deliberate purpose of renewing social contact between the classes. The influence of that contact may well have been greater upon the visitors than the visited. For example, it made the future Labour Prime Minister Clement Attlee into a socialist; he was already at Haileybury House in Limehouse, working for the Independent Labour Party. More generally socialist propaganda, especially where supported by Christian Socialist clergy, had left its mark, while the first systematic poverty surveys of Booth and Rowntree again helped the recognition of working-class needs. And the thinking of some of the Liberal middle-class intellectual minority went much further. During the First World War indeed the most sustained ideological radicalism came as much out of the Liberal as the socialist camp, and included that of Bertrand Russell. It is equally significant of the British political situation that J. A. Hobson, whose *Imperialism* was among Lenin's own sources, and who might have been among the intellectual leaders of the socialist movement, could remain a Liberal.

There was a complementary disposition in the labour movement, again founded upon its historical experience, to work for change within rather than against the social system. Had the labour unrest been met by unbending coercion and resistance, it could well have proved a revolutionary movement. No working class was better organized. Nor should the British working class be underestimated by contrast with the often over-romanticized ideological awareness of its European counterparts. It was the most literate in the world. Many of the early socialists were self-taught intellectuals whose enthusiasms ranged from Marx to Shakespeare. British labour leaders had worked with Marx himself when they founded the First International. Marx's portrait hung with Morris's in many socialist meeting rooms and there was no lack of younger potential revolutionary ideological leaders among the syndicalists and Social Democrats. In a true crisis it would have been possible for working-class political consciousness to draw on this strand of its inheritance. But the potential revolutionary leaders remained unheeded, or at least confined to the industrial struggle, because the rank and file were never driven to the point where they might have called on them. The governing classes neither proved intransigent nor collapsed. Nor did the working classes as a whole become socialist. Indeed, they did not fully support even Lloyd George's moderate social reforms. It was only after he had moved to the right, and fought in alliance with the Conservatives, that he was able to win from the electorate an overwhelming parliamentary majority in the 1918 General Election. The industrial militancy was never effectively carried over into political consciousness.

The paradox of this industrially strong, yet politically disunited and inhibited working-class movement, was founded not merely on its successes in action, but upon its very sources of strength. For example, the support found in many of the chapels for the labour cause, while often a foundation for organization, also tended to limit working-class consciousness. This was true even of the socialists. Many of them shared Nonconformist beliefs in the path of self-improvement through thrift and temperance, which did not have to be rejected like the doctrine of acquiescence in poverty typically preached by Anglican and Catholic clergy. English Nonconformity also had a more indirect influence. By the 1900s, it no longer generally provided much mental training in doctrinal logic. It is noticeable that the Social Democrats were strongest in those regions where there was little or no working-class Nonconformity, as in London, Lancashire and Glasgow; and many of their members had learnt Roman Catholic or Jewish theology as children, and while rejecting these faiths, kept some taste for theory in politics. The less sharp message of the Independent Labour Party echoed more closely that of the chapels. It was the dominant strain in the Edwardian socialist movement: an emphasis on understanding and brotherhood, on class solidarity rather than class conflict. It was a tendency again reinforced, through the part they played in the socialist movement and especially through the Fabian Society, as well as in their own new 'white collar' trade unions, by the sympathy of the new clerical classes, including civil servants. They could advocate social welfare with much more confidence than class struggle. And in the Socialist Sunday

Schools too children were instructed in mutual love but not in class war. It was an ideology which consolidated a working class exceptional in its power of self-defence, but unprepared for attack.

Lastly, the more general changes in working-class culture also affected attitudes in both directions. Literacy was no longer a major social division, but the Chartist movement had run its own schools. If there was never during the Edwardian unrest the widespread millenarian hope of some of the Chartist years, one reason may be the impact of universal education in the Board School mould. And another may perhaps be found in the rising common culture of the music halls and cinemas, with its tolerance, its evasion of political and religious disputes, and its fatalism: the culture of Dan Leno and Charlie Chaplin – of little men chased by angry women and giant foremen.

There was a good deal of sense then underlying our London hatter's view of the Edwardian crisis. To the Liberals the militant labour unrest was certainly a cruel political blow. It forced Lloyd George into final recognition that he could not offer sufficient social and political gains to the labour movement without destroying his support in the middle classes. His wartime transition to coalition with the Conservatives was its logical sequel. It may well have been his understanding of the political consequences of the unrest which also caused him, in common with the less perceptive Edwardian well-to-do, to overestimate its social challenge. There was indeed a *Strange Death of Liberal England* in party politics. In the end Lloyd George divided and destroyed rather than saved his own party. From 1918 onwards, the political battle which counted was between Labour and the Conservatives. But the modification which he secured was otherwise enough. The unrest provided the turmoil, and anguish, through which labour had gained – and accepted – recognition of a new standing in society.

17 War

The outbreak of the First World War, cutting across and twisting the Edwardian domestic crisis, brings us to our last instrument of change. Some social changes are clearly responses to the inner contradictions or logic of a society. Others are responses to new influences from outside: to new creeds, new inventions, new lines in trade, changes in climate and so on. Early twentieth-century examples include the European syndicalist doctrine of the general strike among militant workers, American business techniques such as work study, product standardization and assembly line production, and the development of the new motor car and oil trades. But by far the most dramatic of these external influences was the First World War. In the past, wars had often forced social change on the conquered. Now, because fighting was no longer confined to professionals but involved the mobilization of the whole economy, it brought equally drastic transformations to the victors. In 1914 Britain had presented the classic case of an early industrial capitalist economy, based on free enterprise, free competition and free trade, with the minimum possible state interference. It is true that in a few industries formidable corporations had already appeared like the Lever soap empire; and that to the state protection of workers by sanitary and factory inspectors had been added the recent compulsory state insurance schemes. But these were slight developments when compared with the situation at the end of the war, when the state had assumed the direction of major sectors of the economy such as shipping, the railways, the coalmines, chemicals and engineering and substantial tariffs had been introduced on a whole range of goods. Men no longer had a free choice of job, but could be drafted to military service, or, negatively, to industry through certificates of essential work and consent to job change. Rent control had been imposed on the housing market, and certain essential consumer goods, including sugar, potatoes, meat and coal, were distributed according to state rationing schemes. The state indeed had assumed many of the powers to be associated with totalitarianism, including propaganda techniques such as fake photographs, rumours, lies and the suppression of facts. War news was censored and some papers were at times banned. Industrial strikes were forbidden and some of the most militant trade unionists imprisoned. Those who remained were now more likely to see their chief enemy as the state rather than the individual capitalist:

> 'The state has become the almighty power, regulating and controlling the lives of all ... The centralizing process has been wonderfully rapid. From the inception of the Insurance Act the speed has been cumulative ... We are rapidly approaching the heyday of officialdom in every department of life.'[1]

At the same time the war proved a turning point in millions of individual lives. Men who had never left their own communities were forced to travel, mix in new company and meet new ideas, and sometimes learn a new trade which would become their civilian occupation after the war. They would carry with them the haunting memory of desolation and fear in the trenches, with its intrinsic challenge to comfortable belief in the sense of society and the meaning of life. Paul Nash, whose paintings are perhaps the most powerful visual evocation of the squalor of the battlefront, wrote of it in a letter:

> 'We all have a vague notion of the terrors of a battle, and can conjure up with the aid of some of the more inspired war correspondents and the pictures in the *Daily Mirror* some vision of a battlefield; but no pen or drawing can convey this country ... Evil and the incarnate fiend alone can be master of this war ... Sunset and sunrise are blasphemous, they are mockeries to man, only the black rain out of the bruised

and swollen clouds all through the bitter black of night is fit atmosphere in such a land. The rain drives on, the stinking mud becomes more evilly yellow, the shell holes fill up with green-white water, the roads and tracks are covered in inches of slime, the black dying trees ooze and sweat and the shells never cease. They alone plunge overhead, tearing away the rotting tree stumps, striking down horses and mules, annihilating, maiming, maddening, they plunge into the grave which is this land; one huge grave . . .'[2]

More men were killed in these trenches than have been in any other war; many more than in the Second World War. The British dead and wounded were more than two million. Nearly one in every ten Edwardian men under forty-five was killed, and another one in five wounded. For all these lives ended or maimed there were also parents, wives, lovers and friends, shaken or bereaved. In this atmosphere of danger and shock lives were also created which would not have been in peacetime, as if compensating for those lost: the illegitimacy ratio jumped from 4 to 6 per cent of all births, higher than it was to be again until the 1960s. The war also brought other positive experiences to those at home. Upper-class girls who had never been allowed to walk alone in the street suddenly found themselves, as the result of taking a war job, with the freedom and company of factory girls. One quarter of the 1,600,000 domestic servants took their chance to switch to the new openings for women in munitions and other factories, in transport and on the land. There was also an influx of women into civil service and commercial occupations. Altogether the number of women in industrial work rose from 2,100,000 to 2,900,000.

Perhaps the most astonishing change was in the apparently widespread collapse of sexual caution. The illegitimacy rate was but one sign of this. There were also the new fashions for lipstick, skirts showing the legs, and coloured underwear. There were the innumerable rushed and shotgun marriages and the unrecorded infidelities of lonely married women – 'there seemed to be a sort of moral truce in the absence of the husbands'.

The emotional atmosphere generated by recruiting and by entertaining soldiers on leave made for a new ease in transient relationships.

> ' "Getting-off" was the simplest matter in the world. "Soul-mates" met and linked up with a truly astonishing facility. Love affairs were started anywhere and everywhere, on the underground, in trams, buses, at shops, cafés or in the street. A look was sufficient to break the ice and make two perfect strangers into lovers . . . Practically all sexually mature young women were in a state of perpetual intoxication. They forgot to be indignant when a man in uniform asked to sleep with them. They wanted to have a soldier lover, or a soldier husband, and in their secret minds the thought of widowhood was inevitably present . . .'[3]

There is exaggeration – indeed fantasy – here of course, but the impression itself was a sign of the change in social expectations. In some circles the alarm was such that Patrol Committees were formed to spy on courting soldiers and evict kissing couples from deep doorways and shop entrances, 'a job the police constable did not care to do'. The Women's Police Service, which was set up in 1915, did however specialize in moral patrolling. Local organizers' reports of the activities of the Patrol Committees indicate the manner of their interventions:

> 'A military policeman came up, evidently very perturbed, and said he had been watching a couple (man a civilian) for some time, and would the lady patrols try and get the girl away? They found the couple indicated partly screened by bushes, but with other couples all around and in a disgraceful position . . . [In another case] we came across a young girl one night struggling with a Canadian soldier among some bushes, and were able to save her. With the consent of the Chief Constable I am now ordering such couples to come out into the open, and have met with no refusals or resistance of any kind from the men, who always look extremely ashamed and sheepish. The girls try to brazen it out, but always do as they are told in the end.'[4]

There were many more bushes, however, than lady patrols, and behind some of them their fears were certainly realized. Nor can there be any doubt that the shift of many women from unskilled to skilled work, and the return to work of many others who had been serving their husbands as full-time housekeepers, gave a real boost to the position of women in many a household. Robert Roberts, son of a skilled Lancashire craftsman, remembers one such shock to male assumptions of superiority:

> 'My father was typical. In his cups he was wont to boast that, at the lathe, he had to manipulate a micrometer and work to limits of one thousandth of an inch. We were much impressed, until one evening in 1917 a teenage sister running a capstan in the ironworks remarked indifferently that she, too, used a "mike" to even finer limits. There was, she said, "nothing to it". The old man fell silent. Thus did status crumble!'[5]

In its impact upon attitudes and in the incidents and accidents which it brought there can be no question that the First World War changed millions of individual lives. It is also clear that some of the general changes of the war years anticipated future developments. But does it follow that the First World War therefore hastened these social changes? Historians such as Arthur Marwick have argued that the long-term effect of the war on social attitudes and social structure was profound. Yet it is perhaps more remarkable how slight its permanent impact was upon British society as a whole.

Consider, for example, sexual behaviour and the position of women. When the four years of wartime emancipation and their aftermath had passed, what traces had they left? The one clear gain was the vote. But the case for extending the vote to women had become by 1914 politically almost unanswerable, and the war had simply provided politicians with a face-saving opportunity to grant it. Conversely, it may have ensured that women went to their first parliamentary poll in a less militant spirit than if the activities of the suffragette movement had not been generally suspended for the previous four years. Certainly women had not used the vote to keep their war gains. They were back in their pre-war work situation. As the men had been demobilized, they had quickly ousted the women who had replaced them in industrial work. In 1921 women constituted exactly the 29 per cent of the workforce that they had in 1911. Nor was their participation to increase significantly during the next thirty years. It was perhaps only to the small group of upper-class women that the war brought a new right to work which lasted. It is true that the decline of domestic service was to continue, and especially of living in, but this went back to the 1870s, and the exodus of the war years was in fact compensated by a revival of numbers in the 1920s.

A similar return to pre-war standards and trends can be seen in sexual behaviour. The illegitimacy rate fell to lower levels in the 1920s than those of before 1914, although a part of this reduction may have been due to the beginning of a wider acceptance of contraception. The long-term rise in divorce rates continued, held back by the war itself, shooting up in its aftermath, and then falling again in the late 1920s to the level which might have been predicted without the war's intervention. The new fashions for short skirts and face make-up, like the close-hold ragtime dance style, were innovations of the years immediately before the war and would have spread down the social scale in any case. It is less obvious now than it once seemed that the boyish leggy style of the 1920s was more overtly sexual than the thrusting Edwardian bosom. The war years, anyway, did not see a further shortening of fashionable skirt lengths, but rather a transient phase of military tastes in dress. Similar observations apply to birth control. The war may have spread knowledge of contraception, but the small families of the 1920s could have been expected from the trends of the previous sixty years whether or not there had been a war. The legal reforms of the 1920s which abolished the inequality of standards between husbands and wives in obtaining divorce had been recommended by the Royal Commission which reported in 1911, and again continued a long established current of legal change towards equality between the sexes. Similarly, the Sex Disqualification Act of 1919 which opened all public offices to women was a fruit won by the campaigning of the feminist movement before, rather than during the war. However much the war affected the lives of many individuals, it certainly cannot be said to have brought the social emancipation of women.

It is revealing that nobody has recently argued that the war brought about the emancipation of children, another sphere of change also linked both to the shrinking size of the family and to changes in educated opinion. There can be no doubt that the absence of fathers in the army gave them, as well as their mothers, unexpected liberty. It also gave them new work opportunities. The restrictions on hours were widely overlooked and in many counties the official school leaving age was lowered from fourteen to eleven. The number of children of fourteen or under at work quadrupled, a much more spectacular increase than among women, and girls' and boys' wages also rose faster than those of any other group. Wartime trends here have been ignored by historians because they happen to have been the direct reverse of long-term educational developments, which were immediately resumed in 1918 with the Fisher Education Act enforcing full-time school attendance on all children to the age of fourteen. This Act was not a turning point, but rather a consolidation of Edwardian achievements which had been interrupted by the war. Nor, surprisingly enough, were crime statistics ever concocted to fulfil the gloomy wartime predictions of the criminologist who asked: 'Had we set out with the deliberate intention of manufacturing juvenile delinquents, could we have done so in a more certain way?'[6]

Similar contradictions appear if we consider the assertion that the First World War was the critical factor in bringing participation in power to the working classes. Certainly it presented a traumatic challenge to orthodoxies; but there was no less challenge presented to socialism and to trade unionism than to the doctrines of economic Liberalism such as free trade, or indeed to faith in Christianity. Disasters have more often turned people towards than away from religion, and if the First World War did spread agnosticism (which is difficult to prove), this only indicates the extent to which religious faith had withered. The same can be said for the disintegration of political Liberalism.

The Liberal government faced peculiar difficulties in conducting a war, but failures of one kind and another and splits in the face of them had been the recurrent experiences of both political parties for decades. What is significant is the failure of the Liberals to recover at any level from their wartime experience. They had been a grand coalition of interests who, unlike the new Labour party, could neither rely on the instinctive class allegiance of most working-class voters, nor rally to a coherent political faith for the future.

The labour movement also faced enormous problems in 1918. The socialists were divided between war supporters and pacifists. The Russian revolution introduced another split in opinion. The trade unions had benefited dramatically from full employment, doubling their membership, but at the price of suspending their traditional workshop practices of protective restriction, which had to be reimposed in the much less favourable post-war situation. They had failed to win wage rises as fast as those in prices, so that working-class real wages declined during the war. Like the socialists, they were divided in their attitude to the war, and the participation of Arthur Henderson as the voice of the labour movement in the war cabinet angered many of the militants among them. After the war, moreover, the series of great disputes which culminated in defeat in the General Strike were in a pattern set by pre-1914 national strikes and inter-union alliances. Enthusiasm for workers' control, on the other hand, which had been boosted by the wartime loss of traditional protections, proved much less generally sustained. Both the trade unions and the Labour party undoubtedly emerged in 1920 stronger than they had been in 1910, but their growth was more an indication of their social resilience than of the impact of the war. In 1918 the franchise was extended not only to (some) women, but to all adult men, a change which also helped the Labour party. Had the war not intervened, different elections would have been fought under different franchises in different years, but it is a long step from this to arguing that the old franchise would not have been changed, or that Labour would not have succeeded the Liberals.

The true effects of the war were more particular. Two examples of changing social habits may be given. Firstly, the drastic restriction of public house drinking hours, which the waning temperance movement was hardly likely to have won in peacetime, undoubtedly accelerated the decline in drinking. Convictions for drunkenness fell during the wartime years to a mere fifth of their pre-war level. While deeper social changes undoubtedly account for the long-term decline in drinking habits which had already set in before the war, there can be no doubt that restricted opportunities for drinkers made the inter-war years decidedly more sober than they would otherwise have been.

Secondly, the war brought adjustments to upper-class society, partly through the direct impact of the especially high rates of death and wounding among officers. The old territorial society was already threatened by the gradual rise in taxation and death duties (not yet mitigated by extensive evasion), the very low economic returns to be made by land since the onset of the agricultural depression, and also the effect of the motor car in breaking the localism of social life in the country. It had, however, held together until 1914. During the war many country houses became hospitals and other institutions, and afterwards families had to make a positive decision to re-open them. There was not always either the finance, or the wish, or even a family heir to do this. In other cases death duties were met by selling off land. Large numbers of farmers, who had profited from the temporary subsidizing of agricultural production by the wartime government, were able to buy the land they occupied. As a result there was a critical reduction in the density of country houses and in their hold on rural society both as farm landlords and as employers of servants. There had been several signs before the war of a coming transfer of rural leadership to the farmers. More secure now through statutory protection of their tenancies, farmers rather than landlords had introduced the few agricultural innovations of the depression years. They were being elected councillors, they had secured some curbing of landlords' game rights; they answered the revived farm labourers' trade unionism with the founding of the National Farmers' Union. The disruption of the war hastened their succession.

We can also be specific about the effect of the war upon some aspects of social welfare. By holding up house building for four years it created a housing shortage. One by-product of this was that it became much less easy for working-class families to move than when houses to let were plentiful, and so made for stabler, more consolidated working-class communities, especially in the large cities. At the same time it changed the emphasis of public housing activity, which was already quickening after the 1909 Housing Act, from slum clearance and sanitary improvement to new house building. As a wartime emergency the government had introduced rent control, but now feared the consequences of lifting the control in a situation of housing shortage. The need to provide homes for returning soldiers paved the way for the acceptance of state subsidies for house building. Although the post-war housing campaign proved a failure because more active government intervention – in securing supplies, building labour, sites and so on – would have been essential for success in the confused situation at that time, the provision of state subsidies in the 1919 Housing Act was a critical advance. Some degree of rent control for existing tenants in cheap housing was also kept after the war. The two changes significantly reduced the proportion of working-class income spent on rent in the following decades.

Like other former responsibilities of the Local Government Board, housing was brought together with health insurance under the control of the new Ministry of Health set up in 1919. This Ministry was a response to the demands of Sir George Newman and other Edwardian reformers for a co-ordinated health service, but it did not in fact bring one. The preventive health services of the local authorities were not co-ordinated with the curative services provided under the health insurance system; the insurance system was not extended to cover children, old people or unoccupied women; and no co-ordinated hospital service emerged. Meanwhile, although supervised by the new Ministry, the Poor Law Guardians continued to perform their traditional functions.

For the unemployed too the Guardians remained the last resort, but a more critical change had taken place here. Unemployment itself had been temporarily cured by the feverish industrial activity of the war. The emptying of workhouses and closing of casual wards brought the confidence in which unemployment insurance was extended to a further million workers in 1916, so that it now covered a third of the workforce. This cover was made universal by the decision of the government in October 1918, faced by the inevitable dislocation as the war ended and troops were demobilized, to give both displaced civilians and soldiers an 'out of work donation' equivalent to a paid-up insurance benefit. This 'dole' lasted for between six months and a year, after which application had to be made to the Guardians in the old way. The granting of this less humiliating aid to the able-bodied unemployed, replacing incarceration and 'test' labour in the workhouse, was a major concession to the demands of the labour movement. It assumed that they had a right to help, rather than that they were out of work through their own fault. Before 1914 the provision of relief works for the unemployed under the 1905 Act and the first insurance schemes had marked a partial acceptance of this new view, but only the peculiar economic circumstances of the war made it general. The dole was intended as a temporary expedient, but the political costs of rescinding it were to make the new form of relief permanent. It was, moreover, to prove a critical legacy in shaping the social history of the inter-war years. The pre-war unemployment figures are only partial, based on trade union returns and thus weighted in favour of those in regular work. If they are doubled, they range from 6 to 16 per cent, with over 10 per cent in most years; and even if a smaller multiplier is preferred, it is clear enough that unemployment was no new social problem of the inter-war years. But from 1921 until 1939 it not only ran at a continuously higher level, at best 10 and at worst over 20 per cent, but affected for the first time whole communities of the best-paid industrial working class, the vanguard of the labour movement. Their protest was much more formidable than that of the pre-war unemployed. By softening their experience of hardship, the dole significantly lessened the sharpness of post-war political and social confrontation.

The new patterns of inter-war unemployment lead us to perhaps the most important direct consequences of the war, its impact upon the economy. Some of this impact was positive.

Before the war scientific research had been neglected both because of the dominance of gentlemanly humanities in the universities and through the lethargy of industrialists, and the science-based chemical and electrical industries had been lagging in their development. The war proved a major stimulus to research as a result of the new government support provided through the Department of Scientific and Industrial Research started in 1915. The war also brought direct government aid in the expansion of the chemical and electrical industries, not only for munitions work but also to fill the gaps previously filled by imports from Germany. Wireless manufacture and the aircraft industry were similarly stimulated. The need to raise home food production led to the first considerable use of tractors and also a widespread application of nitrogen fertilizers, although these changes were not maintained when the agricultural depression returned at the end of the war. To meet the needs for armaments and ships, steel production capacity was expanded by 50 per cent. The neglected home ores in the East Midlands were brought into use and new alloys were developed. Shipyards were extended and labour-saving automatic welding became widespread. In engineering, the machine tool industry was expanded and its products standardized, and production by semi-skilled assembly line methods begun in the motor industry. At the same time there were important changes in industrial organization: not only a push towards amalgamation at the top, but also an increased concern with factory welfare and amenities such as canteens, partly because of a paternalistic desire to protect the new women workers in industry. The government urged on these welfare improvements. It also imposed replanned layouts and up-to-date accounting on many firms. By no means all these developments would have come, even in time, without the war.

Some of this stimulus, however, proved of transient benefit. In particular, the war had so widely built up international steel-making and shipbuilding capacity that there was a disastrous post-war overcapacity in both industries. As a result two of the most prosperous groups of Edwardian workers now found themselves among the worst victims of unemployment. The war also created a diversion, which held up some important new economic developments, such as the start of the mass production of private cars. Equally serious was the directly negative effect of its disruption. Before 1914 one of the bastions of British prosperity had been in shipping: as many as 90 per cent of the world's tramp steamers were British. Pre-eminence in shipping brought 'invisible' support to the balance of trade, and a market for British shipbuilders. During the war years nearly a third of British shipping was diverted to military purposes, and more than a third of its total tonnage was sunk. The shipping lost to trade was replaced by that of other countries, and Britain never recovered her former position. Similarly, the disruption of trading patterns proved in some respects permanent. Neutral countries had been able to establish new networks which now had to be competed with. And just as the war had given vital encouragement to some of Britain's own more backward industries, so in other countries home industries had sprung up to fill the place of British manufactures.

Worse still, the post-war British economy had to adapt to this much less favourable international trading situation stripped of the advantages which had ensured a favourable balance of trade in the previous decades. Imports had long exceeded exports, but the returns from shipping, finance and foreign investments easily bridged the gap. Now, besides the shipping losses, Britain had spent her foreign assets in paying for the war. The world's great creditor nation of 1914 had been forced into heavy borrowing. Undoubtedly long-term weaknesses were evident in the British economy well before 1914. The war, however, forced sudden and direct economic changes which not only altered individual lives, through providing different work or no work, but also determined the whole post-war standard of living. The First World War, in short, left the average Edwardian with a little more welfare in a rather less rich country; less likely to become really prosperous, but better protected against penury.

Part IV
The Outcome

18 The Standard of Life

We have already discovered, through assessing the instruments of change in Edwardian society, many of the features of that change itself. But to give a proper measure of the outcome, the fruits of both conscious and unconscious pressures for change, we need to look at the patterns as a whole. We shall examine then, three spheres of general social change, returning through them to the themes of the dimensions of inequality with which we started – in sustenance, in the family, in social class. We begin with sustenance: with the ordinary standard of life.

Before 1900 a critical transition in the standard of living had already been accomplished in Britain. The majority of the population were no longer struggling, as they still were in most of the world, to provide themselves with a minimal subsistence. There was, after the needs for clothing, food and shelter had been met, a small margin for comfort. How small the margin was needs to be emphasized: small enough, for example, for land seizures and the breaking of Scottish farms into subsistence crofts to continue even in the 1920s. Nevertheless, during the twentieth century this margin was to increase, and the numbers without it were to fall steadily. Eventually the whole concept of poverty itself was to be transformed from absolute want to relative deprivation. While relative deprivation has probably diminished little, absolute want has certainly declined. The *New Survey of London Life and Labour*, which reassessed London poverty at the end of the 1920s with the same yardstick that Charles Booth had used forty years earlier, found only 8·7 per cent of the entire population living in poverty, in contrast to Booth's 30·7 per cent. Similarly Rowntree, who had estimated 28 per cent of the York population in poverty in 1901, reported in re-survey figures of 18 per cent in 1936 and 2 per cent in 1950.

In the long run the most important single reason for this reduction of absolute poverty was the rise in real wages. There were, however, other important factors, including the reduction of family size, the extension of social welfare and the decline of drunkenness. Real wages, as we have seen, were stagnant during the Edwardian period, but the operation of the other factors ensured that the improvement of working-class living standards did continue. From 1908 the introduction of state old age pensions for those aged seventy, although minimal and means-tested, helped one small group of the poor. The new unemployment insurance started in 1913 only protected a small sector of the workforce, but it was to lead on to the provision of the general out-of-work dole, and meanwhile the full employment of the war itself helped to reduce the numbers in want.

Health insurance, which through clubs and other schemes had probably covered half the adult male population in 1900, was extended by the national health insurance scheme, also started in 1913, to all workers below the tax limit. As a result, in addition to now covering three-quarters of all adult males, it was now extended to a quarter of the adult female population. Wartime full employment extended its coverage still further, to reach 60 per cent of all adults. The sick benefit took care of the doctor's bills and also provided support for the family during the illness of the chief wage-earner. Insurance did not bring a co-ordination of health activities into a single service, but it was paralleled by other extensions. The total number of hospital beds, for example, increased in the twenty years before 1911 from 113,000 to 197,000. Since middle-class patients still preferred to be nursed and even operated on at home, this expansion principally benefited the working classes. The most rapid growth was in fact of public infirmaries now separated from the workhouses, providing a free treatment which no longer implied the stigma of pauperization. There was also a marked increase in health work by local authorities. School medical inspection and the feeding of undernourished school children was begun by the most progressive authorities under socialist influence in the

1890s, and the Liberal government, with some reluctance, made these national policies. Clinics and milk schemes for infants were also started by some cities. Meanwhile, especially after 1909, when the Local Government Board became much more vigorous in its pressure on neglectful authorities, the general conversion from privies to water closets proceeded with the extension of water and sewage schemes. As a result, not only did the long-term decline in the general death rate which went back to the mid nineteenth century continue, but for the first time infant mortality started to fall. During these two first decades of the twentieth century expectation of life at birth climbed from fifty to nearly sixty. In terms of health, the Edwardian population thus stood halfway between the mid nineteenth century, when life expectancy at birth had been barely forty years, and the present, when it exceeds seventy.

Better health reduced the number of families in poverty in middle life, and conversely the increase in real wages, and so in standards of nutrition, had undoubtedly hastened the fall in death rates. Equally critical had been the improvement of the urban environment. Although towns in the 1900s remained less healthy than the countryside, they were no longer net devourers of population as they had been in the early nineteenth century. Migration from rural into urban districts was in fact effectively complete by 1911, and urban population growth for the future was already self-sustained. In these more settled towns steady improvements were being carried out by local authorities (or by companies with their support), extending beyond water, drainage and slum clearance schemes to tramways, parks, gas and electricity. Electricity was not as yet used in private houses except by the well-to-do, but it became normal in public places such as theatres and cinemas. The spread of gas for cooking and lighting working-class homes was by contrast very rapid at this time. In 1885 there had been two million gas consumers, but none of electricity; by 1920 there were one million of electricity and seven and a half million of gas.

The tramways, and the motor bus services which followed them from around 1910, not only made travel easier for those who had to undertake it, but encouraged working-class travel.

In 1900 transport had been largely a privilege of the middle and upper classes, by private horse or the expensive railway service, although some commuting by workmen's trains into the big cities had begun. By 1920 travel by public transport to work was common in all towns. At the same time the rapid spread of the bicycle both helped the working classes to get to work, and made the countryside more accessible to them for leisure – or the town for country people. Similarly, by making town work accessible to villages, the new transport partly explains the end of migration into the towns. In 1890 the working classes had largely travelled on foot. They had walked to work and walked for leisure. By 1920 not only were they widely using public transport, but the first cheap motor car, which was eventually to squeeze trams, cycles and buses off the roads, had also appeared. The Channel, first crossed by a pioneer flight in 1909, was now bridged by a daily London–Paris air service started in 1919. A new age of mass travelling, faster and further afield, was ahead.

The working classes were travelling more because they now had the slight margin of resources needed to do so; to pay a tram fare rather than move house when they changed work places. This fact was also to help the easing of housing difficulties, by allowing the replacement of overcrowded city-centre housing with subsidized council-built housing on the outskirts. The dense, compact Victorian city could now give way to the sprawling conurbation of the late twentieth century. But in fact the Edwardians were to hand on a physical urban structure which was remarkably little changed. The first Town Planning Act of 1909, purely permissive and affecting new development only, was at first little used. There was no general improvement in housing between 1900 and 1918, because the late Victorian housing boom petered out and then house-building was almost halted by the First World War. The gradual reduction of family size, which helped to cut overcrowding, was therefore countered by a failure to provide even the minimum of new housing to meet population growth. The main advances were thus made through the improvement of insanitary old houses, rather than the provision of new stock with more and larger rooms and amenities such as gas supply and bathrooms. In the long run the raising of standards to an acceptable level could only come through a plentiful supply of new housing. The Edwardian period is consequently chiefly notable more for the pioneering examples of the private garden cities and of council estates such as the London County Council's Millbank flats and cottages at Old Oak Common, and for the slow steps towards the national political acceptance of subsidized housing, than for actual achievement. In 1911 9 per cent of the population were still living more than two to a room, while council housing made up less than 1 per cent of the national housing stock. Today council housing constitutes 30 per cent of the stock and overcrowding has fallen to less than 2 per cent.

The late-nineteenth-century improvement in standards in two other essentials, food and clothing, did however continue up to 1914, although both were temporarily set back by wartime shortages. The practice of buying new ready-made clothing, and its mechanized production in factories, began with boots and best suits for men, and was spreading slowly to women and children, and to everyday wear. In food new consumption patterns were also spreading. The development of cheap imports by refrigerated transport had already brought meat within the means of nearly all families before 1900, although only the artisan could still afford home-reared beef, while the poor would be obliged to rely on cheap 'pieces', bags of bones, old meat and so on. There was some increase in fish consumption, encouraged by the popularity of fish and chip shops. More milk and butter and more vegetables and fruit were bought. Apple orchards were expanding at home, while the importing of bananas developed rapidly. There was also a sharp rise in the buying of confectionery and sweets, much of it very likely by those working-class children who now had pocket money. Adult indulgences were at the same time changing. Beer was being exchanged for the cigarette; and alcoholism and cirrhosis of the liver for lung cancer.

Perhaps the most fundamental change in the standard of life was that affecting leisure. Standard weekly working hours had fallen from sixty or seventy in the nineteenth century to fifty-three in 1910, not much more than the average of forty-eight hours still worked, due to increasing overtime, in the 1950s. Saturday was already a half, if not a whole holiday. There was thus more opportunity as well as more money for entertainment. For the moment the favourite choices for leisure-time activity remained either drinking or religion, but their successors were already on the scene. Holiday traffic and the sale of bicycles were booming; organized sport and its associated betting were also spreading. Newspaper sales and library issues were rising, borne forward by the new general literacy. More music halls were still opening, while cinemas, a novelty in 1900, had become normal in any town by 1920. With entertainment as with travel, and indeed combining in the holiday trade, a new age of mass consumption was opening. The cinema was to reach its peak as soon as the 1930s when twenty million tickets were being sold every week. By the same time six million were betting on football results, and three million subscribed to the *Radio Times*. Public broadcasting did not begin until after the First World War, but the development of radio was essentially an Edwardian achievement. There was already one form, however, in which the new media had already penetrated the privacy of the ordinary home. It was the least insistent, although no less devastating in its impact upon a world which had hitherto made its own amusements. This was the gramophone.

19 Family

The gradual improvement of real earnings and the changes in the standard of life associated with this have made their mark on family life in the twentieth century, if only because the home itself has become more comfortable. A home-centred, more privatized life, perhaps partly moulded by notions of 'respectability' and imitation of middle-class behaviour, has through economic improvement become more generally available. Equally important, however, has been the conscious and unconscious influence of social attitudes and theories.

An example might be the spread of personal cleanliness. This dates back to the mid nineteenth century and can be clearly traced in the decline of typhus, a disease chiefly spread by body lice. The campaign for cleanliness was launched by the professional classes as a response to the worsening health of large towns in the early nineteenth century, and it was carried forward not only through the professional influence of doctors and the public sanitary works which they were able to procure, but also through the social influence of changes in upper-class personal habits. The upper classes first wore underwear and bathed regularly, partly because they had the resources (including water) to do so. By the early twentieth century these habits had so spread that they were now also typical of working-class standards. A Bolton casual labourer's daughter, whose mother took in washing to earn sufficient to keep the family, remembers how 'Mother used to keep us clean. She used to wash practically every day. She were very particular over clothes, very. Like she said, we weren't well off but we had clean clothes.'[1]

There still remained a substantial section among the big-city poor who had not yet adopted such strict standards, but a final push was given by the introduction of school medical inspection. The number of London children found flea-bitten dropped steadily from 30 per cent in 1908 to under 4 per cent in the mid 1920s, and other cities reported similar improvements. Glasgow reported a doubling of attendances at public baths between 1900 and 1920 (although this was a sign of the times rather than an important aid to cleanliness, since even so attendances amounted to less than two a year per citizen). The spread of indoor water taps was much more helpful. But the combination of better facilities and social influence had by 1920 ensured that most British families took care to keep themselves clean. And this in turn offered a basis for other changes in attitude or habit, such as whether the family thought of itself as 'rough' or 'respectable', and what were its standards of parental care.

Some of these changing attitudes were helped forward by conscious campaigns, of which the suffragette movement for the civil equality of women is the best-known. Children too, on at least one occasion, joined to agitate against their public rather than private oppression. During the national industrial unrest of 1911 school children briefly united in a wave of school strikes across the country demanding the abolition of caning. Some also asked for weekly pocket money in return for school attendance. If their protests bore little immediate fruit, they were in line with the trends of informed educational opinion, for the Edwardian period saw not only the founding of private 'progressive' schools, but also a new emphasis in government departmental policy, a turn away from the drilling in the three Rs backed by the stick towards a wider, more flexible curriculum and the development of individual creativity. With education, as with the civil subjection of women, new official policies were only very slowly adopted in practice. It was important, however, that opinion was asserting its imperceptible pressure in a new direction. The same tendencies can be seen in the official treatment of children who were recognized social casualties: the spread of boarding out for pauper children, the progress of the doctrine of the priority of the child's interest in legal disputes between parents, and the setting up in 1907–8 of separate courts and a probation service in the hope of bringing a more individual judicial treatment to delinquent children. All the changes in the twentieth-century family thus took place in the context of a weakening of the formal authority of moral and social hierarchy, and a pervasive official lip-service to the concepts of democracy and individualism.

Equally persistent in its effect during this period was the long-term change in demographic structure. The most important of these has been the reduction in the number of children born to each family. Couples married in the 1860s (the parents of many Edwardians) had on average six children. Those married in the 1900s had three, in the 1920s two. The restriction in child-bearing began among the well-to-do, and spread down the social scale, affecting especially rapidly industrial groups such as the cotton workers with good work opportunities for women. By the 1900s fertility remained high only among the unskilled and also among miners, whose communities provided especially few jobs for women; and even here family size was falling. The reason for this change, as we have seen earlier, was not the spread of contraceptives, for family restriction was largely achieved without their use. It may not be wholly coincidental that the decline in the death rates of older children and adults was simultaneous, so that the survival of children was less of a lottery. By the 1900s, too, there was certainly an awareness in the working class of the connection between too many children and poverty, and also some signs of concern at the dangers to a mother's health. It is a social change of major importance – condemned, however, to remain mysterious, for we can never know the mixture of instinct, reason and circumstance which determined the behaviour of those late-nineteenth-century parents. We can only speak of the consequences of family limitation.

Firstly, it helped on the rising standard of living in all classes. In his classic discussion of *Prosperity and Parenthood*, J. A. Banks argued that the cost of maintaining servants was one major reason for the progress of family restriction among the professional classes. But since the fall in the proportion of female domestic servants only set in after professional families began to have fewer children, and it was the custom to take on more servants as the number of children grew, it seems more likely that the limitation of children caused the reduction in domestic service than vice versa. Family restriction accelerated the rise in middle-class living standards by reducing household labour costs. Consequently more resources and care could be given to each child. By the 1900s the young middle-class mother, with only two children, could give each substantial individual attention. This was the demographic background to the 'progressive' theory of child-rearing which was becoming increasingly fashionable. A parallel change, less directly encouraged by professional manuals, was taking place in ordinary working-class families. With fewer children the home was less likely to be overcrowded, cleanliness was easier, there was more time for individual affection and less need for regimental discipline, and as spare resources increased it became possible for working-class parents to convey affection through material generosity, as through giving birthday presents. The gentle, home-centred working-class family of two or three children already existed in the early twentieth century, and was to become increasingly common. At the same time some of the customary resorts of children outside the home were to become less congenial. Edwardian legislation restricted street trading by children and inhibited them from entering public houses. From 1918 they were no longer able to leave school before the age of fourteen. The advent of the motor car had made many streets in small towns and villages for the first time dangerous for play; while for those who remained on the streets the more careful attentions of juvenile court magistrates and probation officers, which were replacing the Edwardian policeman's informal flick across the ear, were paradoxically a much more serious social danger just because they marked a child more effectively. Lastly, less drunkenness, and thus less parental violence, further reduced the minority of children who kept out of home for their own safety. Whether corporal punishment is less generally used is a more difficult question. It is possible, for example, that individualism and flexibility have brought more punishment for children, and that Edwardians could more often claim that they were 'never hit' by their parents because they received fewer encouragements to question parental rulings. Nottingham, the city of the Newsons' invaluable studies of contemporary child-rearing, represented only a part of the Edwardian scene, and may be equally unrepresentative today. We need more information before a history of twentieth-century childhood becomes a possibility.

This is equally true of the social history of youth. Once again, some of the most interesting questions remain speculative. What was the impact, for example, of the freer attitude to sexual experience in literature which goes back to the 1890s, of Ibsen's plays, of Edward Carpenter's philosophy, of a novel like Grant Allen's *The Woman who Did*? Is there any general significance in the fact that the first English translations of Freud were published in our period? Or of the manuals which appeared arguing in favour of 'wild oats' for women and trial marriage? We can be certain at least that their influence never reached the daughter of a Midland market stallholder, an uninhibited man himself who had nine children and betted, drank and fought with spirit. She never married, like many of the women born in the 1890s, and one reason was a fear of sexual expression based upon pure ignorance:

> 'The first boy I went with he said, "May I kiss you?" So I said, "Yes, just here." And he kissed me on my cheek and I thought if he kissed me on the lips I'd have a baby. You see, none of us knew. I used to say to myself, "I won't let any man touch me." He had to keep away from me. I was frightened to death.'[2]

We can only guess that such a handicap may have been less common among girls born after 1910, and that if change was taking place the cinema and perhaps women's magazines were a more potent influence than fashionable literature. Yet one sensitive index, the illegitimacy ratio, suggests that astonishingly little change was to occur in sexual mores for another two generations, despite the decline in religious practice, the spread of belief in sexual expressiveness and fulfilment, and the increasing availability of contraceptives. Apart from wartime fluctuations, it was only in the 1950s, beginning in London and especially among middle- and upper-class girls, that illegitimacy ratios were to show a significant rise. In Scotland indeed the ratio had continued to fall until that date, so that there was much *less* illegitimacy in the 1950s than in the 1900s.

For the moment the only sure sign of general change was demographic: the average age of marriage had begun its gradual decline from the Edwardian all-time peak, of twenty-six years for women, to the twenty-three years of today. At the same time, the proportion of women who remained permanently single began to shrink, from as many as 20 per cent among Edwardians to a mere 5 per cent now. In one sense this represents a definite gain for youth, but at the same time it has probably intensified the difficulties of this transitional phase in the life cycle by shortening it. Not only has the marriage age fallen, but the school leaving age has risen. The average Edwardian adjusted, over a period of more than twelve years, first to work, then to courting and finally to setting up an independent household. Today there are only six years between starting work and marriage. Moreover, since the age of puberty has also fallen, courting is more likely to start in the incongruous context of school restrictions. For Edwardian women the average age at menarche was fifteen, while in the 1960s it was thirteen. The ordinary Edwardian schoolgirl, unlike her successors today, was never physically capable of conceiving an illegitimate child. Some aspects of contemporary tension between adults and youth are related to this fact alone. But when these various changes of phasing in the life cycle are remembered, perhaps the continuity of twentieth-century youth culture is more striking than new developments. Those at work have more resources than their Edwardian predecessors, but then fewer teenagers are allowed to work. They now more often meet at dances than in the street, while church and chapel activities have become of little importance to them, but they are the only age group which has not become predominantly home-centred in their leisure activities since 1914. So far from being a modern phenomenon, youth culture remains obstinately Edwardian.

Marriage too has probably changed much less than is often suggested. Take, for example, the widely read primer of the sociologist Ronald Fletcher on *The Family*. He writes:

> 'In the modern marriage, both partners choose each other freely as persons. Both are of equal status and expect to have an equal share in taking decisions . . . They live together permanently and intimately in their own home and in relative independence of wider groups of kindred . . . The modern marital relationship, to a far lesser degree than the Victorian, has no authoritative "blue-print" in custom, morality, and law of expected family relationships . . . It is therefore a matter of personal initiative, exploration and . . . personal love.'[3]

The assumption underlying this description of modern marriage, which is itself largely a speculation based upon an absence of evidence, is an equally imaginary past in which marriage was formal and authoritarian, spouses were chosen by parents, and an unloving couple resided with their extended family. In Britain, at any rate, we can assert with confidence that for at least three hundred years most couples have chosen each other 'as persons' and set up independent nuclear rather than extended households. There has always been variety in the balance of authority within households, which is certainly not equal today, and is in critical respects *more* divided than it was when the family was an economic as well as a domestic unit. We are still a long way – to cite another recent sociological title – from *The Symmetrical Family*.[4] Nor is there any reason for believing that formal rules rather than personal qualities were the essence of past marriage. Certainly the Victorian marriage as conceived by these authors bears little resemblance to the experience of the typical Edwardian, and is a very unsound basis for any assessment of the direction of change during the twentieth century.

What can be said with any confidence is much more limited. Because men and women now live longer, marry earlier and have fewer children than their Edwardian predecessors, far more married women are in a position to work after a brief early phase of child-rearing. They are, moreover, now essential to the labour market because earlier marriage and later school leaving have drastically reduced the numbers of single working women. At the same time the male working-class occupational distribution has also changed, with a decline in the proportions working in both heavy industrial labour and service jobs, neither of which were conducive to home-centred attitudes. Combined with increasing home comfort, the attractions of the new media and the distractions of fewer children, there has consequently almost certainly been a further shift towards the more privatized type of married family life which was already, it should be emphasized, extremely common in the Edwardian period. Whether working-class wives receive more help from their husbands in the house than they did is less easily determined, for we have little reliable modern information on this. We only know that with the advent of domestic machinery, and the reduction of children, women have needed and probably received less help from other members of the family or from neighbours in general. The primary responsibility for such tasks has certainly remained with women, and there is some indication that through rising standards, as in house cleaning and child care, the hours spent on them have changed surprisingly little. The most striking changes in marital roles may well have occurred principally in the middle classes who can no longer secure the aid of domestic servants. But we cannot from this infer with Rhona and Robert Rapoport that the rare *Dual Career Families* today should be taken for the pattern of the future; or still less that 'many more men than ever before in Western society are washing up, cooking, doing housework, shopping, and caring for babies'.[5]

Whatever its changes in character, marriage today lasts longer than it did. Edwardians who married in 1911 had on average twenty-eight years ahead of them; the modern couple more than forty. Better health has so far easily outpaced the effects of increasing divorce. It has ensured that many fewer children are forced, through the death of a parent, to depend on the extended rather than the nuclear family for their upbringing.

Yet this has happened at a time when, paradoxically, better health has made the three-generation family much more common. Grandparents are no longer a rarity. Demographic change has transformed the position of the old in the twentieth century perhaps more than any other group in the family. The old are now treble the proportion of the British population that they were in the 1900s. They are still poor, but they live much longer. Even if fit, they are likely to have been retired from work, and the dwindling of unmarried young workers in need of lodgings has almost eliminated one of their former chief sources of supplementary income. Despite the fact that a probably increasing number of younger married couples take widowed parents into their own households, the proportion of old people to be found in institutions has grown still more rapidly. This is not because the role of family in assisting the old has declined but simply because far more of them need to be assisted. Many who leave their homes for institutions do so through no positive wish, but simply because society has not chosen to find the means to support them at home. Brought up as children to respect the old, they can now find themselves in their own old age more disadvantaged even than either women or children. Many of them wait for death sitting listlessly around the walls of former general wards of (renamed) workhouses, successors of Edwardian paupers.

The fate of the old might be seen as one consequence of the more general decline of traditional authority in the family and society. This would be mistaken. The old were chronically poor and underprivileged in 1900, and the help which they receive from both kin and from the state has actually increased. What is more relevant is that the factors which have progressively lifted the majority of the population above the level of absolute poverty, reducing the need of most families for the exchange of help with neighbours and making possible a home-centred social and leisure life, have separated the nuclear family of parents and children from the experience of less self-sufficient groups. Not only the old, but also young unmarried adults, who equally depend upon the wider society rather than the private family, have been left increasingly isolated. Often they have no choice but to walk, vulnerable or discontented, streets from which others have withdrawn. The twentieth century has seen a strengthening rather than a disintegration of the family in Britain, but it is a strengthening which has brought very unequal benefits.

20 Class

Few Edwardians were unaware that they lived in a class society. Certainly their experience varied. Southern towns with their large middle-class professional presence and the English countryside with its upper-class country house gentry provided a direct and personal experience of social hierarchy. Those who lived in the solid working-class districts of the cities, or relatively homogeneous industrial communities such as mining settlements, or rural equivalents like the crofting townships, were more likely to see themselves as ordinary people, more or less equal, but subjected to economic burdens by landowners, coal-owners and other outside magnates. There were some Edwardians who disapproved on principle of class distinction and tried to treat all with whom they came into contact, even the destitute, as equals. But nearly all working-class Edwardians, at some moment in their lives, would have faced the feelings which came to one Essex farmworker's boy as he observed Sunday worship in the Church of England:

> 'One thing as a boy I didn't like and it sticks in my mind today. I came to the conclusion that church-goers were something like the railway carriages were at one time – first, second and third class. You see, my mother was a person of the lower class, was a poor woman, and she and her friends were all poor, but they were great church-goers, regular church-goers, kindly gentle people. But . . . they had to sit in the back pews. In the middle of the church were the local shopkeepers and people who were considered to be a little bit superior to the others – better educated, perhaps. And right at the top of the church, behind where

the choir used to sit, were the local farmers, the local bigwigs, you see. Posh people. And when people left the church, although as I said he was a nice old kindly vicar, he didn't seem to have any time for the lower classes. Mother and her friends would pass out of the church door, the vicar would stand near the church door, and he would just nod and smile, perhaps not that, even. But when the higher class people came out he would shake hands and beam to every one of them as if they was somebody far superior to my mother ... And I didn't like that. I thought my mother was worth a handshake as well as the rich ...

'I used to discuss this sort of thing with my mother ... I said it wasn't right, it wasn't proper. I said she shouldn't go to church. She said, "Nothing will ever stop me from going to my church."'[1]

Railway trains and churches were but two of innumerable common situations in which Edwardians were made to feel their precise station in life. There were the socially graded bars into which public houses were divided; distinctions of clothing and accent; the cleaner conditions and later hours of work of the better paid; the separate educational systems of elementary, grammar and private schools; separate entrances in the houses of the well-to-do, and even in some shops, for middle- and working-class visitors. Above all, there were immense and obvious divergences in standards of living. In Britain today, while the achievement of a classless society may still seem remote, some at least of these distinctions have become blurred. The social display of Sunday church parades has dwindled as rapidly as personal domestic service, while the fine grading of first, second and third class carriages, and workmen's trains, has given way to a mere two classes of travel. And such symbolic changes have come with a wide sense that British society is indeed less classbound than it was.

The explanation of this change in atmosphere is less easy than might generally be expected. There has not, as we noticed earlier, been any marked trend towards social mobility; simply an alteration of its channels. It is arguable, indeed, that after the age of twenty an Edwardian had rather more chance of social mobility than his successors today. More surprising perhaps is the lack of any convincing evidence of a substantial change in the unequal distribution of resources between the classes. We know much less about the distribution of wealth today than in the 1900s because of the rapid growth of tax evasion, and no recent analysis has overcome the difficulties in comparison revealed by R. M. Titmuss in his *Income Distribution and Social Change*. It is clear that the need to evade tax has caused a considerable dispersion of wealth, previously held by the family head, among the younger members of wealthy families. This partly explains one oddity when the distribution of national capital is calculated from death duty returns (which despite their admittedly growing unrepresentativeness are still the most general available statistics): while the share of the richest 1 per cent has shrunk, that of the remainder of the top 10 per cent has actually grown since the Edwardian period (Table 7).

Table 7. Distribution of national capital derived from estate duty statistics [2]

Percentage of population aged 25 and over	*Percentage of National Capital owned* 1911–13	1924–30	1936–8	1960
Richest 1%	69	62	56	42
Richest 10%	92	91	88	83
Richest 2–10%	23	29	32	41

These figures hardly suggest that there has been much overall dispersion of capital wealth between the social classes, as opposed to dispersion within families. It is true that there have been some shifts in the areas of concentration. The ownership of housing and, until very recently, of farmland by private landlords has declined. On the other hand there can be little doubt about the concentration of ownership in commercial land and in industry. Perhaps the most striking indication that the distribution of wealth has changed little during the twentieth century is that of the fastest growing sector of the national capital, company stocks and shares: the top 10 per cent now hold 98 per cent.

We have a clearer picture of the relative distribution of incomes. Turning back to Table 2 on page 24, it can be seen immediately that the position of manual workers as a whole has not improved, nor that of women in relation to men. The most important redistribution has occurred *within* the middle classes, from professional to business managerial occupations. Nor is it merely a coincidence that this shift of advantage has happened just as social mobility into the professions has become easier and mobility within industry more difficult.

Inequality of resources is thus no less characteristic of Britain today than it was in the Edwardian period. The key to change in the sphere of class lies rather in the effect of the continuous rise in the average earnings of all classes. The rising cost of wages in relation to materials and other factors has gradually eliminated a whole series of luxury trades, as the profitability of production for the mass working-class market has at the same time increased. The effect upon clothing has been especially critical. Edwardians were socially stratified into those who wore tailor-made clothes, those who wore new ready-mades, and those who wore only other people's cast-offs. The British people are no longer visually divided in this obvious way, because the great majority of all classes now buy new ready-made factory clothing. And they no longer need to feel such special respect for service jobs – shop, domestic, railway, postal or military – just because of the uniform. Similarly the motor car, once the leisure privilege of the Edwardian rich, is now so ubiquitous that its ownership no longer brings any class distinction at all. Nor is it only the well-to-do who can afford foreign travel. Again, with the advent of the package tour, the structure of the market has changed, and the advantages of the wealthy minority lessened. As the resources of the majority have increased, so have the choices within their reach; and as a result, even though the resources of the rich have increased still more, their exclusive luxuries have been reduced.

This has itself contributed to another key change: the disintegration of local society. This is not to suggest that there has been any lessening of the regional inequality of class distribution in Britain, for the reverse may be the case. Analyses of tax returns, investment income and entries to *Who's Who* all show an overwhelming concentration of the wealthy today in the south-east. The northern industrial areas retain their environmental disadvantages in terms of housing and health (especially in infant mortality), yet they have lost their early twentieth-century near monopoly of high industrial working-class earnings. Regional class differences have thus tended to simplify and consolidate.

The effect of this has been reinforced by the breakdown in the *local* character of social hierarchy. Outside the cities, where residential segregation and commuting were developing, local communities were directly linked to work places. Edwardians were not – as is often believed – immobile, but they soon met new neighbours at work. This was how class solidarity developed quickly in new mine settlements. The classic 'traditional' proletarian community is often quite modern. But the working-class pattern of the future lay towards the cities, and the attenuation of the links between the family and the occupational class community. Similarly, at the other end of the social scale, the Edwardian aristocracy was still a territorial presence. And in general, with a diversity immediately reflecting local occupational structures, social superiors and inferiors in Edwardian Britain acknowledged their relative social standing in regular personal encounters: at work, in the shops, at church. This contact was given heightened social significance by the personal nature of employment. Middle- and upper-class families employed personal domestic servants. Shop assistants were employed by local shopkeepers, craftsmen and labourers by local builders and manufacturers. Today the growth of multiple trading and industrial corporations has brought employers to the cities, where they never meet most of those who work for them. A shrinking proportion of families employ domestic servants. With the closing of country houses and the selling off of a large proportion of farms, the old upper class have ceded much of their control of the countryside to their former tenants, the farmers. The contemporary rich are international in their pursuits. Their increased mobility has loosened the foundations of social deference.

Linked both to rising earnings and to the increased mobility of the wealthy is a shrinking in the scale of the establishments of the well-to-do. While the Edwardian middle and upper classes employed innumerable servants to supply them with hot water, fires and clean rooms, the rising cost of labour in relation to machinery has made household equipment such as central heating a decisively cheaper way of securing the same services. Many of the service wings added to older houses in the nineteenth century have consequently been pulled down again in the twentieth. Other large houses have been divided into flats. At the other end of the scale overcrowding has been reduced. The private landlord sector has shrunk from 90 per cent to 20 per cent, in the face of the growth of both council tenants and mortgage-paying owner-occupiers – now a third and a half of all householders respectively; and this has brought about some convergence in the standards of new housing. As a result, although housing types still present a clear index of social class, the extreme ranges of scale, both in the number of rooms and the members of the household, has diminished. At the same time it has ceased to be the custom for a third of all occupied women to work in the peculiarly deferential situation of domestic service, or for the families of the middle and upper classes to receive the daily practice in class command which service ensured. Like working-class families, the middle classes have become more privatized, and in losing personal service their own lives have become in certain ways also less restricted. Grace Fulford, for example, the daughter of a London professional family among our Edwardians, was to experience a drastic reduction after marriage from the service to which she had been brought up. But she did not remember the change as all loss:

> 'Poor things . . . They'd be in the house, oh yes . . . Not only was it a big responsibility, but you also never had your house to yourself. I mean, if you got a luncheon party or dinner party you had to stop talking when they came into the room, because you might be talking about something you didn't want them to particularly know. And of course gossip was rampant. All passed on and exaggerated of course.

But really the majority of people I knew who had servants were glad really when more modern [labour-] saving devices came in and they were able to do without them living in. So as you could do with daily labour . . .'[3]

This decline in the personal and local power of the upper and middle classes could have had a much more drastic effect upon British society if it had not been counterbalanced by a slowly widening diffusion, along with rising living standards, of concern for social 'respectability' – the democratization of the once exclusive ideal of the gentleman. But this concern also reflects the growing importance in the class structure of education.

Education has been the last key factor in bringing a diminution of overt class distinction in the twentieth century. The British educational system still provides a powerful reinforcement of inherited class inequality. The continued existence of a private sector, and especially of the public schools, has helped to preserve middle-class chances of entry into the universities, professions and business management. But the working of state education itself, by selecting and discriminating between children at an age when the advantages of middle-class comforts and culture at home are critical, also favours those with the most support from their social background. The increasing use of educational achievement as a criterion by employers, and the widening of educational opportunity itself on a selective basis, have made this effect of education as a social class determinant much more important today than it was before 1914. On the other hand, for the minority of working-class boys who are successful as scholars, the broadening and lengthening of the scholarship ladder has provided important new chances. In 1907 only a quarter of all places for grammar school entrants had just become free. The number from working-class backgrounds who went on to Oxford and Cambridge or the higher professions was still insignificant. A bare 1 per cent of the children of semi-skilled and unskilled manual workers even reached secondary schools. The transition to the present situation of universal secondary education of some kind, and general university student grants, has taken place very gradually along with the systematization of selection. Its most important effect on the social class structure has not been to provide more general social mobility, for as we have seen there is little evidence of generally increased movement. More important is the training in culture and manners which is offered through education to the socially mobile. Promotion through work did not provide such lessons in social behaviour. Today you can no longer, as you could before 1914, feel any more certain of a man's social origins from his accent and tastes than from his possession of a cheque book. And conversely, as the acquisition of middle-class accents and tastes has been made relatively easy, they have ceased to carry such weight. Men in the professions and clerical work, where expansion has provided the best chances of advancement through education, have benefited less from the general rise in real incomes than other occupational groups. Hence the dilemma of *The Blackcoated Worker*.[4] Educational opportunity has undermined overt class distinction from two directions.

Lastly, even where class distinctions are observed, it has become less the convention to exploit them or comment on them. This is partly because the distinctions have themselves become less clearly meaningful. It also reflects an increasing mutuality of social power. At the personal level the middle class can no longer call on abundant cheap labour to supply the services they need, nor are they the customers who matter most. Working-class labour and custom have been revalued. So has the collective voice of the working class. During the Edwardian unrest major unions such as the railwaymen had still to gain recognition from their own employers. Today governments regularly consult the Trades Union Congress as part of national economic planning. The Labour party, which only elected its first MPs in the 1900s, had by the 1920s supplanted the Liberals. The social influence of the fact that from then onwards Labour shared the government of Britain with the Conservatives may have been as pervasive as any egalitarian legislation. The middle classes are more likely to respect the working classes, if only from self-interest.

The Edwardians thus stood at the edge of a change as significant as the lifting of the majority of the population out of poverty: the blurring of overt class distinction. It took them by surprise. The same farm-worker's boy who observed class discrimination at church experienced the humiliations of never having new clothes too:

> 'They considered themselves so far superior to us, you know. They were well dressed. Shopkeepers' kids were well dressed then; farmers' kids, bricklayers' kids. But the farmworkers' kids didn't have any of those [new clothes], only home-made ones, and we did feel it then . . . Hurt that our parents hadn't got more money to buy new clothes. I should think I was fifteen before I ever had a new suit . . .
>
> 'And one more thing about that. Living next door to the Post Office we used to take telegrams for the post mistress; I've gone over to Little Bentley or Bromley for sixpence, you see. And one Sunday morning I had to take a telegram to the local baker . . . And this was the first Sunday I had this new suit on, and when I took this telegram he said, "Let me see, your name is Hills I think, isn't it?" I said "Yes, sir." We always called them "sir", we were brought up to call men like that "sir", the doctor and the vicar whom we thought were rich, even the local baker we thought was important. "Ee," he said, "I see you've got a new suit on, it looks like a new suit to me. Good gracious me," he said, "some of you people are going to be as well dressed as we are."
>
> 'I've never forgotten that. That's what we had to put up with from the so-called rich and intellectuals.'[5]

21 Theory and Practice

We have so far sketched in broad outline the main dimensions of social change in early twentieth-century Britain. In so doing we have implicitly used theories of social change. In concluding we need to discuss some of these briefly. We cannot of course hope to settle such fundamental issues as the factors of social change or the role of the individual in history in the paragraphs which follow, and some readers may prefer to skip them. But we can at least indicate the theoretical position from which this book began and to which – hopefully – it leads, and in so doing suggest some possible avenues for further exploration. After this we shall return finally to the raw material upon which both the description and analysis of social change must ultimately rest, the life experience of ordinary people.

Because general trends are not easily perceived, social change is mostly recognized through particular and often arbitrary incidents. There is, moreover, much social change experienced in a single lifetime which is quite independent of any alterations in the general social structure. Individuals change their occupations, move up or down the social scale or between differing communities, gain or lose faiths or friends. The normal life cycle brings not only rises and falls in prosperity but expansions and contractions of community. Because children make new friendships more quickly than adults, it is normal for those who move from one area to another to feel that people are less neighbourly than when they were young. Old people who are now both alone and poor may be quite justly nostalgic for their earlier days. The middle-aged and elderly have for generations believed that in *their* youth family and neighbours were friendlier, children more respectful of adults. Their feeling of loss is reasonable, but it is a loss as easily explained by the life cycle as by change in society. Thus much confusion about recent social change can be avoided by a more precise delineation of its direction, sphere and level.

Long-term trends need to be separated from repetitive changes normal to the social system, such as life cycles or trade cycles. Changes also need to be seen from the perspective of different levels. A minor adaptation of the overall social structure may require the construction of totally new institutions; it may or may not affect the working of the family; it will transform some individual lives.

Let us take a single incident. We can return to Grace Fulford, one of our Edwardians brought up in a well-to-do London household. She had now married, to a husband who was never able to achieve the prosperity of her professional father. In an attempt to recover some of her previous standard of living she took advantage of the occupational opportunities for women temporarily created by the First World War and became a civil servant. As she still had three young children she engaged a 'housekeeper', a single servant who was expected to perform a task which normally would have occupied two or three living-in servants in the 1900s. The result was a confrontation which might be taken as a symbol of the changed relationship of the middle and working classes in the early twentieth century:

> 'I had one, an absolute gem . . . I was sorry when she went. She went because her own mother was ill, lived down in the country and she went back. Then I got another one. Oh dear. She was like a Grenadier Guardsman. And I came in one day unexpectedly. Oh I was horrified . . . And she was sitting on those [scullery] steps eating her dinner off the floor. I never saw such a state that my baby was in with a great lump of bread and jam in her hand and all over her face, all over the pram. Oh it was terrible. Of course I gave her notice, dismissed her immediately. Told her to pack her things and go the next day. And I remember her coming in, coming to me in the morning, standing over me, just like a Grenadier Guardsman, I was so small and she

> was so big. And I just told her what I thought of her and she said to me, "I've never had such a character in all my life." She said, "I've a good mind to punch your husband on the nose." She didn't, but she had to go. Oh I was determined.'

But Grace Fulford's own career suffered as much from the breach as that of the servant who had lost her 'character'. Her husband secretly sent in her own resignation. 'It was accepted, I got a letter to say it was accepted. I was furious. Of course I couldn't do anything about it because he was part of the Ministry, it would have been washing your own affairs in public, that.'[1]

We have here not only an illustration of the declining power of the middle-class lady as an employer. In the making of this incident, long-term trends in general social values, and a temporary general change in the occupational structure, intersect with the downward social mobility of an individual, the expectation of domestic service of a middle-class mother at a particular stage in the family life cycle and the occupational careers of three women. The incident also shows that changes in husband–wife roles do not necessarily follow when married women take up paid work.

In arguing from the particular to the general, which is the task of the historian and the sociologist concerned with social change, caution and precision in defining change are thus essential. Historians have perhaps taken too little notice of the theoretical work on this aspect of social change by sociologists such as Sorokin, McIver and Moore.

Rather more attention has been given by historians to the grand generalizations of various schools of what may be called trend sociology. Indeed, these include some of the best-known names and concepts of sociology: the supreme law of progress of Comte, the cycles of growth and decay of Sorokin, or the social transformations caused by urbanization and industrialization as set out by Durkheim, Toennies, or more recently 'modernization' theory. But in fact the value to the historian of these interpretations is surprisingly limited. Although set forward as theories, they are more properly crystallizations of history, presented as change between an ideal model of society past and an ideal model present. As such, they provide some measure from which to begin a comparative historical analysis, but little understanding of the actual dynamics of change. They are, moreover, parasitic upon history itself, and so have proved vulnerable to changes in historical interpretation of the past, and to the realization of the future. Durkheim and Toennies, like the 'modernization' theorists, assumed a consistent trend from the – allegedly – stable, unspecialized and close-knit societies of the past, personal and family-centred, to an anonymous industrial urban world of specialized organization, decision by impersonal criteria, and constant change. But with the passing of time much of their empirical basis has been undermined. For example, in twentieth-century Britain the stabilizing of urban working-class neighbourhoods and the general shift to a more family-centred social life are both reversals of the trends observed by Toennies and Durkheim. Similarly, the disintegration of the compact early-twentieth-century city has made nonsense of the ideal types of rural and urban society, closely related to the ideal past and present of Toennies and Durkheim, which formed the theoretical framework for the fascinating empirical studies of Robert Park's Chicago school of urban sociology. Such polarities of past and present are increasingly recognized as an untenable base for any satisfactory theory of social change.

Although with some justice more often ridiculed than taken seriously by historians, the more recent functionalist school in American sociology has surprisingly proved more fruitful. This is not because, as expounded by Talcott Parsons or followers such as Smelser, it has fitted the facts of social change any better. The general functionalist theory was based on the analogy of society with a living creature, in which all the parts performed interdependent functions in maintaining the life of the organism, and in neutralizing both internal and external threats. The essence of a society was thus what held it together, and its tendency was always towards the maintenance of its social structure, the assertion of 'common' values, towards equilibrium rather than conflict. Change was brought, when equilibrium was disturbed as by technological change, through a process of 'differentiation' in the social structure – like the splitting up of activities once carried out within the family into schools, factories, hospitals and so on. Unfortunately as it happens the waning significance of the family as a consequence of 'structural differentiation' is a sociological myth, one might say a piece of intellectual folklore, of similar value to the conventional opinions of the elderly on the same subject. From the evidence one could as easily argue the very reverse: leisure, for example, in Britain is more family-centred and socialization is more parent-centred in the 1970s than it was in the 1900s. Moreover, the functionalist assumptions that change was largely caused by factors external to a society, and that societies were based upon a consensus of shared values, has been revealed as absurd, even in the American context.

Nevertheless, functionalism has had one great merit: it has focused more attention on why major social changes do *not* always take place. And for early-twentieth-century Britain, given the dimensions of inequality which we have described, it is perhaps more remarkable how slight a social change has taken place, how strong the basic social structure has proved, than that there have been certain limited if critical transformations. The functionalist sociologists drew attention to the means by which changes could be neutralized and social equilibrium maintained. This has led other sociologists back to the analysis of conflict in society with new understanding.

For the functionalists themselves to have incorporated conflict into their general theory would have brought a central position not only to the issue of social class, but also to the theories of Marx. For both political and intellectual reasons this was an improbable step. The development of a *conflict theory* of social change has indeed suffered from crudely simplified versions of Marxism. In particular, there have been recurrent presentations, sometimes said to be Marxist and sometimes anti-Marxist, of single-factor economic or technological determinism as a theory of social change. (The recent 'convergence' theory that the logic of industrial technology is bringing the same kind of social hierarchy and state control to all societies is an 'anti-Marxist' example.) Such notions are, of course, useless in the face of the complex reality of social change in the past. We have assumed throughout our discussion that social changes are caused by the conjunction of a multiplicity of factors, both external and internal: military, demographic, economic, political, ideological and so on. Furthermore, since these factors mould change in conjunction rather than separately, and while the development of each separately may be logical their intersections can be haphazard, the history of each society will be in some respects unique. Consequently, while we can hope to analyse the past, our explanations cannot provide any *certain* predictions for the future.

More important, for our purposes, is the subtlety with which conflict theorists, and especially Marx himself, not only in such classics as *Capital* but also in the earlier writings only published from the 1920s, analysed the connections and discordances between the political, economic and ideological structures of society, and the social struggles through which these were resolved. It was a return to such an approach for which Ralf Dahrendorf called in his recent *Class and Class Conflict in an Industrial Society*; but a return with one important difference in emphasis. Marx had written with the assumption that, despite reversals and betrayals, the political organization of the working class would lead to the intensification of social conflict, and eventually to social revolution. By the mid twentieth century it is clear enough that the organization of the working class does not always have such effects. Dahrendorf, influenced by functionalism, emphasized the reverse aspect of working-class movements: how organization leads to institutionalization, and a share of power to the containment of conflict. In the case of early-twentieth-century Britain a two-sided interpretation of working-class politics, both as a form of conflict forcing forward change and as an institutionalized softening of demand, makes good sense. But we should emphasize that the eventual outcome was certainly not an inevitable one. The conflict could always have become less sharp, and brought about lesser social adjustments than those achieved through the Edwardian crisis. There also remained within it the possibility – given another conjunction of factors, a changed context or a different response – that it might break its bounds.

How does this leave the question with which we started this book: the extent to which social change in these years was the fruit of conscious effort? We have seen how some of the most important changes were not the results of conscious political demand. This is particularly true of developments in the family and in the economy, upon which the rising standard of living chiefly depended. But we should not underestimate the essential contribution of ordinary Edwardians. The spheres of change were interconnected in manifold ways. One example is the way in which the Edwardian economic doctrine of thrift was linked, not only to family budgeting conventions in the ordinary working class, but also to sexual behaviour; and how the switch to an emphasis on consumption has subsequently affected all three. Similarly, there was mutual reinforcement between the collective pressure for social advance and individual ambition for self-improvement. Collective pressure secured the Edwardian advances in social welfare and the civil emancipation of women. Through trade unionism it protected the working-class share in real earnings. But we cannot limit the achievements of Edwardian radicals, socialists and labour organizers and supporters to this. Without enthusiasm, their willingness to fight for a collective advance, the social situation of ordinary Edwardians would not so much have edged forward, as fallen back. Collective pressure for increased earnings was, moreover, one of the motive forces of economic change, upon which the future prosperity of all classes rested. And it fed, as well as fed upon, the individual pressures for self-improvement, which were manifested in decisions to change jobs or change investments, to move or improve a house, or not to have too many children. The changing twentieth-century family and economy were shaped by the aggregate of such conscious individual decisions.

We can thus return to the individual Edwardian: to the fusion of theory and practice in real lives. We shall finish with the stories of Alice Richards and Alice Towey, two Edwardians who both fought for change, collectively or individually, more and less successfully. Here are the springs of change. Each of these two lives is in some ways representative and in others unique, and in this, each is characteristic of the obstinately rich human material from which history and sociology must be shaped.

Alice Richards

The Richards were East Londoners. They lived in a neighbourhood of streets which were at that time the edge of the city, half a mile from the Royal Albert Docks, with the great Beckton gasworks a mile further out across the Thames marshes. The family moved a number of times between various houses. Sometimes they rented just one floor, sometimes a complete house with parlour, kitchen, living room and two bedrooms above, turning the parlour into a third bedroom for an aunt or at one time letting it to a young couple 'in difficulties'.

Mr Richards was a skilled man, a plumber, who had served his apprenticeship. He worked on ships for one of the eastern lines, and very occasionally had to go out to Malta or India for them. He also had other talents, for he would earn extra money in the evenings as a part-time music hall singer and step-dancer. 'He danced with Dan Leno and Lottie Collins.' He attributed this musical ability to the fact that his own parents had migrated to Stepney, his birthplace, from Wales.

Mrs Richards also came from Stepney and her parents were first generation immigrants to the city too, although they came from the English countryside. Her father had had his own shoe shop, while her mother ran the home as a 'tailoring works' with daughters and sisters for labour. Mrs Richards thus came from quite a prosperous background, perhaps occupationally more correctly described as lower-middle rather than upper-working-class. She worked as a tailoress at home until she married, in her early twenties. Since her husband could not have earned as much as her father, her married life would in any case have been less comfortable than her childhood; but her fortunes, and those of her new family, were to be much more seriously affected by ill-health.

She had altogether eleven children. The eldest died as a young child and four others as infants. Worse still, after her third child was born she herself suffered a paralysis which affected the whole of one side of her body. Although she adapted remarkably to this handicap, she thereafter relied considerably upon the support of her family. Her mother, for example, retained one of the children sent to her during the initial illness, and this second child was therefore brought up permanently by her grandmother. The third went into service as soon as she left school. Another went to live with an aunt. As a result she never had more than three girls to look after herself. She was also helped with the making and mending of boots and clothes by the grandparents. She contrived, aided by a child, to do some dress-making herself. 'She would have the material laid on the table and she would draw the shape on it and I would have to cut it out. And she would pin the material to her dress and sew it that way.'

She was able to get about quite well too, although she needed the help of a child to hold the bag if she went shopping, and the company of Mr Richards if she was to get on to a tram. Similarly she managed the housework without any paid help, taking an understandable pride in her standards.

> 'Of course there were some things she couldn't do. She couldn't climb on a chair. But she would clean – it was amazing how she would hold the flannel and wring it – same with the washing you know. She used to do her washing. The washing was beautiful too and her home was spotlessly clean ...
>
> 'But you see, from a very young child we were all trained to do something in the home. I mean my first job was to clean the knives ... And if they wasn't clean I had to do them again. The prongs of the forks were all examined to see that they were all clean ... We all had set jobs. And my mother had a meat dish cover ... and there was tins on the mantelshelf for tea and I had to clean them. Little

things came along as I got older. Then you had to start, I suppose about eight years of age, washing up and wiping. And then my mother started teaching me how to clean the floors . . .

'Yes, she taught us, yes. And she was thorough in her teaching, it wasn't just slapdash. Corners had to be gone into and if the corner wasn't done well you done it again. And the edge of the lino was picked up to see that you wiped the dust from underneath. And then I started cleaning windows. I could sit out of a window upstairs when I was nine years of age and clean the windows outside.'

Nor was it only the three daughters who helped. Although Mr Richards's views on the position of married women were conventional enough – 'A woman's place was in the home and that was it' – in practice he shared many of the household tasks himself. He helped mend clothes, sewing and putting on buttons. On Saturdays he went shopping with his wife. Every morning before setting out to work he would light the fire and take her up a cup of tea. 'He'd clean windows and all that sort of thing and then get down and scrub the floor if necessary. He'd wash up, yes.' He would look after the children, read to them and take them out for walks. He also talked to them about the events in the news, elections and strikes, and even the Edwardian theory of the atom. As a father he 'made a great fuss of us kids. I missed him terribly when he died because he used to sit and explain such a lot to me.' He would read frequently to his wife too, for Mrs Richards herself could not read.

Mr Richards was an intelligent, public-spirited working man, whose views were an interesting mixture of the conventional and unconventional. Although 'the only time he ever went to church was to a wedding or a funeral', he was very strict in his insistence on Sunday observance. Even stitching was forbidden in the house, and the children were not allowed to play outside. They went to church three times on Sundays, principally to the Church of England, but also to various other activities, some on weeknights, such as a Presbyterian PT club and a Congregational mission choir. 'I used to go round to different other churches, you know, to sing cantatas.' At home grace was always said at meals, and strict manners were observed. The children were not allowed to talk and food had to be finished: 'You sat there till you ate it.' They kept their set places and 'this even happened after my mother died, my mother's place was left'. The newspaper, which was only taken on Sundays, was not intended to be read by the children. 'If I wanted to read the newspaper, I'd sneak it out.' Probably Mr Richards wished to protect his daughters from some of the seamy stories reported from the courts. He certainly insisted on an avoidance of any visual intimacy between himself and his daughters. He never bathed them or undressed them as children, and kept them away when he was bathing himself.

> 'Never. No. Was very particular about that. He would come in of an evening time and go into the back kitchen and he'd shut the back kitchen doors and strip to the waist and have a good wash. But none of us were allowed to go out there while he was washing.'

Mr Richards was thus a strict man. 'We had to be very obedient, and we couldn't speak until we were spoken to.' In contrast to his wife, who was very lenient, he was prepared to smack his daughters for disobedience. But he was also an affectionate father, and indulgent enough to buy his children a Sunday morning present of sweets each week. He shared a bond with them in the help which they all gave to Mrs Richards. 'We were a very close family.' She was herself a demonstrative mother. 'I was very attached to my mother, very much so.' When Mr Richards had to be out in the evening, the eldest girl would always stay up with her mother until he returned. The children thus grew up in an atmosphere which, despite some rather formal rules, was on the whole warm and even spontaneous. Unlike many Edwardian working-class children, the girls had birthday parties and presents. Mr Richards read to them all, and played cribbage and dominoes and snap. They were a musical family and 'we used to sing around the house'. Despite the ban on newspapers, the girls were encouraged to read books from the library. The whole family sometimes went together to a music hall. Above all, the girls were allowed to play freely outside the house, without restrictions as to their playmates. They took full advantage of this. Besides the usual girls' games such as skipping and hoops, they joined in boys' sports. 'Oh I played football with the boys and cricket when I was a kid. I was a tomboy . . . I could run like a hare.' They also explored the marshes, fished in the ditches and went into the fields to 'pick buttercups and daisies. Fancied we was in the country . . . listening to the birds singing.'

The girls' freedom to choose their own playmates was characteristic of Mr and Mrs Richards's social attitudes. They lived in a poor neighbourhood with no 'higher class' residents at all and a good many families so poor 'that they would pack into one room, you'd get two or three families probably living in one house'. Although Mrs Richards could not get out easily, she had quite a regular social life both with her relatives and with neighbouring friends. One of these was a woman who would have been shunned by many artisans' wives because she drank. 'She was a woman that did drink. She was a very nice woman but unfortunately this was her failing. And mother, rather than see her get into trouble with her husband, sent me in to clean up for her you know.'

Mr Richards was a man of very clear social views. 'He was very much of a socialist . . . and he was a staunch trade unionist, he was in trade unions from the time I can remember. He was constantly fighting for better conditions for working men.' He belonged to the gas workers' Number One branch, and supported the socialists at elections. He was not only an active trade unionist, attending union meetings, but also went every week to a friendly society meeting, the Buffaloes. At the pub where this met he was also secretary of a farthing thrift club 'that was held upstairs'. As far as possible, moreover, he brought up his daughters to share in his views and activities. 'If a man had been ill a long time or out of work or met with an accident, they would get what they called a benefit concert up, and probably father would be doing a turn, of course mother and I would go when he was going.' Occasionally the girls would go to pay his union dues for him. He also encouraged them to follow his own generosity towards poorer children. 'My father was a man who would bring anybody in if he thought they needed a meal. And it was nothing for me . . . to take kiddies in and they would be fed at the table and given a meal. Oh yes, yes.'

Above all, Mr Richards brought them up to reject the social gestures through which class hierarchy was acknowledged. 'He wouldn't have no class distinction at all.' They were never to curtsey: 'You bow the knee to no man.' In the same spirit he was against his daughters working in service, although in this case he was prepared to respect their own independence. 'He didn't believe in his children being servants to other people. He was against it, but [my sister] was so keen on going that he provided her with her clothes and let her go.' On their respecting others, however, he insisted absolutely.

> 'We were taught that everybody was equal and if it was a tramp knocked at the door for a glass of water, I couldn't go in and say to my father, "There's a man", or "There's a tramp, knocking at the door". He was "a gentleman". We were taught this. And if it was a poor old woman hawking something, coming along with a basket, perhaps a little bit of cotton and stuff in, and knocked at the door, I had to say there was "a lady" at the door. And we were brought up very strictly in that way.'

While Mr Richards was in full health, he and the children could afford to be generous to those who were less privileged. As he got into his late forties, however, his health began to fail, first from rheumatic gout and then from bronchitis. Instead of new clothes, the family had to find second-hand garments. There was less food at the table for all, Mr Richards included. 'We had to sit down at the table together and we had to share. If there wasn't sufficient for my mother he wouldn't have his.' The situation became much worse, however, during the 1912 dock strike, when he had no earnings for weeks. Appeals by the unions raised some funds for food vouchers, and the local churches supplied breakfasts for young children, but adults were reduced to semi-starvation. Under this strain Mrs Richards's health finally broke. 'People were starving, there was no question of it, they were starving . . . I know the day my mother was taken ill she never had a crust of bread in the house.'

Alice, the eldest of the daughters at home, took her mother's place as housekeeper. The funeral had a certain splendour, with feathers on the horses and the hearse itself, black velvet draping, and the family in black dresses, black earrings, necklaces and brooches. They wore mourning for a year. Three years after the funeral, Alice saw Mr Richards buried in turn.

She was to take up his fight for the underprivileged. Her own start in adulthood had not been auspicious. She had got used to work before leaving school, taking tailoring work to the shop for her aunt and also carrying 'a couple of lads' dinners down to the factory'. But after leaving school she could not settle. She tried two sweet factories. Then she was 'apprenticed to tailoring of all things and I detested it. Hated it. Yes. And I was there six weeks . . . My aunt lived in the same house as us and I used to sit at the machine turning the pockets out of the trousers and the straps and I saw more trousers in my life than I ever wanted to see. I didn't want to know.' Eventually, against her father's advice, she too went into service. 'I was only there a month when I wanted to come home. Three months I had in service.' It was a six-roomed house quite near by. She had to do all the cleaning.

> 'And there was some cleaning to do believe me. And there was three children and they were little horrors. Well I suppose I'd been brought up strict and these kids wasn't. And I was given half a day off a week on a Monday, and I got half a crown a week . . .
>
> 'I slept in the same room as the mistress's sister. The mistress helped in the house of course. But I did the rough work . . . She did the cooking. I did no cooking at all. The food was good. [I ate] with them most of the time, but if they had any company well, they had it in their parlour . . .

She was a little bit on the snobbish side. You know, he had a business . . . Wasn't much to do of evening time . . . I used to sit in the living room and they probably would sit in their front room. And I was only home a month or six weeks when mother died.'

Her mother's death ended her father's hope that she could attend evening classes and so find more suitable work. She did work again during the war in a rubber factory, 'of all things making golf balls while war was on, yes. But I was doing a man's work you see.' But by this time she had married. She had met her husband years earlier, when he was serving in a local shop and she was a schoolgirl. They married in 1915, immediately after her father died. 'It wasn't very much of a wedding . . . A soldier, sailor and a fireman were married that morning, three of us together, and they were all in uniform.' Her husband went back to the front, while she moved in with her mother-in-law. Then ill-health began to strike again, just as it had maimed her family in her childhood. Her husband was severely wounded, and her first child left blind and partly paralysed by illness. Nevertheless, indeed perhaps stimulated by these setbacks, Alice was to carry on the collective fight for change: in the Labour party and the Co-operative movement, for special causes such as the blind and the mentally ill and the unmarried mother; as a town councillor, and eventually as mayor. The Richards were not a typical working-class family; but they may fairly stand for those who led its collective progress.

Alice Towey

Our second story is of an individual struggle. It was less fruitful, but in some ways more representative of ordinary experience, at least in the most deprived section of the working class. Here is the underside to the springs of change.

The Toweys were Midlanders, living in one of the pottery towns which now form Stoke-on-Trent. They lived in a series of houses, decent enough with usually two bedrooms, two main rooms and a scullery, but never a permanent home because they could not keep up the rent for more than a few successive weeks.

> 'We must have had eight houses, up to when I was five . . . They wouldn't pay the rent. They wouldn't. No idea of it. My father and mother as well, she was as bad. Because you know there was empty houses, hundreds of them. That's all you've got to do, go and give 'em sixpence for a key. Cos one of the neighbours had the keys. You gave her sixpence, that was it . . . So when they'd been in so long and they didn't pay the rent – they got made to move. We never dared have a fire on the Mondays when the landlord was round. We didn't. No. Cos he never knew which house we were in.'

They were forcibly evicted several times, once with a ten-day-old infant who died after the family had spent the night in a coalhouse. Altogether of Mrs Towey's ten children only four girls were to survive until adulthood.

The root of the family's problems was the irregularity of Mr Towey's income. He was a locally born man, a labourer now in middle age, who alternated between bricklayer's labouring and pit haulage work, and was frequently out of work altogether. He would start work hungry, have to ask for an advance of wages to feed himself, and soon find himself too exhausted to carry on. The winters were particularly difficult because there was less building work and often he could not face the pit.

> 'And you couldn't condemn a man for being frightened of pit could you? Not really. Well in the winter-time there was no labouring going on, there wasn't much building. The only building more or less them days was the repairs of ovens or kilns or pot banks. See? And he used to go scouting round for that . . . So there's no surety of our food. No surety whatever.'

Although quite affectionate to his children, and not without friends in the pubs, Mr Towey was not a sympathetic husband. Even when he was not working, he did nothing to help in the house. 'He'd sit in the chair, smoking his pipe. Never saw him doing nothing about the house ... By gum he didn't. He wouldn't know which way to do it. No. Oh no.' He did nothing for his children either. 'There was only one thing he was there for and that was get 'em.' Even that was the fruit of Saturday night drinking rather than of love. 'Me mother thought a lot about him. But I never saw my father return any. No ... he didn't come down to earth as a husband and father. And I think that's what me mother wanted, she couldn't get understanding ... When they got a big family it was left to the woman to have all the troubles. They walked out of it.' So estranged had Mr Towey become from his wife that their only emotional contact took the form of fighting:

> 'Oh, they used to fight like dogs ... He used to come in drunk ... They used to fight vicious ... Wasn't a very big woman but she was strong. He never could beat her you know. Only by kicking ... And I saw 'em one night, both of 'em, they were in their night attire on the table fighting like lions. Horrible.'

Part of Mrs Towey's bitterness against her husband sprang from the fact that she had not been brought up to expect this kind of life. Although born in the Potteries, she came from a prosperous Catholic Irish farming family. Her father had come to England after falling in love with one of the family's maids. 'He was banished. They cut him off see.' Mrs Towey, however, had fallen still further through her marriage, for her brother was still middle-class in both manner and occupation, an insurance inspector whom the Towey children thought a gentleman 'because he used to dress so nice'. But they saw little of him. 'Me mother's people, they were a pretty proud lot. And they just wouldn't bother with her. Cos they thought she was as bad as me father.'

Mrs Towey had nevertheless kept some of her own self-respect. Her children had few illusions as to their social standing. 'We were in a low grade. Well if a mother and father don't pull together, that's it, isn't it?' Even so, Mrs Towey felt herself superior to families who swore – despite the fact that she had begun to swear mildly herself. She would refuse to let her children accept food for running errands for neighbours. 'You see, that's where the independence came in ... She'd walk about the house as though she'd tons of money ... We were very poor but proud. And strict.'

The discipline which she imposed on her children provided one vent for her anger against her husband. Although she did not impose respectable standards by, for example, restricting the children's choice of playmates or insisting on table manners, she punished her children frequently with 'hidings' and 'punchings'. She showed little affection to the girls. 'She was more regimental ... Well to be truthful I was frightened of her, my mother. I was terribly frightened of her.'

Such was the front with which Mrs Towey faced her unequal struggle to bring up her children. When some money was coming in she could rise to feeding them with rabbit and vegetable stew, bacon broth, or cow's hearts for dinner, and bread and tea for other meals. But very often the children had to rely on free school meals. 'We had nothing, many, many, many a morning.' When they came home, they would be sent straight to bed. '"If you go to bed you won't feel half so hungry" ... Many's the time I've filled myself with orange peel.'

Before the birth of the last girl, parents and children all shared the same bed. 'Nancy was the little one, she slept at the top of the bed, against the wall. And me mother next and me Dad next, and then me and Lou were sleeping at the bottom. Well if we got a bed we wouldn't have enough bedclothes for two ... We only had one sheet on the bed, one over us and one under us, and then there was a bed cover and all the others were coats. That we begged.' Apart from two chairs and a table, the bed was the only furniture in the house. Even when the family rose at one stage to seven, there were only two chairs. The rest ate their food standing, taking it from the one plate on the table and eating with fingers or spoons. They had no knives or forks and only the single plate. They did not even possess a bath tub. Instead, they washed in a bucket. 'But she was clean, will say that. She saw that we did it.' The stairs were scrubbed too, and the grate polished. 'And the table was as white as snow.'

The children were sometimes able to obtain new shoes from school. Otherwise they wore the cheapest second-hand footwear available, odd shoes 'as near as you could get 'em'. For dresses 'we used to beg jackets and she'd make us frocks out of them. Take the buttons off and the buttonholes, stitch 'em up. That was it, it was a frock.' Once a year, however, money saved through a clothing club would be used to buy new white frocks and slippers. 'We daren't kneel down when we went to Corpus Christi in case you dirtied 'em, because they had to go to pawn shop next day. We never saw 'em again.'

Although nominally Catholic, Mr Towey never attended church and Mrs Towey only once a year. They did not trouble to send the children to catechism. Nor did they have any interest in politics. There was never a newspaper in the house before 1914. Their poverty also cut them off from social life. They could not invite neighbours in, for they had neither chairs nor food to offer them. 'Oh no, no. Life was very primitive then.' If a neighbour died, they could not attend the funeral, for they 'didn't have any clothes'. For the same reason they never went out visiting. Mrs Towey never had a coat and had only men's boots. She did not even go to the shops, but sent her children instead. The children lived a similarly bare life. They enjoyed no games, music, books, pets or hobbies of any kind in the home, or theatre, cinema, walks or outings outside of it. Very often they could not even go to school, for lack of clothing, or because they were needed to pick up coal. Christmas was marked by fighting rather than presents, while 'the only difference in a birthday was, me mother never hit you that day'.

For the Toweys the outbreak of the First World War brought immediate change for the better. Mr Towey enlisted. This not merely interrupted his fights with his wife, but brought the family a regular income for the first time. They were able to settle down in one house. At the same time Alice, the eldest girl, left school and began full-time work in the potteries.

Her first job was as a handle-maker. After a few weeks she moved to paper print cutting in a small workshop with her mother's sister and brother-in-law. She stayed at this work for about two years, until her ambition was stirred.

> 'I heard me uncle Herbert talking about somebody working in the clay that they got more money . . . And it just struck me on the idea, thought myself, "Oh dear, can get more money in the clay. I can get another job. I shall do" . . . So, when I went they said, "Would you like to go scolloping?" . . . And I said, "I'll accept it but I won't be able to do it very quick." Said, "No, you mustn't try to."
>
> 'Of course when I went to work in the shop I saw these 'ere other women on these lathes . . . I got talking to the girls in dinner hour and they said as they got twelve bob a week. So I asked him, I said, "If there comes a vacancy could I go to work lathe treading? Twelve shillings a week." He said, "Oh you'll have to earn piecework." I said, "Oh I'll work hard." That's how I went, got this 'ere twelve bob. Well I'd only been on it a week or two when I went and got a head lathe, for a pound a week . . . I treaded the lathe and I sponged the cups at the same time. You worked with your hands and feet . . . and the man used to shape it, but it had to go round very very quick . . . I worked terribly hard for it. But work didn't come into it. It was what I achieved with it that I wanted. Well it was a big income that was you know. It was. And it really put me mother on her feet.'

If it was ambition which first attracted Alice Towey to lathe treading, she was to find that she had looked for a ladder in a treadmill. First of all her mother began to blossom out on the fruits of her labours in a way which simply repeated the earlier habits of Mr Towey. 'Me mother was having a bit of a good time then you know. She never went to work . . . She wouldn't get up and do her cleaning. We had to do that at night.' She began to buy clothes and go out drinking, 'lots of women together, soldiers' wives'. Although Alice was now earning, she demanded that she performed songs to her boozing friends, and humiliated her in other ways.

> 'She stood at the front gate talking to the neighbours. You daren't pass her. You'd have to stand there when you came in from work, you'd wait. She'd stand there deliberate. Just to make you know that you'd got to do it. Then she'd say, "You can pass now."'

At intervals Mr Towey also appeared on leave, very much in his old form. After one of his visits Mrs Towey developed a fatal cancer, which was attributed to one of his kicks. Alice buried her mother a few months before her father returned from the war.

She now found herself both housekeeper and breadwinner to the widowed Mr Towey. Her situation was as bad as her mother's. Before long she was provoked to a second, and equally futile, break for a better life.

> 'I only stuck it until just before I was twenty. And me father was at home, he was courting this woman. And started drinking. And I've got a photograph of me mother over the [fireplace] ... And I was putting these [clothes] over the line and this woman that was going about with me father, she says ... "You're exactly like your mother." She didn't like me. I could tell she didn't like me 'cos I didn't give her no encouragement, I didn't like the idea of it. And I said, "Well is there any fault you can find here, other than you've got her husband? Aren't you satisfied?" And then me father said, "Don't you talk to her like that." I said, "I am twenty," I said, "and I'm allowed to speak in this house. It's as much mine as yours." Cos I was doing the working. She says, "If I was him I'd bang you on the bloody ear'ole." So I turned round and banged her instead. And I could hit as well, them days. And it knocked her straight up. She stood up, see. So I hit her, it knocked her, and she fell and the chair broke under her. Of course I had to shift. I daren't stop there ... I shot.
>
> 'And it'd be half past eleven at night And I run across the banks, and I thought to myself, "Whatever am I going to do now?" Got nowhere to go. Cos a thing I'd never done

before you know, never experienced it. And there was a young woman there, and she was with a fellow. She said, "Alice, whatever are you doing out here?" Well I told her. I said, "Well I've nowhere to go." So she said, "I'll find you somewhere." So I said, "Where? I haven't got me coat nor nothing." Well she said, "I'll take you across to Mary Harding's." It was across the road you know. I didn't know this woman. Anyway I went in. She says, "Yes, come in," she says, "I've only got the one bed. You'll have to sleep with me and the two children." So I said, "Oh I'll fix myself up somewhere, later on."

'But anyway I stayed there, about a month, and we got another bed. Her husband and her were parted. She had a baby while her husband was in the forces and they'd parted, so she was all alone. And this Friday night she'd gone fetch her babies from nurse like. And there was a mirror like over her grate, high up. And I was cleaning this and singing. All of a sudden I just saw the reflection of somebody in the doorway. He was a smart soldier. When I turned I said, "Who are you?" And he started laughing. I said, "I'll ask you again," I said, "who are you?" He said, "I'm Mary's brother." "Oh," I said, "you'd better come in then if you are. By the way," I said, "what were you staring at?" He said, "I was looking at your legs. Looking at your legs," he says, "and now I've seen your face," he says, "it's nicer than ever." I said, "You're a bit forward aren't you?" You know, I was frightened of him really. Anyway I said, "Wait here a minute," I said, "I'll go and fetch her." I couldn't get out quick enough That's how I met me husband.

'Well, Mary came in with the children, said, "What are you doing here?" Said, "I'm off for four days." Said, "Why only four days?" Said, "Oh I'm going to India." Said, "Oh," she said, "that's a bit sudden isn't it?" He said, "Yes." Well anyway, we sat talking. So I said to Mary, "I'll get in your bed and let him lie in that other spare bed." He said, "Oh no need," he said, "I'm not tired." I said, "Well I am, I've got to go work, Saturday you know." We sat up talking till two o'clock. He was telling me all his life, at first he was telling me all about his life, he'd got no home nor nothing. And – I told him how I come to be there. So anyway, he said "Oh," he said, "I told you from the first that I liked you, soon as you turned your face round." "Well," I said, "what does that imply?" He said, "Well what would you say if I asked you to marry me?" The same night, yes. I said, "I'm not that bad off you know," I said, "I know I haven't got a home. I've still got me pride. I don't want to get married."

'He said, "Well I shan't be able to see you again," he said, "for seven years . . . and I've got no home," he said, "and, if I could put me trust in you, could you trust me?" I said, "No, I don't want to be married," I said, "I've just had enough of married life with me sisters you know." So Mary says, "Well why don't you marry him?" she said, "I can guarantee he's a good boy. He isn't anybody's you know Alice, no more than you are. You've neither of you got a home. You can't call this home. Why don't you make it up and get married?" So I said, "Well it's a big chance." I said, "It isn't a love marriage," I said, "it is a marriage of convenience, and I'll take your sister's word," I said, "I will." We were married three days later. And we never went bed. Never went bed. We were married two o'clock and he took the Stoke train quarter to four.'

She was to follow him to married quarters in India. 'Leave everything behind. Start life afresh.' But the gamble failed. Within months he was invalided home, a chronically sick man, unable to work again. She nursed him, married another soldier, and brought up five children from her two marriages. But she was never able to stop working. She trod the lathe for more than forty years.

'Lathe treading? I liked it because it was a lot of movement in it. But that was all right while I was single. But when I got having children, I didn't like it. But I'd got no other choice, I couldn't do anything else. So I had to stay. Stay put. It's been a terrible hard life. But they don't do it now you know. It's all done by machinery . . . I'm happier now than I've ever been in my life . . . It seems a shame you've got to work until you're seventy, before you can enjoy life.'

Note on Further Reading

General

George Dangerfield, *The Strange Death of Liberal England*, 1935, for the pre-war crisis; Arthur Marwick, *The Deluge*, 1965, for the war itself. Of other general books on the period R. C. K. Ensor, *England 1870–1914*, 1936, and E. Halévy, *History of the English People: Epilogue*, 1926–32, are classics which have lasted well. S. Nowell-Smith (ed.), *Edwardian England*, 1964, and E. Royston Pike, *Human Documents of the Lloyd George Era*, 1972, are also useful.

Beyond this, there is also a rich literature in political history which can be read as background to social history, including H. M. Pelling, *The Social Geography of British Elections, 1880–1910*, 1967, and there is much excellent recent work in the field of trade union and political labour history. Bibliographies of this are published by the *Bulletin of the Society for the Study of Labour History*, but special mention may be made of E. J. Hobsbawm, *Labouring Men*, 1964, H. M. Pelling, *Popular Politics and Society in Late Victorian Britain*, 1968, the History Workshop Pamphlets (Bob Gilding, *The Journeymen Coopers of East London*, 1971, Dave Douglass, *Pit Life in County Durham*, 1972), and Christopher Storm-Clark, 'The Miners, 1870–1970: a test case for oral history', *Victorian Studies* (XV), 1971, 49–74.

Most other topics are poorly dealt with in recent work, and as a result the footnotes in the text provide a good indication of the best primary sources for further reading.

Sustenance and the Standard of Living

On actual social conditions, Booth, Rowntree and Parliamentary Papers referred to in footnotes remain the best sources, but there is a good literature on state activity: Bentley B. Gilbert, *Evolution of National Insurance in Great Britain*, 1966, and *British Social Policy 1914–39*, 1970, B. Abel-Smith, *The Hospitals, 1800–1948*, 1964, T. Ferguson, *Scottish Social Welfare, 1864–1914*, 1958, Brian Simon, *Education and the Labour Movement, 1870–1920*, 1965, and G. A. N. Lowndes, *The Silent Social Revolution*, 1937. For private education, E. C. Mack, *Public Schools and British Opinion since 1860*, 1941. There are some other remarkable contemporary sources, such as B. S. Rowntree and B. Lasker, *Unemployment: a Social Study*, 1911, Mary Higgs, *The Tramp Ward*, c. 1904, Montague Lomax, *Experiences of an Asylum Doctor*, 1922, E. Holmes, *What is and What Might Be*, c. 1912, and S. Hobhouse and F. Brockway, *English Prisons Today*, 1922, whose perspective is the experience of poverty, education and institutions rather than its administration.

The Family

For childhood, Thea Thompson, *New Society*, 5 October 1972; for youth, F. Musgrove, *Youth and the Social Order*, 1964; for adulthood, P. F. Cominos, 'Late-Victorian sexual respectability and the social system', *International Review of Social History*, (8), 1963, and Sheila Rowbotham, *Women, Resistance and Revolution*, 1972, and *Hidden from History*, 1973. Of contemporary literature referred to, C. Hamilton, *Marriage as a Trade*, 1909, is outstanding; C. E. B. Russell is an especially good observer of youth, and see Booth and Loane generally. Stephen Reynolds, *A Poor Man's House*, 1909, M. Pember Reeves, *Round About a Pound a Week*, 1913, and Lady Florence Bell, *At the Works*, 1907, are also notable, and there are a number of excellent books on women's work, such as E. Cadbury, Matheson and Shann, *Women's Work and Wages*, 1906, and Clementina Black, *Married Women's Work*, 1915. On family limitation, besides the first census statistics in 1911, there is E. M. Elderton, *Report on the English Birthrate*, 1914.

There is little notable recent material on leisure, or on the social history of the arts except for E. E. Mackerness, *Social History of English Music*, 1964, and A. L. Lloyd, *Folk Song in England*, 1967. Religion is much better served with Robert Currie, *Methodism Divided*, 1965, Roger Lloyd, *The Church of England in the 20th Century*, 1946–50, Owen Chadwick, *The Victorian Church*, 2, 1970, and Hugh McLeod's *Class and Religion in the Late Victorian City*, 1974. Of contemporary sources, Booth is outstanding, and R. Mudie-Smith, *The Religious Life of London*, 1904, is also exceptional as a survey.

The Economy

There is no up-to-date account of the whole period for the general reader to replace Sir J. Clapham, *Economic History of Modern Britain*, Vol. 3, 1932. For the last years see S. Pollard, *Development of the British Economy 1914–50*, 1962. Also important are P. Deane and W. A. Cole, *British Economic Growth 1688–1959*, 1962, J. B. Jefferys, *Retail Trading in Britain 1850–1950*, 1954, H. J. Habakkuk, *American and British Technology in the 19th Century*, 1962, P. J. Perry, *British Farming in the Great Depression*, 1974, and for the general perspective, E. J. Hobsbawm, *Industry and Empire*, 1968.

Class and Community, Country and Town

In addition to most of the previous reading, Glass's *Social Mobility*, 1954, is important. For a general perspective, Hobsbawm's *Industry and Empire* is again perhaps the best starting-point. There is also a rich literature of local studies, including recently J. Littlejohn, *Westrigg*, 1963, J. M. Lee, *Social Leaders and Public Persons*, 1963, D. Jenkins, *The Agricultural Community in South West Wales at the Turn of the 20th Century*, 1971, George Ewart Evans, *Where Beards Wag All*, 1970, S. Pollard, *History of Labour in Sheffield*, 1959, Gareth Stedman-Jones, *Outcast London*, 1971, and L. P. Gartner, *The Jewish Immigrant in England*, 1960. Of contemporary literature, in addition to Booth and Lady Bell, special mention may be made of A. Paterson, *Across the Bridges*, 1911, C. B. Hawkins, *Norwich, a Social Study*, 1910, H. Rider Haggard, *Rural England*, 1902, and M. Kendall and B. S. Rowntree, *How the Labourer Lives*, 1913.

Autobiography

There is an abundance to choose from, especially for the middle and upper classes. A series of working-class autobiographies is collected in J. Burnett, *Useful Toil*, 1974. A choice of good titles giving a social cross-section might be: Sonia Keppel, *Edwardian Daughter*, 1959, Katherine Chorley, *Manchester Made Them*, 1950, Fred Willis, *A Book of London Yesterdays*, 1960, Alfred Williams, *Life in a Railway Factory*, 1916, Frank Richards, *Old Soldier Sahib*, 1936, Robert Roberts, *The Classic Slum*, 1971, Pat O'Mara, *Autobiography of a Liverpool Irish Slummy*, 1934, Patrick MacGill, *Children of the Dead End: the Autobiography of a Navvy*, 1914, Angus McLellan, *The Furrow Behind Me*, 1962, and Spike Mays, *Reuben's Corner*, 1969.

Novels

Especially good for these years: D. H. Lawrence, *The White Peacock*, 1911, *Sons and Lovers*, 1913, and *Women in Love*, 1921; Robert Tressall, *The Ragged Trousered Philanthropists*, 1914, Walter Greenwood, *Love on the Dole*, 1933, and H. G. Wells, *The History of Mr Polly*, 1910; J. Galsworthy, *The Forsyte Saga*, 1906–21, and E. M. Forster, *Howard's End*, 1910; V. Sackville-West, *The Edwardians*, 1930, and Henry James, *The Golden Bowl*, 1904.

Notes

In these notes PP stands for Parliamentary Papers, Int for Interview (with Edwardians).

Introduction

1 Int 34, pp. 7–8.
2 E. Durkheim, *Suicide*, trans. 1952, p. 37; very effectively evaluated in this respect by Jack Douglas, *The Social Meanings of Suicide*, 1967.
3 *Oral History* (I, 4) 1973, pp. 1–47. This journal is published by The Oral History Society, Department of Sociology, University of Essex, Colchester, Essex.

1 Money

1 Chiozza Money, *Riches and Poverty*, 1905, p. 52.
2 A. B. Atkinson, *Unequal Shares*, 1972, p. 21.
3 Int 406, p. 27.
4 Guy Routh, *Occupation and Pay in Great Britain 1906–60*, 1965, p. 107.
5 Routh, op. cit., pp. 4–5.

2 *Sustenance*

1 G. R. M. Devereux, *Etiquette for Men*, 1902, p. 22.
2 B. S. Rowntree, *Poverty, a Study of Town Life*, 1901, p. 171.
3 Ibid., pp. 167–8.
4 Int 347, p. 52.
5 Int 298, p. 13.

6 Rowntree, op. cit., pp. 297, 321, 340, 343.
7 A. Ponsonby, *The Camel and the Needle's Eye*, 1910, pp. 153–5.
8 Int 261, p. 53.
9 Int 398, p. 28.
10 PP 1902, XXVI, p. 717.
11 Land Enquiry Committee, *The Land*, Volume II, 1914, pp. 37–9.
12 C. F. G. Masterman, *The Condition of England*, 1909, p. 72.
13 A. Goodrich-Freer, *The Outer Isles*, 1902, pp. 152–3.
14 PP 1917–18, XIV, p. 368.

3 Country and Town

1 Int 41, p. 35.
2 Op. cit., pp. 7–8, 22–4, 151.
3 PP 1908 CVII, p. 591.
4 Int 203, p. 19.
5 Ibid., p. 36.
6 Int 189, p. 41.
7 Int 128, p. 19.
8 Int 362, pp. 51–2, 78, 102.
9 Int 47, p. 37.
10 Int 134, p. 43.
11 Int 54, p. 27.
12 Int 27, pp. 2, 8.
13 PP 1903, XII, p. 226.
14 Plymouth: Robert Sherard, *The Cry of the Poor*, 1901, pp. 24–5.

4 Childhood

1 Int 99, pp. 29.
2 Int 225, p. 79.
3 Int 278, p. 18.
4 Int 125, p. 57.
5 Int 134, pp. 15, 19.
6 Ibid., pp. 5, 30, 38.

7 Int 416, pp. 8, 43.
8 Int 203, p. 39.
9 Walter Greenwood, *There Was a Time*, 1967, p. 43.
10 Int 140, p. 33.
11 J. and E. Newson, *Patterns of Infant Care in an Urban Community*, 1963, p. 221.
12 Int 269, p. 16.
13 Int 1020.
14 Int 18, p. 60.
15 Int 181, p. 31.
16 Int 132, pp. 5, 9, 23.
17 Int 220, p. 16.
18 Int 126, pp. 12, 16, 26, 58.
19 Newson, op. cit., p. 225.
20 Int 118, p. 41.
21 Int 134, pp. 10, 22.
22 Int 18, p. 58.
23 M. E. Loane, *From Their Point of View*, 1908, pp. 99–108.
24 Charles Booth, *Life and Labour of the People in London, 1892–1903*, I, p. 160.
25 Int 208, pp. 14, 32.
26 E. H. Cooper, *The Twentieth Century Child*, 1905, pp. 107–8.

5 Youth

1 Int 334, p. 119.
2 W. H. Davies, *Beggars*, 1909, pp. 85–7.
3 Charles Russell and Lilian Rigby, *Working Lads' Clubs*, 1908, p. 12.
4 Sally Alexander, *St Giles's Fair*, 1970, History Workshop Pamphlet 2, p. 24, quoting *Oxford Times* as early as 1888.
5 Int 145, p. 16.
6 Int 132, p. 41.
7 Int 141, p. 14.
8 Int 22, p. 69.
9 Int 38, pp. 21–2.
10 PP 1910, XXVIII, p. 60.

11 Thomas Burke, *Nights in Town* (1915), 1925 edition, pp. 79–80.
12 Charles Booth, op. cit., Series 3, Vol. I, pp. 55–6.
13 Int 30, p. 20.
14 Royal Commission on Population, *Papers*, 1949, 1, *Report on an Enquiry into Family Limitation*, pp. 7–8.
15 Robert Roberts, *The Classic Slum*, 1971, p. 38.
16 Spike Mays, *Reuben's Corner*, 1969, pp. 66, 148.

6 Men and Women: Adulthood and Old Age

1 Int 138, p. 51.
2 Int 334, pp. 90–1.
3 BBC Sound Archive, 24 May 1948.
4 D. H. Lawrence, *Women in Love*, 1921, pp. 48–9.
5 Int 320, p. 73.
6 Int 261, p. 51.
7 J. and E. Newson, *Infant Care in an Urban Community*, 1963, p. 133.
8 Int 181, pp. 10, 30.
9 Int 350, pp. 11–12, 24.
10 R. Page Arnot, *The Miners: Years of Struggle*, 1953, pp. 147–8.
11 PP 1904, XXXII, p. 133.
12 Int 203, pp. 9–10.
13 Int 18, p. 21.
14 James Corin, *Mating, Marriage and the Status of Women*, 1910, p. 128.
15 George Lansbury, *My Life*, 1928, pp. 135–6.

Edwardians

1 Birthdates are not given, to protect confidentiality. The only stories taken beyond 1918 are Emmie Durham's and Richard Morgan's, which are both brought to 1920.
2 Mrs Davies's father and husband both had the same surname, and so did her husband's employer, although they came from different families. Such confusing situations are

not uncommon in Welsh and Scottish communities; one reason for their more frequent use of nicknames, patronymics, family tee-names, etc.

12 The Economy

1 P. Deane and W. A. Cole, *British Economic Growth*, 1962, p. 142.
2 G. Routh, op. cit., pp. 4–5.
3 Int 261, pp. 40, 45.
4 Int 94, pp. 38, 40, 42.

13 Escape

1 Tony Parker and Robert Allerton, *The Courage of his Convictions*, 1962, pp. 27–9.
2 Sam Larner, 'Now is the Time for Fishing', Folkways Records 1961, FG 3507.
3 City of Edinburgh Charity Organisation Society, *Report on the Physical Condition of 1400 School Children . .*, 1906, p. 22.
4 PP 1909 XXX, p. 663; PP 1909 XLIII, p. 21.
5 M. E. Loane, *The Common Growth*, 1911, p. 72.
6 A. Freeman, *Boy Life and Labour*, 1914, p. 152.
7 A. Paterson, *Across the Bridges*, 1911, pp. 144–5.
8 C. B. Hawkins, *Norwich, a Social Study*, 1910, p. 312.
9 Op. cit., I, pp. 113–14.
10 Lady Bell, *At the Works*, 1907, pp. 10, 132–3.
11 Lawrence, *Women in Love*, p. 102.
12 Op. cit., series 3, I, p. 102.
13 Booth, op. cit., 3, I, pp. 82, 89.
14 George Haw (ed.), *Christianity and the Working Classes*, 1906, p. 75.
15 Booth, op. cit., 3, I, pp. 24, 80.
16 B. G. Orchard cited in R. B. Walker, 'Religious changes in Liverpool in the 19th Century', *Journal of Ecclesiastical History* (XIX), 1969, p. 204.
17 W. H. Hudson, *The Land's End*, 1908, p. 199.

18 Rev J. V. Morgan, *The Welsh Religious Revival*, 1909, pp. 45, 112–13, 135, 139, 233.
19 *Northern Daily Telegraph*, 26 September 1900.

14 Solidarity

1 PP 1914 XXX, pp. 393–4.
2 Int 369, pp. 23–7.
3 A.S.E. *Monthly Report*, August 1905.
4 Written in 1893: S. and B. Webb, *History of Trade Unionism*, 1894, pp. 456–8.
5 R. P. Arnot, *South Wales Miners*, 1967, p. 185.
6 Dock, Wharf, Riverside and General Workers' Union, *24th Annual Report*, 1913, pp. 8–9.
7 Report of conference on fusion, December 1911.
8 C. L. Goodrich, *The Frontier of Control*, 1920, p. 12.
9 R. Hyman, *The Workers' Union*, 1971, p. 223.

15 Politics

1 Int 58, p. 13.
2 Int 143, p. 39.
3 P. F. Clarke, *Lancashire and the New Liberalism*, 1971, p. 343.
4 Int 42, p. 57.
5 Int 56, p. 15.
6 Int 32, p. 21.
7 Int 277, p. 33.
8 Int 51, p. 20.
9 Int 22, p. 57.
10 Int 347, p. 50.
11 Stephen Reynolds, *Seems So!*, 1911, pp. 6–12.
12 *Manchester Guardian*, 27 January 1910.
13 Int 17, p. 74.
14 Int 45, p. 19.
15 Frank Gray, *The Confessions of a Candidate*, 1925, pp. 9–10.
16 Ibid.
17 Edward Marsh, *A Number of People*, 1939, p. 150.

18 W. S. Churchill, *Liberalism and the Social Problem*, 1909, p. 82.
19 18 November 1910.
20 November 1900 (XXXVI), p. 331.
21 A. L. Lowell, *The Government of England*, 1908, p. 509.
22 George Lansbury, *My Life*, 1928, p. 78.
23 *Looking Backwards – and Forwards*, 1935, pp. 237–8.
24 Flora Thompson, *Lark Rise*, 1939, p. 100.
25 Robert Tressall, *The Ragged Trousered Philanthropists*, 1914, p. 14.

16 The Edwardian Crisis

1 *A Book of London Yesterdays*, 1960, p. 135.
2 C. F. G. Masterman, *The Condition of England*, 1909, pp. 120–1.
3 Lewis did not in fact intend 'The Crowd' to portray a revolutionary multitude. It represents the dominance of machinery over workmen. The revolt which broke out in the hitherto notably staid English art world was important only as yet another addition to the pre-war atmosphere of disturbance. Critics were horrified by the direct sexuality of Epstein's early sculpture; by Futurist lectures accompanied by concerts of noises like 'dead cats in a foghorn'; pictures like Nevinson's 'Portrait of a Motorist' with bits of glass and real buttons stuck in; and the aggressive propaganda issued from *Blast* and the Rebel Art Centre. But although the art rebellion gave 'the Modern Medievalist and the Fat Man of the Renaissance' in the art establishment good cause for anxiety, it was far from revolutionary in its social aims. The new artists wanted recognition that Britain was an industrial rather than a natural world; and, more important, the right to speak in a professional language, rather than the traditional realism generally preferred by the wealthy patrons on whom they depended. 'I look upon *Nature*, while I live in a *steel city*,' wrote David Bomberg in an exhibition catalogue. 'My object is the *construction of Pure Form*.' 'People are invited,' wrote

Lewis in another, 'to entirely change their idea of the painter's mission, and penetrate, deferentially, with him into a transposed universe, as abstract as, though different to, the musician's' (quoted in Richard Cork, *Vorticism and Its Allies*, Arts Council 1974, pp. 12, 18–19). The demand for deference from the public here sums up the social objective of this particular revolt. In its hymn to machinery – which was to achieve its nemesis with the destruction of the art rebellion itself by the First World War – *Blast* mocked the proletariat along with the rich.

4 *Woman and Labour*, 1911, p. 201.
5 p. 122.
6 Cicely Hamilton, *Marriage as a Trade*, 1909, p. 41.
7 1909, pp. 93, 113, 171, 220.
8 Hamilton, op. cit., pp. 185–9.
9 1913, pp. 26, 40, 61, 80.
10 *Woman and Labour*, pp. 55, 279–80.
11 M. M. Bird, *Woman at Work*, 1911, p. 22.
12 Stephen Reynolds, *Seems So!*, p. 15.
13 *The Great Scourge and How to End It*, 1913, p. 98.
14 C. W. Saleeby, *Woman and Womanhood*, 1912, pp. 15, 20.
15 Hamilton, op. cit., pp. 51, 279.
16 Int 134, p. 34.
17 D. Lloyd George, *Better Times*, 1910, pp. 151, 174–5.
18 *Liberalism and the Social Problem*, pp. 361–2.
19 J. J. Horgan, *The Complete Grammar of Anarchy*, 1919, pp. 3–4.
20 *The Times*, 29 July 1912. Those who believe retrospective memory to be peculiarly unreliable may note that contemporary sources give differing versions of the wording of this unusually important public speech.
21 Viscount Esher, *Journals and Letters*, 1938, III, p. 135.
22 *The Times*, 29 November 1913.
23 27 July 1914.
24 *Seamen's Torch*, 1938, p. 228.
25 6 January 1912.
26 *Collected Works*, 18, p. 468.
27 *The Times*, 25 March 1914.

28 PP 1917–18 XV, p. 155.
29 James Hinton, *The First Shop Stewards' Movement*, 1973, p. 115.
30 *Lenin on Britain*, 1934, p. 147.
31 *Industrial Problems and Disputes*, 1920, pp. 149–50.
32 Ibid., p. 348.

17 War

1 *Solidarity*, March 1917.
2 Paul Nash, *Outline*, 1949, pp. 210–11.
3 H. C. Fischer and Dr E. X. Dubois, *Sexual Life During the World War*, 1937, pp. 89, 100, 142.
4 Quoted by David Mitchell, *Women on the Warpath*, 1966, pp. 212–13.
5 *The Classic Slum*, p. 160.
6 Cecil Leeson, in I. Andrews, *Effects of the War upon Women and Children in Great Britain*, New York, 1918, p. 159.

19 Family

1 Int 36, p. 8.
2 Int 419, p. 42.
3 (1962) 1973 edition, pp. 139–40.
4 M. Young and P. Willmott, 1973.
5 Op. cit., p. 304.

20 Class

1 Int 22, pp. 24–5.
2 A. B. Atkinson, *Unequal Shares*, 1972, p. 21.
3 Int 178, pp. 10–11.
4 David Lockwood, 1958.
5 Int 22, p. 28.

21 Theory and Practice

1 Int 178, pp. 136, 151.

Index